SACRED ECOLOGY
Traditional Ecological Knowledge
and Resource Management

SACRED ECOLOGY
Traditional Ecological Knowledge and Resource Management

Fikret Berkes

TAYLOR & FRANCIS
· Founded 1798 ·

USA	Publishing Office:	TAYLOR & FRANCIS
		325 Chestnut Street
		Philadelphia, PA 19106
		Tel: (215) 625-8900
		Fax: (215) 625-2940
	Distribution Center:	TAYLOR & FRANCIS
		47 Runway Road, Suite G
		Levittown, PA 19057-4700
		Tel: (215) 269-0400
		Fax: (215) 269-0363
UK		TAYLOR & FRANCIS
		1 Gunpowder Square
		London EC4A 3DE
		Tel: +44 171 583 0490
		Fax: +44 171 583 0581

SACRED ECOLOGY: Traditional Ecological Knowledge and Resource Management

3 4 5 6 7 8 9 0

Cover design by Norm Myers.
Cover photo: Travelling on the James Bay coast, Quebec, Canada, in early June. See chapter 7. Photo: Fikret Berkes.

A CIP catalog record for this book is available from the British Library.
∞ The paper in this publication meets the requirements of the ANSI Standard Z39.48-1984 (Permanence of Paper).

Library of Congress Cataloging-in-Publication Data

Berkes, Fikret.
    Sacred ecology : traditional ecological knowledge and resource management / Fikret Berkes.
        p.   cm.
    ISBN 1-56032-694-8 (case : alk. paper).—ISBN 1-56032-695-6 (pbk. : alk. paper)
    1. Environmental sciences—Philosophy.   2. Human ecology. 3. Social change.   4. James Bay—Traditional Knowledge—Case studies.   I. Title.
GE40.B45   1999
179'.1--dc21   98-43381
                                                                         CIP

1-56032-694-8 (case)
1-56032-695-6 (paper)

Contents

PART II: PRACTICE

PART III: ISSUES

List of Figures,
Tables, and Boxes

FIGURES

TABLES

BOXES

Preface

When I started to write this book, I had to remind myself of the oft-repeated conventional wisdom that the amount of knowledge in the world has been doubling every decade in recent times. Aside from the questions of just who measured the amount of knowledge and how, the obviously rapid pace of the growth of information all around us is sobering to anyone interested in traditional ecological knowledge. Has ancient knowledge perhaps become irrelevant, or has it simply been swamped by modern knowledge and reduced merely to a footnote? Just what can the study of traditional knowledge contribute to the contemporary world? This volume tries to answer these questions somewhat along the lines of the quotation attributed to the British philosopher Bertrand Russell: "One of the troubles of our age is that habits of thought cannot change as quickly as techniques, with the result that as skill increases, wisdom fades."

The interest in indigenous systems is not merely academic. The lessons of traditional knowledge, especially of the ecological kind, have practical significance for the rest of the world. There is a growing line of thought, as this volume documents, that we are moving in the new millennium toward different ways of seeing, perceiving, and doing, with a broader knowledge base than that allowed by modernist Western science. For many of us, the science of ecology has a historic role to play in this process. As Theodore Roszak observed in his 1972 book, *Where the Wasteland Ends*, "ecology already hovers on the threshold of heresy." Some three decades ago, ecology held a great deal of promise to step across this threshold, and "in so doing, revolutionize the sciences as a whole. . . . The question remains open: which will ecology be, the last of the old sciences or the first of the new?" (Roszak 1972, 404).

It may be an exaggeration to say that the science of ecology as a whole has such a momentous choice to make. No doubt much of ecology will continue as conventional science, and at least for the foreseeable future, such ecology will have a role to play in the advancement of knowledge. The fact of the matter is, an overwhelmingly large part of ecology tries to adhere to the tenets of conventional science. It tends to be quantitative, reductionistic, and not at all sacred or spiritual, seemingly bent on dashing Roszak's hopes, as Evernden (1993) later noted. But for me the more interesting kinds of ecology are the unconventional ones–if not quite "heretical," certainly at the edge of scientific respectability! Thomas Kuhn's (1970) *The Structure of Scientific Revolutions* argues that new scientific paradigms arise at the peripheries of mainstream science. New ways of looking at phenomena come about as the conventional paradigm proves less and less capable of explaining observations. A case in point is the replacement of Newton's mechanistic model of the universe by Einstein's relativity principle. Does traditional ecological knowledge represent some such paradigm change (in a small way) in the field of ecology? Only time will tell.

Before entering the world of traditional ecological knowledge, let me explain how I came to develop an interest in it. I first became involved in the human ecology of an indigenous group, the Cree Indians, in 1971, but I did not start my field studies in James Bay in subarctic Canada until 1974. At the time, I had just finished my Ph.D. work as a marine scientist and applied ecologist, and I had spent much of my graduate student years practicing being a "good scientist," always skeptical and always questioning the evidence. I also believed that all phenomena could be studied by the use of the scientific method. This latter belief was shaken somewhat in 1972 when I first started to teach at McGill University in Montreal. The course was about environmental studies and social change, taught by a team led by John Southin and Wade Chambers, themselves unconventional thinkers. I was exposed to a great many new ideas, and for the first time, to philosophy of science. Now this was a new field for me; science students (and scientists) almost never read philosophy of science! One book, perhaps the earliest one that forced me to take a broader view of knowledge, was R. G. H. Siu's *The Tao of Science*.

By 1974, I was in James Bay fishing with the Cree. I had turned down an excellent opportunity to do a postdoctoral fellowship with a leading marine ecologist, to work instead with my anthropologist colleague, Harvey Feit, a move considered quite suicidal professionally by many of my scientist friends. My early studies of human ecology, fisheries, and environmental assessment in James Bay actually went very well. I had a little innovative twist in my study plan. Instead of setting my own nets and sampling my own fish as scientists normally do, I was accompanying Cree fishers to go to *their own* fishing areas and collecting the usual biological data from their catch, as well as collecting data on the Cree fishery itself. The reason for the unusual study design was only in part deliberate as a study of *human* ecology; in part it was dictated by the limitations of my budget.

I was comfortable with the collection of "objective" and quantitative data, and the Cree fishers and their families were quite content that I was not the kind of researcher who was always asking questions. We did a lot of fishing; the fishery was not a commercial one but subsistence, carried out only for household and community needs. One year I calculated that with my puny research grant, I had outfished (outsampled) the government research team, which had a quarter-

million-dollar budget to conduct fisheries assessment in the same waters. But it
was really the Cree who were doing the fishing. I was only the guest and inept
helper, as they effortlessly set nets and pulled in the fish, zipping up and down
the most complicated coastline you could ever imagine, where the configuration
changed at each phase of the tide. I was beginning to develop a healthy respect
for their knowledge and capabilities.

Twice I thought I would wrap up the James Bay project, once in 1978
and again in 1982, but somehow I ended up going back. I was finding that
the more research I did in James Bay, the more interesting research questions
presented themselves. Many were questions I had not asked at the start of my
research, such as, "With no government regulation, how come the Cree did
not overfish, and how come the resources did not suffer from the tragedy of
the commons?" The answer was that the Cree had community-based resource
management, and the analysis of common property resources became my main
line of research (e.g. Berkes 1989a). There were other questions as well, some
of which I did not get to until quite recently. Traditional knowledge is one of
them. I had made considerable progress in describing and analyzing traditional,
community-based resource management of the Cree. But this analysis had been
based on *my* academic interpretation of the system, what some anthropologists
would call the *etic* view. (Chapter 7 gives a detailed account of that work.) I had
not given much thought to the *emic* view or how the Cree themselves saw their
systems, nor did I think the unique Cree worldview of nature, as documented
by an earlier generation of anthropologists, was particularly relevant in James
Bay of the 1980s. I was soon proven wrong.

It started with a comment by one of my Cree associates. He said, "Now that
you have been doing work here (on and off) for ten years, you must have learned
something of our hunting and fishing. How about doing something useful for the
community, writing down for us some of our rules and practices to help educate
the younger generation?" We had an unwritten agreement about the conditions of
my research in the community: I would come back and be accountable (they did
not approve of researchers who disappeared with the data after a year or two),
and I would help put the information to the use of the community as needed.
Now my associate was taking me up on it. A promise is a promise, although
I should admit, I initially regarded the task as free consultancy, or worse, as a
secretarial/editorial job, but in any case the request was consistent with the Cree
practice of reciprocity and therefore impossible to refuse without losing face.

My fears about the drudgery of the job were quickly dispelled when I
started meeting with the self-selected task force organized by my associate,
George Lameboy, and by the head of the Chisasibi Cree Trappers Association,
Robbie Matthew. It was a group of brilliant, humorous, and wise people. I found
myself as the invited scribe in a latter-day "Black Elk Speaks" (Brown 1953),
with an internal check and consensus mechanism thrown in, because I had not
one elder but a whole group with me! We proceeded Cree-style, slowly and
deliberately, with many digressions and much good humor. They set the agenda;

I made the notes, and edited and brought them to the next meeting. Then they went over each line, translated back to Cree for the benefit of the members who did not speak English, and they made sure, as only meticulous hunters can, that I eventually got everything right. This process continued though five meetings in 1984, and at the end of the year I presented the group with the final report. It was later turned by the Cree into a small book, *Cree Trappers Speak* (Bearskin et al. 1989). Chapter 5 of the present volume borrows heavily from the report, and chapter 6 gives a flavor of the Cree-style discourse that led to it.

The slow pace of the proceedings meant that I could keep up with the notes and not have to use a tape recorder, which many of the older Cree dislike as a symbol of white man's technology. It also meant that I had time to absorb the discussion and seek clarification every now and then. Here was a group of elders and experts, speaking without the prompting of a meddlesome researcher, about their views of life, spirituality, rituals in the bush, uncomfortable relations with missionaries (Berkes 1986b), the cycling of animal populations, the proper ways to hunt caribou and geese, and on and on. In my ten years, I had never asked questions about these things, and some of these matters I did not think they would talk about at all.

Out of the discussion emerged a worldview different from the mainstream Euro-Canadian one, a worldview in which nature pulsated with life, compelling in its spiritual ecology. In one of the stories Cree elders told, a famous and influential missionary of the James Bay coast of the 1930s was quoted as repeatedly telling the Cree, "there are no spirits in the bush." The Cree elder sighed and added, "No matter how much he repeated that, we all knew that the land was sacred and full of spirits." Here we were, in 1984, on the sacred land where the animals determined the success of the hunt. Violate rules of respect and reciprocity, you came back from the hunt empty-handed. Many of the Cree believed that; some of the younger hunters were skeptical but not willing to take a chance either (although many others violated the rules nevertheless).

Somewhat to my surprise, I found myself comfortable with the Cree view of nature, even though, by virtue of my Western education and scientific training, I was heavily inclined to resist it. My generation had grown up with the marvels of the space age and the glorification of science and technology. Later, the environmental movement of the 1960s and the 1970s had provided a devastating critique of the misapplications of science and technology, but we were short on prescriptions, especially of the nonscientific kind. The standard view of ecosystems on which I had been brought up was rather machine-like. The influential ecologist, Eugene Odum (1971), for example, characterized ecological cycles as giant wheels powered by the energy of the sun. In this mechanical ecology, there was little room for the discussion of ecological ethics and even less of the sacred.

There were other views of ecology, but they were not a part of the discussion among ecologists. As Paul Shepard once observed, although ecology is a science, its greater and overriding wisdom is universal. That wisdom can be approached mathematically, experimentally, or it can be danced or told as myth. It is in Australian aborigines' "dreamtime" and in Gary Snyder's poetry. I discovered Aldo Leopold's (1949) "land ethics" only in the 1970s. Among the exceptions to conventional ecology was the work of Ian McHarg. He was writing about nature and environment, not as an ecologist but as a landscape architect and planner, inspiring dissatisfied ecologists such as myself to widen our radius of intellectual search. The chapter "On Values" in his *Design with Nature* (1969) talked about Iroquois bear rituals preceding a hunt. The hunter talks to the bear and assures the bear that the killing is motivated by need; at the same time, the ritual reminds him of his ethical obligations. McHarg observed, "Now if you would wish to develop an attitude to prey that would ensure stability in a hunting society, then such views are the guarantee." The science of ecology did not discuss such views, but Siu, Leopold, McHarg, and later Bateson (1972) mentally prepared me to be receptive to a traditional ecology that did.

A large number of people (academics, resource managers, and practitioners) contributed to the development of this volume by sharing their ideas and insights and by sending material. I am grateful to them all. They include Arun Agrawal (Yale University), Upali and Mala Amarasinghe (Kelaniya University), Mac Chapin (Native Lands), Johan Colding (Stockholm University), Ian Davidson-Hunt (University of Manitoba), Jocelyn Davies (University of Adelaide), Roy Dudgeon (University of Manitoba), Nick Flanders (Dartmouth College), Carl Folke (Stockholm University), Milton Freeman (University of Alberta), Madhav Gadgil (Indian Institute of Science), Anne Gunn (Government of the Northwest Territories), Chris Hannibal-Paci (University of Manitoba), Jeff Hutchings (Dalhousie University), Bob Johannes (consultant, Tasmania, formerly CSIRO), Stephen Kellert (Yale University), Gary Kofinas (University of British Columbia), Allice Legat (consultant, NWT), Robin Mahon (consultant, Barbados), Henrik Moller (University of Otago), Barbara Neis (Memorial University), Garry Peterson (University of Florida), Dick Preston (McMaster University), Kent Redford (Wildlife Conservation Society), Yves Renard (CANARI), Mere Roberts (University of Auckland), Allan Smith (CANARI), Frank Tough (University of Alberta), Ron Trosper (Northern Arizona University), Nancy Turner (University of Victoria), Marty Weinstein (consultant, B.C.), and Elspeth Young (Australian National University). I would like to pay a special tribute to Mike Warren (Iowa State University) who passed on prematurely in 1997; his enthusiasm and generous friendship will be sorely missed.

A large number of people shared their traditional and local knowledge with me, in Quebec, Ontario, Manitoba, Northwest Territories, British Columbia, Newfoundland, and Labrador (all in Canada), the Caribbean area, Turkey, India, Bangladesh, and Sri Lanka. I cannot possibly name them all and do justice, but I am nevertheless much indebted to them. In regard to the three chapters on the James Bay Cree, the key people who influenced me include George and James

Bobbish, William and Margaret Cromarty, George Lameboy, Robbie Matthew, John Turner, and their families.

For chapter reviews I am thankful to Frank Tough, Yves Renard, Allan Smith, Kent Redford, and my wife, Dr. Mina Kislalioglu Berkes. My son, Jem Berkes, assisted a great deal with the technical production. Prabir Mitra drew the figures, except figure 10.1, which was drafted by Alun Hughes. The assistance of the Taylor & Francis team, especially that of Alison Howson, Catherine Kovacs, and Elizabeth Cohen was greatly appreciated.

SACRED ECOLOGY
Traditional Ecological Knowledge and Resource Management

Part One

Concepts

Chapter One

Context of Traditional Ecological Knowledge

Most of us have lost that sense of unity of biosphere and humanity which would bind and reassure us all with an affirmation of beauty. Most of us do not today believe that whatever the ups and downs of detail within our limited experience, the larger whole is primarily beautiful.

—Gregory Bateson, *Mind and Nature*

Ecological awareness will arise only when we combine our rational knowledge with an intuition for the nonlinear nature of our environment. Such intuitive wisdom is characteristic of traditional, nonliterate cultures, especially of American Indian cultures, in which life was organized around a highly refined awareness of the environment.

—F. Capra, *The Turning Point*

We live in a world densely populated by humans in close communication with one another over the surface of the earth. More and more, the world looks like a single society, a "global village." But in fact, human society consists of a great many groups, as different from one another as the city dwellers of New York, rice farmers of India, and aboriginal hunters of northern Canada. People of our global village differ not only in their daily occupations and material wealth, but also in the ways in which they view the world around them. This multitude of perceptions is directly related to cultural diversity around the world, a diversity that is rapidly shrinking. Surrounded by the built landscape, it has become difficult for people to relate to the environment. This alienation from nature has contributed to the environmental problems of the contemporary world. But at the same time, it has triggered a search for new ways of relating to nature.

The science of ecology, or at least one school of ecology that takes a broader holistic view, provides a new vision of the earth as a system of interconnected relationships. Emerging out of the discourse of ecology is a view of human society as part of a web of life within the ecosystem. Researchers are discovering, in the words of Berry (1988), "a universe that is dynamically alive: a whole system, fluid and interconnected.... Science is discovering a new version of the 'enchanted' world that was part of the natural mind for most of human history." This view is a radical departure from the static, mechanical, disembodied view of the world formulated by Descartes, Newton, and other thinkers of the Age of Enlightenment, and which has dominated our thinking.

The land ethics of Aldo Leopold (1949), deep ecology (Naess 1989), Gaia (Lovelock 1979), a sense of place, bioregionalism, topophilia or love of land (Tuan 1974), and biophilia or love of living things (Kellert and Wilson 1993; Kellert 1997) are some of the ways in which people concerned with environmental ethics have searched for the personal and spiritual element of ecology that has been missing in scientific ecology. Yet others have explored Eastern religions and Native American worldviews for insights (Callicott 1994; Bruun and Kalland 1995). These efforts are very much a part of the broader context of the interest in traditional ecological knowledge, since it represents experience acquired over thousands of years of direct human contact with the environment.

The term *traditional ecological knowledge* came into widespread use only in the 1980s, but the practice of traditional ecological knowledge is as old as ancient hunter-gatherer cultures. Although this book is about traditional *ecological* knowledge in *resource management*, the study of other types of traditional knowledge is valued in a number of fields. In fact, in comparison to some of these fields, the study of indigenous knowledge in ecology is relatively recent.

The earliest systematic studies of traditional ecological knowledge were carried out by anthropologists. As part of this endeavor, ecological knowledge was studied by ethnoecology, an approach that focuses on the conceptions of ecological relationships held by a people or a culture (Toledo 1992). Ethnoecology is a subset of ethnoscience (folk science), defined by Hardesty (1977, 291) as "the study of systems of knowledge developed by a given culture to classify the objects, activities, and events of its universe." As the definition indicates, much of the early research in ethnoscience was concerned with folk taxonomies. Pioneering work by Conklin (1957) documented, for example, that traditional peoples such as the Hanunoo of the Philippines often possessed exceptionally detailed knowledge of local plants and animals and their natural history, recognizing in one case some 1,600 plant species.

Various kinds of indigenous environmental knowledge have come to be accepted and used by scientific experts in a number of areas. For example, there has been growing recognition of the capabilities of traditional agriculturalists (Warren et al. 1995), pharmacologists (Schultes 1989), water engineers (Groenfelt 1991), and architects (Fathy 1986). Increased appreciation of ethnoscience, ancient and contemporary, paved the way for the acceptability of the validity of traditional knowledge in a variety of fields. In the area of ecology, various works showed that indigenous groups and other traditional peoples in diverse geographical areas, from the Arctic to the Amazon, had their own understandings of ecological relationships and systems of managing resources. The feasibility of applying traditional ecological knowledge to contemporary resource management problems in various parts of the world was gradually recognized in the international arena, as reflected in the following quotation from *Our Common Future*, the report of the World Commission on Environment and Development:

Tribal and indigenous peoples' . . . lifestyles can offer modern societies many lessons in the management of resources in complex forest, mountain and dryland ecosystems [WCED 1987, 12]. . . . These communities are the repositories of vast accumulations of traditional knowledge and experience that link humanity with its ancient origins. Their disappearance is a loss for the larger society, which could learn a great deal from their traditional skills in sustainably managing very complex ecological systems. (WCED 1987, 114–15)

DEFINING TRADITIONAL ECOLOGICAL KNOWLEDGE

There is no universally accepted definition of traditional ecological knowledge. The term is, by necessity, ambiguous since the words *traditional* and *ecological knowledge* are themselves ambiguous. In the dictionary sense, traditional usually refers to cultural continuity transmitted in the form of social attitudes, beliefs, principles, and conventions of behavior and practice derived from historical experience. It is cumulative and open to change (Nakashima 1998). Hunn (1993a, 13) explains: "New ideas and techniques may be incorporated into a given tradition, but only if they fit into the complex fabric of existing traditional practices and understandings. Thus traditions are enduring adaptations to specific places. . . . Traditions are the products of generations of intelligent reflection tested in the rigorous laboratory of survival. That they have endured is proof to their power."

For some, *tradition* and *change* are contradictory concepts, and it is difficult to define just how much and what kind of change would affect the labeling of a practice as "traditional." Worse, as Lewis (1993a) points out, the traditional "may be dismissed or denigrated because the custodians of such knowledge are no longer considered 'traditional' by outsiders, particularly those in positions of power and authority." This is one of the reasons why some scholars avoid using the term *traditional* and instead favor the term *indigenous*, thus avoiding the debate over tradition, as Warren (1995, 13) explains:

In 1980, David Brokensha, Oswald Werner and I were struggling to find a term that could replace "traditional" in the designation "traditional knowledge." In our view, "traditional" denoted the 19th-century attitudes of simple, savage and static. We wanted a term that represented the dynamic contributions of any community to problem-solving, based on their own perceptions and conceptions, and the ways that they identified, categorized and classified phenomena important to them. At the same time Robert Chambers and his group at Sussex were struggling with the same issue. Independent of each other, we both came up with the term "indigenous."

There is some logic in this, although for many others traditional does not mean an inflexible adherence to the past; it simply means time-tested and wise. In particular, for many groups of indigenous people the word tradition carries many positive meanings. For example, when the Inuit (Eskimo) participants in a 1995 conference were asked to describe traditional knowledge, there was consensus on the following meanings: practical common sense; teachings and experience passed through generations; knowing the country; being rooted in spiritual health; a way of life; an authority system of rules for resource use; respect; obligation to share; wisdom in using knowledge; using heart and head together (Emery 1997, 3).

The term *ecological knowledge* poses definitional problems of its own. If ecology is defined narrowly as a branch of biology concerned with interrelationships in the biophysical environment, in the domain of Western science, then *traditional ecological knowledge* becomes a problematic term. If, on the other hand, ecological knowledge is defined broadly to refer to the knowledge, however acquired, of relationships of living beings with one another and with their environment, then the term becomes tenable. It is what Levi-Strauss (1962) has called the *science du concret*, the native knowledge of the natural milieu firmly rooted in the reality of an accumulation of concrete, personal experiences, as opposed to book-learning.

In this context, *ecological knowledge* is not the term of preference for many traditional or indigenous peoples themselves. In the Canadian North, for example, aboriginal peoples often refer to their "knowledge of the land" rather than to ecological knowledge. *Land* to them, however, is more than the physical landscape; it includes the living environment. For example, the Dogrib Dene (Athapascan) term *ndè* is usually translated as "land." But its meaning is closer to "ecosystem," except that *ndè* is based on the idea that everything in the environment has life and spirit (Legat et al. 1995). Interestingly, in the history of the science of ecology, *land* was also often used as a synonym for *ecosystem*, as in the "land ethic" of Leopold (1949).

To arrive at a definition of traditional ecological knowledge, it is necessary to sift through the various meanings and elements of the concept through the development of the fields of ethnoscience and human ecology (see chapter 3). The study of traditional ecological knowledge begins with the study of species identifications and classification (ethnobiology) and proceeds to considerations of peoples' understandings of ecological processes and their relationships with the environment (human ecology). Implied in the concept is a component of local *knowledge* of species and other environmental phenomena. There is also a component of *practice* in the way people carry out their agriculture, hunting and fishing, and other livelihood activities. Further, there is a component of *belief* in peoples' perceptions of their role within ecosystems and how they interact with natural processes. Boxes 1.1 and 1.2 illustrate the idea that purely ecological aspects of tradition cannot be divorced from the social and spiritual. Stories and legends are part of culture and indigenous knowledge because they signify meaning. Such meaning and values are rooted in the land and closely related to a "sense of place." As Butz (1996, 52) notes, indigenous "ecological knowledge and activities (are) symbolically and instrumentally embedded in

---

BOX 1.1
THE TRADITION OF COYOTE STORIES

"Traditions include ideas of religion, patterns of artistic expression, and familial relationships, for example, in addition to knowledge of economically valuable resources. However, closer examination will reveal that it is not possible to divorce the ecological aspects of a tradition from the religious, the aesthetic, or the social. For example, among native American people of the Columbia Plateau of north-western North America, moral precepts are inculcated by means of a body of 'Coyote stories,'" explains Hunn. An elder from the Columbia Plateau tribes may know more than sixty such stories, each one constituting a full evening's performance. "To appreciate the meanings these stories convey requires an intimate knowledge of the local natural environment, local animals and plants being the main characters and local places the stage on which they act out the human drama. Children learn the moral precepts that will guide them in their social and ecological relationships by listening to their elders tell these stories. Thus religion, art and ecology are one. Traditions are thus ecological in the sense that they represent a complex and integrated system of practices and beliefs."

Source: Hunn 1993a, 14

BOX 1.2
A CREE LEGEND OF FLOOD AND ORIGIN OF THE EARTH

According to archaeological evidence, the Cree have been living in the James Bay area for thousands of years. According to native beliefs and legends, the Cree have lived on this land "from the beginning," since time immemorial. They lived through major floods that destroyed the rest of the earth.

After the flood, according to the legend, the Cree trickster-hero, Wesakachak, found himself floating helplessly along with otter, beaver, and muskrat. The Creator gave Wesakachak the power, not to create, but to remake the world if only Wesakachak could bring up some earth from underneath the flood waters. Wesakachak turned to his companions for help. First, he called on the otter to dive down and bring up a piece of the earth. But the otter failed. Wesakachak then asked the beaver to do the same, but the beaver was also unsuccessful. Finally, Wesakachak, in desperation, turned to the muskrat. Small as he was, the muskrat had a strong heart and he tried very hard. Twice he dove and twice he failed. On the third attempt, he dove so deep that he almost drowned. But when he came up, against his breast in his forepaws, he held a piece of the old earth. . . .

Source: Traditional. There are many versions of this popular legend; this one is from the Moose Factory area of western James Bay (Mushkegowuk region). In some Mushkego (West Main) Cree legends, Wesakachak is the first human in the world. In others, he is the creator of all things. He is a teacher but also a fool who finally puts a barrier between all the earth's creatures so that they can no longer talk to one another. The older Chisasibi Cree hunters still refer to the ancient "time when humans and animals talked to one another."

the places and life worlds out of which they developed and which they help constitute."

Putting together the most salient attributes of traditional ecological knowledge, one may arrive at a working definition of traditional ecological knowledge as *a cumulative body of knowledge, practice, and belief, evolving by adaptive processes and handed down through generations by cultural transmission, about the relationship of living beings (including humans) with one another and with their environment*. This definition, evolving from our earlier work (Berkes 1993; Gadgil et al. 1993; Berkes et al. 1995), is the operational definition used in this volume. Traditional ecological knowledge is both cumulative and dynamic, building on experience and adapting to changes. It is an attribute of societies with historical continuity in resource use on a particular land. By and large, these are nonindustrial or less technologically oriented societies, many of them indigenous or tribal, but not exclusively so. Some nonindigenous groups, such as inshore cod fishers of Newfoundland (Neis 1992) and users of Swiss Alpine commons (Netting 1981), no doubt also hold traditional ecological knowledge.

Local knowledge is the term of choice of some scholars "because it is the least problematical" (Ruddle 1994a, 161); it can be argued that indigenous ecological knowledge is a subset of local ecological knowledge (Jesse Ford, pers. comm.). But the term local knowledge conveys neither the *ecological* aspect of the concept, nor a sense of the temporal dimension and cumulative cultural transmission. In this volume, *local knowledge* is used when referring to recent knowledge, as in the nontraditional knowledge of some Caribbean region peoples discussed in chapter 8. The term *indigenous knowledge* (IK) is more broadly defined as the local knowledge held by indigenous peoples or local knowledge unique to a given culture or society, consistent with Warren et al. (1995).

Of course, much of the IK literature is not about ecological relationships but about many other fields of ethnoscience including agriculture, ethnobotany (Schultes and Reis 1995), ethnozoology (Clement 1995), ethnopharmacology, irrigation systems (Mabry 1996), soil and water conservation (Reij et al. 1996), soils or ethnopedology (Pawluk et al. 1992), ethnoveterinary medicine (Mathias-Mundy and McCorkle 1995), and ethnoastronomy (Ceci 1978). There is even a literature on indigenous knowledge and classification of snow (Pruitt 1984), freshwater ice (Basso 1972), and sea ice (Nelson 1969; Freeman 1984; Riewe 1991).

Some of these other areas of ethnoscience, for example, ancient erosion control techniques (Pawluk et al. 1992) and water conservation (Reij et al. 1996), are directly related to ecological knowledge, but others (e.g., ethnoastronomy) are less so. The terms *traditional ecological knowledge* and *indigenous knowledge* have often been used interchangeably. But in this volume, the use of *traditional ecological knowledge* is limited to more explicitly *ecological* knowledge and is considered a subset of indigenous knowledge.

TRADITIONAL ECOLOGICAL KNOWLEDGE AS SCIENCE

There are both similarities and differences between traditional science and Western science. Bronowski considers the practice of science (including magic) as a fundamental characteristic of human societies: "to me the most interesting thing about man is that he is an animal who practices art and science and, in every known society, practices both together" (Bronowski 1978, 9). Both Western and indigenous science may be considered, along with art, the result of the same general intellectual process of creating order out of disorder.

More controversial is the question of the existence of curiosity-driven inquiry among traditional peoples. Opinions differ, but there is a great deal of evidence that traditional people do possess scientific curiosity, and that traditional knowledge does not merely encompass matters of immediate practical interest. In his classic study, *The Savage Mind*, Levi-Strauss (1962) argues this point on the grounds that ancient societies could not have acquired such technological skills as those involved in the making of watertight pots without a curiosity-driven scientific attitude and a desire for knowledge for its own sake. As Levi-Strauss (1962, 3) states it, "the universe is an object of thought at least as much as it is a means of satisfying needs."

Levi-Strauss's work is groundbreaking in part because he avoids Western society's long-standing prejudice against non-Western cultures, especially those of "primitive" societies. He prefers to call the latter " 'prior' rather than 'primitive' "; "it was no less scientific and its results no less genuine. They were secured ten thousand years earlier and still remain at the basis of our own civilization" (Levi-Strauss 1962, 16). The worlds of the shaman and the scientist are two parallel modes of acquiring knowledge about the universe, "two distinct though equally positive sciences: one which flowered in the neolithic period, whose theory of the sensible order provided the basis of the arts of civilization (agriculture, animal husbandry, pottery, weaving. . .)." However, the two kinds of sciences are fundamentally distinct in that "the physical world is approached from opposite ends in the two cases: one is supremely concrete, the other supremely abstract" (Levi-Strauss 1962, 269).

Even though clear delimitations are difficult to make and exceptions exist, traditional ecological knowledge is generally thought to differ from Western scientific ecological knowledge in a number of substantive ways. Traditional ecological knowledge is often an integral part of the local culture, and management prescriptions are adapted to the local area. Resource users themselves are the "managers"; they identify themselves as members of a local community and not as individual scientists or resource managers answerable to their peers or to an anonymous government agency. Traditional systems tend to have a large moral and ethical context; there is no separation between nature and culture. In many traditional cultures nature is imbued with sacredness, in Shepard's (1973) sense of *sacred*. It is " 'sacred ecology' in the most expansive, rather than in the scientifically restrictive, sense of the word 'ecology' " (Knudtson and Suzuki 1992, 15).

Banuri and Apffel Marglin (1993) use a systems-of-knowledge analysis, in which the philosophical and anthropological background go back to Weber and Nietzsche, to contrast indigenous and Western scientific knowledge. According to this analysis, indigenous knowledge systems are characterized by embeddedness of knowledge in the local cultural milieu; boundedness of local knowledge in space and time; the importance of community; lack of separation between nature and culture, and between subject and object; commitment or attachment to the local environment as a unique and irreplaceable place; and a noninstrumental approach to nature. These features contrast, respectively, with Western scientific knowledge systems, which are characterized by disembeddedness; universalism; individualism; nature:culture and subject:object dichotomy; mobility; and an instrumental attitude (nature as commodity) toward nature.

The distinction between the two kinds of knowledge "is a difference of degree (quantitative) rather than of type (qualitative)," as Giarelli (1996) puts it. Many other, sometimes simplistic, distinctions have been offered by various authors, including the alleged *inability* of traditional systems to use controlled experiments, to collect *synchronic* (simultaneously observed) data, and to use quantitative measures. These generalizations simply do not hold up to evidence. Examples are available, in fact, to show that traditional knowledge experts are capable of carrying out controlled experiments (see chapter 7, the Cree fisher's experiment on species selectivity of gill nets). Some traditional management systems are based on *synchronic* data collected over large areas, rather than merely *diachronic* data, or a long time-series of local information. An example is the Dene Indian system of monitoring caribou movements over a broad front across the subarctic region of central Canada (see chapter 6).

As well, examples are available to show that quantitative thinking can be part of traditional systems of management. The case in point is Barnston's nineteenth-century estimate of goose populations, which must surely be one of the earliest published uses of traditional knowledge for resource management. Barnston (1861) was one of the first biologists/naturalists to attempt an estimate of wild goose populations in North America. Based on a field survey that indicated that the Cree Indians of James Bay killed some 74,000 geese per year, and an elders' rule of thumb that "for every goose killed, 20 must leave the Bay," Barnston came up with a total goose population figure of 1,200,000 for the region. This is an entirely plausible figure and well within modern population counts, which give a range of one to two million geese that use James Bay as a flyway, including two species, Canada geese (*Branta canadensis*) and lesser snow geese (*Anser caerulescens*).

DIFFERENCES: PHILOSOPHICAL OR POLITICAL?

The relationship between Western science and traditional science is complex, and the differences should not be overemphasized. Considering that there are

a number of different traditions of Western science, and a range of indigenous knowledge systems, caution is necessary in generalizing about differences.
Agrawal (1995a) argues that finding clear demarcations between indigenous and
Western knowledge is futile, given the failure of philosophers of science to find
satisfactory verification criteria to distinguish science from nonscience. Further,
Agrawal (1995b) points out that "it is difficult to adhere to a view of indigenous
and western forms of knowledge being untouched by each other." He examined
supposed differences between indigenous and Western knowledge with respect
to substantive, methodological, and contextual matters and found less than a
clear-cut separation.

According to some scholars, the philosophical differences between the two
kinds of science are not sharply defined; rather, it is our reductionist analysis
that tends to exaggerate the differences (Cordell 1995). Some of these issues
are explored further in the concluding chapter from a political ecology point of
view in which indigenous knowledge is treated as a challenge to the dominant
positivist-reductionist paradigm in Western science. Suffice to point out that
the sources of conflict between practitioners of Western science and traditional
science often have to do with power relationships between Western experts
and aboriginal experts, who have different political agendas and who relate
in different ways to the resource in question. Keith and Simon (1987, 219)
emphasize the issues of authority and legitimacy:

> It is important to understand that conflicts between northern peoples and those seek-
> ing to implement conservation strategies are not merely philosophical. The behavior
> of public officials—most notably of wildlife biologists and marine biologists—in
> conservation debates and disputes often displays a detached arrogance, offensive to
> northern aboriginal peoples by its insistence on Western scientific methods as the
> sole measure of accuracy, and a thinly veiled disdain for traditional knowledge of
> northern people.

Johannes (1989, 5), a biological scientist himself, observes that "the attitudes of many biological scientists and natural resource managers to traditional
knowledge have frequently been dismissive." Consider for example the contrast-
ing views of two tropical forest ecologists, Janzen and Gómez-Pompa. According
to Janzen (1986), only biologists have the competence to decide how the tropical landscape should be conserved. As "representatives of the natural world,"
biologists are "in charge of the future of tropical ecology" and have the expertise to "determine whether tropical agrospace is to be populated" by humans or
whether it should also contain "some islands of the greater nature"—that is, a
landscape without humans. By contrast, Gómez-Pompa and Kaus (1992a) point
out that "the concept of wilderness as untouched land is mostly an urban perception" and has little to do with the reality of tropical forests in which the current
composition of mature vegetation is the legacy of human use over millennia.

> The first step is to recognize that conservation traditions exist in other cultural
> practices and beliefs that are separate from Western traditional conservation. . . .

The view of the white ashes of forest trees that have been felled and burned for
an agricultural plot may appear to an urbanite outsider to be a desecration of the
wilderness, but a farmer may see it as an essential stage of renewal. (Gómez-Pompa
and Kaus 1992a)

As Lewis (1989) comments, "It is difficult for people from 'advanced'
cultures to accept the idea that people from 'primitive' cultures might know
something scientifically significant, or even know more about a subject within
the fields of natural science, in this case fire ecology, than do scientists." These
observations are echoed in the critique of Feyerabend (1987) of the intolerance
of many scientists toward knowledge and insights that originate outside insti-
tutionalized Western science. Scientists tend to dismiss understandings that do
not fit their own; this includes understandings of other scientists using different
paradigms. Feyerabend's analysis provides one explanation for the contemptu-
ous attitude of some scientists toward traditional ecological knowledge. Many
scientists would probably lean toward another explanation: it is the duty of the
scientist to remain skeptical, especially when confronted with an area like traditional knowledge, which does not easily lend itself to scientific verification.
Hence the issue is complex, even if one agrees with Feyerabend and Levi-
Strauss, among others, that Western scientific methodology is merely one way,
and not the only way, to acquire knowledge (Nakashima 1998).

This is not to say that tradition is necessarily virtuous. Obviously, many
traditional practices and belief systems are not, or were not, adaptive. For example, Taoist sages in the third century recommended ingesting cinnabar, a
toxic ore of mercury, for a long life. Some Chinese traditional medicine still
prescribes potions of bear gallbladder, ground-up tiger bone, and rhino horn.
A conservation ethic may be lacking among some traditional groups with detailed environmental knowledge (Redford and Stearman 1993; Callicott 1994).
For example, New Guinea natives possess remarkably detailed knowledge of
plants and animals, but their practices nevertheless have a heavy impact on
the native biota (Diamond 1993). Exaggerated claims of indigenous wisdom
have hurt the study of traditional ecological knowledge (for more on this, see
chapter 9).

As well, misapplications of indigenous knowledge have caused problems.
With regard to overeager and ill-conceived attempts to replicate Mexico's traditional *chinampa* agriculture, Chapin (1988, 17) writes, "we become blinded by
the beauty of the conceptual model [*chinampa*] and lose our bearings, mistaking
it for reality itself. We end up seducing ourselves." That is a caution that is no
doubt relevant to many potential applications. But in general, indigenous knowledge holds much promise for insights and applications, provided care is taken
not to use it out of context. The accomplishments of traditional societies that
carry on to the present in such fields as agriculture are not easily deniable, as
almost all domesticated animal and plant species we depend upon today predate
Western science.

KNOWLEDGE-PRACTICE-BELIEF:
A FRAMEWORK FOR ANALYSIS

Many authors have noted that traditional knowledge may be considered at several levels of analysis, consistent with the description of traditional ecological knowledge as a *knowledge-practice-belief complex*. According to Lewis (1993a), traditional ecological knowledge begins with local knowledge at the level of taxonomic systems and then proceeds to the understanding of processes or functional relationships. Kalland (1994) identifies three levels, starting with empirical or practical knowledge. The second level is "paradigmatic knowledge," or the interpretation of empirical observations to put them in a context, and the third is "institutional knowledge," or knowledge embedded in social institutions. Orlove and Brush (1996), following Nabhan (1985), make a distinction among three levels, different from Kalland's: indigenous environmental knowledge; management practices based on this knowledge; and religious beliefs about and ritual uses of plants and animals. Stevenson's (1996) "interrelated components" of traditional ecological knowledge are also three in number but different again: specific environmental knowledge; knowledge of ecosystem relationships; and a code of ethics governing appropriate human-environmental relationships.

In the present volume, traditional knowledge is considered at four interrelated levels (see figure 1.1). First, there is the local knowledge of animals, plants, soils, and landscape. This level includes knowledge of species identifications and taxonomy, life histories, distributions, and behavior. Based on empirical observations, all such knowledge has obvious survival value. But local knowledge may not be sufficient by itself to ensure the sustainable use of resources. At the second level of analysis, there is a resource management system, one that uses local environmental knowledge *and also includes* an appropriate set of

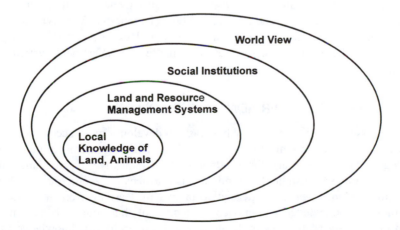

Figure 1.1　Levels of analysis in traditional knowledge and management systems.

practices, tools, and techniques. Those ecological practices require an understanding of ecological processes, such as the functional relationships among key species and an understanding of forest succession. This second level of analysis is comparable to the second level of Orlove and Brush (1996). Third, a traditional system of management requires appropriate social institutions, sets of rules-in-use, and codes of social relationships. For a group of interdependent hunters, fishers, or agriculturists to function effectively, there has to be a social organization for coordination, cooperation, and rule-making to provide social restraints and rule enforcement (Berkes 1989a).

Finally, a fourth level of analysis is the *worldview*, which shapes environmental perception and gives meaning to observations of the environment. It is comparable to Kalland's (1994) "paradigmatic knowledge." As Whitehead (1929) argued, knowledge has components of *observational order* and *conceptual order*. The first of these orders is constituted by our direct perceptions and observations. The second is constituted by our ways of conceiving the universe. The concepts supplied by our conceptual order, the worldview, invariably provide the interpretation of our observations of the world around us. The fourth level includes religion, ethics, and more generally, belief systems, and rounds out the knowledge-practice-belief complex that describes traditional knowledge.

Figure 1.1 shows the four levels of analysis as concentric ellipses, with the management system including local knowledge, the institutional level enveloping the management system, and all three levels embedded within a worldview or belief system. However, it must be emphasized that the four levels are not always distinct. In particular, the management system and the social institution that governs it are often so closely coupled that the distinction between them may seem artificial (Berkes and Folke 1998). One might argue that the management system and the institution are one and the same. It must also be pointed out that there are feedbacks among the levels, and the linkages are in dynamic relationships. Local knowledge may grow; both management systems and institutions may adapt, change, and fall apart and may be renewed. Worldviews shape observations and social institutions but may themselves be affected by changes occurring at the other levels, such as the collapse of management systems, as illustrated in chapter 6.

OBJECTIVES AND OVERVIEW OF THE VOLUME

A major issue of our times is how humans can develop a more acceptable relationship with the environment that supports them. Growing interest in traditional ecological knowledge since the 1980s is perhaps indicative of two things: the need for ecological insights from indigenous practices of resource use, and the need to develop a new ecological ethic in part by learning from the wisdom of traditional knowledge holders. The objective of this volume is to explore both of these ideas together by treating traditional ecological knowledge as a knowledge-practice-belief complex.

The book examines a diversity of traditional knowledge systems and discusses the usefulness of traditional ecological knowledge in terms of providing an understanding, not merely information, which is complementary to scientific ecology. At the same time, the book explores a diversity of relationships that different groups have developed with their environment. Here the approach is evolutionary, with emphasis on the dynamics of relationships between societies and their resources.

The volume is organized in three parts that deal with concepts, practices, and issues, respectively. Chapter 2 builds on the concepts and definitions introduced in this chapter to discuss the emergence of the field of traditional ecological knowledge and its significance, both for indigenous cultures and more broadly for humankind. The intellectual roots of the discipline in ethnobiology and human ecology and the expansion of the meaning and range of traditional knowledge are the subjects of chapter 3.

Part 2 contains substantive material on how traditional ecological knowledge and management systems work. Chapter 4 provides an international context for the practice of traditional knowledge, followed by three chapters on one indigenous society living in the eastern subarctic of North America. Of these, chapter 5 deals with the distinctive Cree Indian worldview of nature and animals and quotes Cree hunters extensively to provide insights into a culture "from the inside." Chapter 6 is about the *actual* behavior of hunters, and it tells the story of how the Cree learned to deal with the experience of declining caribou, based on historical evidence and contemporary observations of cultural evolution in action. Chapter 7 provides a detailed analysis of the Cree system of fishing and its interpretation from the point of view of resource management science, especially as adaptive management.

Part 3 deals with a number of issues regarding the nature and use of traditional ecological knowledge and making indigenous knowledge applicable to contemporary problems. Chapter 8 is about the development of local knowledge and management systems in a nontraditional society, the islands of the West Indies, which provide a laboratory-like setting for the study of local knowledge. Chapter 9 examines critical perspectives of traditional ecological knowledge, its limitations, and the debate over indigenous conservation and explores some possible ways in which conservation ethics develop. Chapter 10 starts with the political ecology of traditional knowledge, examines traditional knowledge as a challenge to the positivist-reductionist paradigm in Western science, and finally discusses the potential of traditional ecological knowledge to inject a measure of ethics into the science of ecology and resource management, thereby restoring the "unity of mind and nature" (Bateson 1979).

Chapter Two

Emergence of the Field

Ethnobiology was for many years an esoteric subject. Work by Conklin and others showing the potential for the application of traditional biology to agricultural development was done nearly half a century ago. Why is it then that traditional ecological knowledge is receiving so much attention lately?

Traditional ecological knowledge transcended academic circles and spilled into the popular media in the 1990s. One sure sign of its popularity was the cover story in *Time* magazine devoted to "Lost tribes, lost knowledge" (Linden 1991). There has been an increasing number of international symposia and workshops, and a rapidly expanding list of books and other publications on the subject. But this in itself cannot be the sole explanation of increasing attention to traditional ecological knowledge. Scholarly discovery of new findings is not a one-way transfer of information from an objective nature to receptive minds. The process is reciprocal and interactive: minds must be sufficiently receptive to receive the information in the first place, in turn stimulating new research and understanding, and these in turn stimulating greater receptivity.

There are probably several factors involved in the increased attention accorded to traditional ecological knowledge: the presence of a dedicated core group of scholars producing not only academic material but also feeding information into international policy circles; parallel developments in other interdisciplinary, policy-relevant fields such as environmental ethics, common property resources, and environmental history; and public dissatisfaction with the outcomes of modernist analysis in fields such as resource conservation and management. Perhaps it is the case that the accumulation of a "critical mass" of knowledge in the subject area happened to coincide with a search by the public, policy makers, scholars, and professionals for *alternatives* to a materialist tradition in ecology and environmental science.

This chapter starts with a review of the emergence of traditional ecological knowledge in the international scene since the 1980s, and its complementary relationship with three interdisciplinary fields: environmental ethics, common property resources, and environmental history. It then proceeds to explore the cultural significance of traditional ecological knowledge for indigenous peoples themselves, and how the subject has necessarily become politically volatile in recent years. Indigenous people have begun to assert control over their knowledge as intellectual property, sometimes related to cultural revitalization movements. The chapter explores the reasons why it is important for indigenous peoples to control the research conducted on their knowledge, and a number of ways in which their voices have been heard. Indigenous control of indigenous knowledge has to be balanced against the need for its practical use for humankind in a number of areas: biological and ecological insights, resource management, protected areas, biodiversity conservation, environmental assessment, social development, and environmental ethics.

EVOLUTION OF INTERNATIONAL INTEREST

Following the classical work in ethnoscience (see chapter 3), a number of international organizations developed an interest in indigenous knowledge. Active from 1984 to 1989, the Traditional Ecological Knowledge Working Group of the International Conservation Union (IUCN) was founded on the idea that traditional ecological knowledge for natural resource conservation and management had been undervalued. The IUCN had already been receptive to the idea (McNeely and Pitt 1985), and the group published a newsletter and stimulated further interest through workshops and publications (Johannes 1989; Freeman and Carbyn 1988; Williams and Baines 1993). Since about 1993, IUCN's Inter-Commission Task Force on Indigenous Peoples has assembled materials to assist governments, development agencies, and other groups to work more effectively with indigenous peoples toward sustainability (Posey and Dutfield 1997).

Several international initiatives were undertaken through the United Nations system. One was UNESCO's program in traditional management systems in coastal marine areas (Johannes et al. 1983; Ruddle and Johannes 1985; Ruddle and Johannes 1990). A second was UNESCO's Man and the Biosphere (MAB) Program, part of which resulted in scientific investigations of traditional systems (e.g. Ramakrishnan 1992). A third was the work undertaken by the United Nations Research Institute for Social Development (UNRISD), which included an examination of the role of indigenous knowledge in the context of participatory management, for example, in protected areas (Pimbert and Pretty 1995).

There is a global network of indigenous knowledge resource centers, focusing mostly on agriculture and sustainable development (rather than ecological knowledge per se). It is coordinated by the Centre for International Research and Advisory Networks (CIRAN/Nuffic), The Hague, Netherlands. Since 1993, CIRAN/Nuffic has also produced a newsletter, *Indigenous Knowledge and Development Monitor*. The predecessor of the *Monitor* was *CIKARD News*, published by the Center for Indigenous Knowledge for Agriculture and Rural Development at Iowa State University. In addition to CIRAN and CIKARD, two other international centers (in Canada and the Netherlands), and two regional centers (in Nigeria and the Philippines), there exists a global network of twenty-seven national centers as of 1998, listed below.

Bangladesh Resource Centre for Indigenous Knowledge
Brazilian Resource Centre for Indigenous Knowledge
Burkina Faso Resource Centre for Indigenous Knowledge
Cameroon Indigenous Knowledge Organisation

Centre for Advanced Research on Indigenous Knowledge Systems, India
Centre for Cosmovisions and Indigenous Knowledge, Ghana
Centre for Indigenous Knowledge, Sierra Leone
Centre for Indigenous Knowledge in Farm and Infrastructure Management,
    Nigeria
Centre for Indigenous Knowledge on Indian Bioresources, India
Centre for Indigenous Knowledge on Population, Resource, and Environ-
    mental Management, Nigeria
Elliniko Resource Centre for Indigenous Knowledge, Greece
Georgia Resource Center for Indigenous Knowledge
Ghana Resource Centre for Indigenous Knowledge
Indigenous Resource Study Centre, Ethiopia
Indonesian Resource Center for Indigenous Knowledge
Interinstitutional Consortium for Indigenous Knowledge, U.S.A.
Kenya Resource Centre for Indigenous Knowledge
Maasai Resource Centre for Indigenous Knowledge, Tanzania
Madagascar Resource Centre for Indigenous Knowledge
Mexican Research, Teaching, and Service Network on Indigenous
    Knowledge
Nigerian Centre for Indigenous Knowledge
Philippine Resource Centre for Sustainable Development and Indigenous
    Knowledge
Russian Resource Centre for Indigenous Knowledge
South African Resource Centre for Indigenous Knowledge
Sri Lanka Resource Centre for Indigenous Knowledge
Uruguayan Resource Centre for Indigenous Knowledge
Venezuelan Resource Secretariat for Indigenous Knowledge
            (Source: *Indigenous Knowledge and Development Monitor.*)

All of these activities have resulted in a substantial and rapidly growing body
of literature. Table 2.1 provides selected examples, by ecosystem and resource
type, from major works dealing with traditional knowledge and resource management systems. Some of these examples are examined in more detail in chapter 4
and elsewhere. In addition to those source books cited in table 2.1, there are a
number of other major works on indigenous knowledge concerned with tropical
forests (Redford and Mansour 1996), grassland or savanna ecosystems (Leach
and Mearns 1996), island ecosystems and coastal resources (Freeman et al.
1991), northern ecosystems (Freeman and Carbyn 1988), and water resources
management (Mabry 1996; Reij et al. 1996). Others deal with conservation
(Morauta et al. 1982; McNeely and Pitt 1985), development (Brokensha et al.
1980; Warren 1991a; Warren et al. 1995), ethnobiology (Alcorn 1984; Berlin
1992), intellectual property rights (Posey and Dutfield 1996), and indigenous
environmental ethics (Knudtson and Suzuki 1992; Anderson 1996). Guides for
indigenous knowledge researchers are also beginning to appear (Grenier 1998).

    This critical mass of literature may be appreciated more fully when consid-
ered alongside other interdisciplinary areas sympathetic to traditional ecological

Table 2.1 Examples of traditional knowledge and resource management systems from selected ecosystems and resource types.

System	Description
Tropical Forests	The Mareng of New Guinea practice shifting cultivation and plant gardens mimicking the diversity of the tropical forest (Rappoport 1984). Similar shifting cultivation (swidden) systems are found in Asia, Africa and South America as well (De Schlippe 1956; Spencer 1966; Redford and Padoch 1992; Ramakrishnan 1992). Groups such as the Runa of Ecuador and the Huastec of tropical Mexico manage the natural process of ecological succession to produce a sequence of food crops and other useful products (Alcorn 1984; Posey and Balee 1989).
Grasslands	Many traditional herding peoples of the African Sahel, such as the Maasai and Turkana of Kenya, have elaborate grazing sequences which involve rotation and alternation of areas used by the herds (Niamir 1990). The Fulani of northern Nigeria say that they must move at least four times in a season to prevent overuse. Many herders move their animals to wet season pastures at the edge of the Sahara, mimicking the seasonal migration of wild ungulates. The Il Chamus of Kenya use two types of dry season reserves successively depending on the elders' decisions (Niamir 1990).
Mountains	Terracing as a soil and water conservation method seems to have been independently discovered by mountain cultures of the Mediterranean, South Asia, Philippines, South America, and perhaps elsewhere. Communal pasture use systems in the Swiss Alps follow traditions at least five centuries old (Netting 1981). Migratory herders who use high mountain pastures in the summer months and who return to lower elevations in the winter are found in many mountainous regions worldwide (Galaty and Johnson 1990).
Temperate Ecosystems	Tribes of the Pacific Northwest of North America maintained a diversity of access control mechanisms, rules for proper harvesting behavior, and rituals to regulate resource use, for example, in the opening dates of the salmon fishing season (Williams and Hunn 1982). Resource management practices of native Californians included land tenure systems and tribal territories, soil and water conservation techniques, and the use of fire for landscape management and succession control (Blackburn and Anderson 1993).

(continued)

Table 2.1 (*Continued*)

System	Description
Tropical Fisheries	Customary restrictions by species, seasons and area help prevent overfishing in many parts of Oceania (Klee 1980). An overharvested resource was declared *tabu* until it was ready to harvest again (Anderson 1996). A diversity of locally adapted reef and lagoon tenure systems are found throughout the Asia Pacific (Ruddle and Johannes 1990; Freeman et al. 1991). The traditional knowledge held by master fishers of Palau, Micronesia, is in some ways more detailed than the published scientific information available to tropical marine ecologists (Johannes 1981).
Waters	Temple priests and rice farmers of Bali, Indonesia, have devised a water distribution system called *subak*. These *subaks* are not autonomous local units but part of a water temple system that manages an entire regional terrace ecosystem. The effectiveness of the *subak* system has been demonstrated by the application of computer modelling techniques (Lansing 1991). Traditional irrigation systems include the *zanjera* of the Philippines, a derivative of the *huerta* irrigation system presently in use in Spain that dates back to ancient Arabic rule in Iberia (Maass and Anderson 1986).

knowledge. This chapter examines three such areas. One of these fields is environmental ethics (Callicott 1989; Engel and Engel 1990; Callicott 1994), which developed a discussion around the subject of indigenous cultures, especially those of American Indian peoples, as a possible source of inspiration for a new environmental ethic (Callicott 1982; Hughes 1983). However, exaggerated claims of American Indians as "the original ecologists" invited refutations and caused scholars to become skeptical of source materials and interpretation. A case in point is the speech of Chief Seattle, which was a hoax knowingly perpetrated by some (see chapter 9 for the story). Scholarly skepticism gave way to the acceptance of a new subfield but only after many comparative studies were carried out.

Many of these studies documented the existence of a generalized reverence for life, a "community-of-beings" worldview, representing the wisdom of many cultures in many parts of the world (White 1967; Gadgil and Berkes 1991; Worster 1988; Callicott 1994), yet certainly not a universal traditional ethic (Dymond 1933; Callicott 1994). Another stream of the literature emphasized religion, or religious ethics, as a prescription for encoding wise management (Rappaport 1979). Anderson (1996, 166) argued that "all traditional societies that have succeeded in managing resources well, over time, have done it in part through religious or ritual representation of resource management. The key point is not religion *per se*, but the use of emotionally powerful cultural symbols to sell particular moral codes and management systems."

A second related field is common property resources, and the investigation of the role of traditional communal property institutions in resource management. A large literature base developed in this area, mainly from the mid-1980s onward, documenting that some traditional social organization and property-rights systems were capable of avoiding the dilemma of the "tragedy of the commons" and leading to sustainable resource use (McCay and Acheson 1987; Berkes 1989a; Bromley 1992). Traditional knowledge was initially of secondary, perhaps even marginal, interest in the commons literature. The primary concerns were institutions and property rights relations. There was a need, however, to document property rights systems that had persisted over historical time, that is, those that were sustainable. Two schools of thought developed on historically rooted common property institutions.

Perhaps not wishing to get embroiled in the debate over the semantics of the term *traditional* (see chapter 1), one school of thought chose its examples from Western societies. For example, the book by Ostrom (1990) relies on examples such as the *huerta* irrigation system in Spain (Maass and Anderson 1986) and the Swiss Alpine commons (Netting 1981), both of which have historical roots that extend well beyond five hundred years. Other literature, however, concentrated on traditional knowledge and management systems of indigenous peoples, not as mere "traditions" frozen in time as anthropological curiosities but as *adaptive responses* that evolved over time (e.g. Johannes 1978; Berkes 1989b; Dei 1992). Recognizing traditional knowledge as the source of ecological adaptations, some studies explicitly and deliberately sought for examples of non-Western resource management systems for their insights (Colding and Folke 1997). The rationale was that indigenous groups may offer practices and adaptations that may expand the range of the rather limited set of Western resource management prescriptions, with its roots in the mechanistic, linear Newtonian science. Thus, the search for alternatives for resource management came to include traditional management systems and their common-property institutions (Berkes and Folke 1998).

A third related field is environmental history, which started to develop a dynamic view of ecological change, with a fresh look at the root causes of environmental problems (Cronon 1983; Turner et al. 1990). Discussion centered on such themes as how, after the great transformation generated by the industrial revolution, ecological relations became more destructive as they became more distant, providing a larger context for the appreciation of traditional knowledge and worldview (Worster 1988). Environmental historians developed interests not only in interpreting ancient landscapes but also in making ecological sense of the ancient peoples and their resource use practices that *resulted* in these landscapes. For example, Cronon's (1983) study of the colonization of New England states and European-Indian relationships conveyed a sense of two competing economies. One of them, the Indian economy, took what we would today call an ecosystem approach and treated the environment as a portfolio of resources and services that supported livelihoods. The other economy, that of the colonists, turned the environment into commodities, exploited sequentially one resource after another following market demands, and caused depletion and environmental degradation in the process.

Similar inquiries in environmental history from diverse geographic and cultural areas, as far apart as California (Blackburn and Anderson 1993) and India, revealed ecologically sensible traditional practices being displaced by the push for commodity production. For example, throughout much of India, forest resource use followed a sequence of exploitation from the more valuable (such as teak) to the less valuable species, and from the more accessible to the less accessible areas (Gadgil and Guha 1992). Under colonial rule, there was a general change from the production of a wide variety of goods for local needs to the production of a few commodities for export (Gadgil and Thapar 1990).

In summary, the development of interest in traditional ecological knowledge is related to major changes in perspectives among scholars, policy makers, and the public. Dissatisfaction with a science that places an artificial divide between mind and nature (Bateson 1972), as discussed in chapter 1, and a reaction to the materialist tradition in ecology, economics, and resource management (Norgaard 1994) are part of the driving forces. Interest in traditional ecological knowledge can be interpreted as a search for alternatives in human-environment relationships and in resource stewardship (Berkes and Folke 1998).

CULTURAL AND POLITICAL SIGNIFICANCE FOR INDIGENOUS PEOPLES

In searching for alternative solutions for global issues, there is always the risk of abstracting traditional knowledge from its cultural and historical context. Ecological knowledge held by a group is only one aspect of their overall culture. However, in contrast to Western science, there is little or no separation between such knowledge and other spheres of culture. Knowledge of the biophysical environment is embedded in the social environment. Many researchers in the past have tried to document traditional ecological knowledge for the sake of cultural preservation. It has been persuasively argued, though, that traditional ecological knowledge can only be conserved in situ; much of indigenous knowledge makes no sense when abstracted from the culture of which it is a part (Agrawal 1995a, 1995b). The questions of the cultural and political significance of traditional ecological knowledge involve a series of linked issues, including worldviews, cultural survival, ownership of knowledge or intellectual property rights, empowerment, local control of land and resources, cultural revitalization, and self-determination.

Traditional ecological knowledge may best be seen as an integrated package that includes the local knowledge and classification systems of the groups in question; their environmental practices and management systems, if any; their social institutions that provide the rules for management systems such as tribal territories; and their worldviews that constitute the ideological or ethical basis of these systems. Among many North American aboriginal groups, hunting is not merely the mechanical use of the local knowledge of animals and the environment to obtain food, it is a religious activity (Preston 1975; Tanner 1979). Speck (1935, 72) said it well many decades ago: "To the Montagnais-Naskapi ... the animals of the forest, the tundra, and the waters of the interior and the coast exist in a specific relation. They have become the objects of engrossing magico-religious activity, for to them hunting is a holy occupation."

Even for contemporary hunters in northern Manitoba, long acculturated and converted to Christianity, hunting continues as a spiritual activity in which "you got to keep it holy" (Brightman 1993, 1). The use of traditional ecological knowledge to make a livelihood sustains the distinctive cultural ideology of the group, as well as the very important social relationships within the group. It helps maintain social identity and provides a source of values. Social relations of cooperation, sharing, gift-giving, gender-role maintenance, and all-important reciprocity (with both humans and animals) are part of what Fienup-Riordan (1990) calls "the broader question of the relation of ideology to adaptation." Knowledge, values, and identity are transferred to succeeding generations through the annual, cyclical repetition of livelihood activities based on traditional ecological knowledge (Freeman 1993a).

Just as the hunt carries symbolic meaning for hunting groups of North American aboriginal peoples, the shifting cultivation (*milpa*) cycle carries symbolic meaning for the indigenous people of Northern Mexico (Alcorn 1984). For the aboriginal people of Australia, ancestors have provided songs, dances, narratives, ceremonies, sacred objects, and paintings in order to maintain the bond between land, people, and totemic beings (Wilkins 1993). "The landscape painting is the country itself," as phrased by traditional elder Wenten Rubuntja (see box 2.1). The spiritual domain of dreaming can, however, also serve a conservation function, as in the case of red kangaroo taboo sites in Central Australia (Newsome 1980).

It is clear enough from the above considerations that the broader social and cultural aspect of traditional knowledge is a very serious matter for many indigenous peoples. Partially for this reason, dealing with traditional ecological knowledge has become politically volatile: knowledge is an intensely political matter. "Although studies on indigenous peoples, societies and communities continue to be carried out, researchers no longer have *carte blanche* to work independently from the people themselves. Nor can they treat the data that they collect as if it was a value-free product which can be extracted and used at will" (Inuit Circumpolar Conference 1992).

Politically organized groups of indigenous peoples are beginning to assert control over their knowledge systems for at least two reasons. First, especially in the area of medicinal plants, some indigenous groups have seen how their knowledge and biological resources have been turned by others into profit-making

BOX 2.1
"ONE FLESH–ONE SPIRIT–ONE COUNTRY–ONE DREAMING":
THE AUSTRALIAN ABORIGINAL CONCEPTION OF THE ENVIRONMENT

Wilkins explains that the Dreamtime is the unifying thread binding social relations, land, and totemism among the Australian Aborigines. *Dreamtime* is the Aboriginal concept that refers to the spiritual domain or dimension in which ancestral totemic beings arose from beneath the uninhabited and unshaped land and, through their actions and movements and their very existence, created, and continue the creation of, the physical, spiritual, cultural, and social world that now exists and that must be perpetuated through continuing all the practices handed down from the ancestors during this time. Because the land is a living record of Dreamtime events, Aborigines perceive their environment in a very different way from Anglo-Australians. For example, in discussing Aboriginal art, Sutton goes so far as to claim that for Aboriginal Australians "there is no geography without meaning or without history. . . . The land is already a narrative—an artifact of intellect—before people represent it."

One should question, Wilkins points out, whether Australian Aborigines themselves would articulate these matters in the same way as anthropologists have, and, he says, it is very clear that they do. Wenten Rubuntja, a respected elder within the Mparntwe Arrernte community and a well-known artist, makes the following pertinent observations:

These rocks we've got to worship. The rainmakers, the caterpillars, or the kangaroos, emus, we got to pray for it. In this country, and every other country, we were looking at worship, before the settlers came here. When the settlers came here they started cutting trees. We shouldn't be cutting trees. We shouldn't be getting rocks, making holes in the country. . . . Country was pretty and country was *tywerrenge* (something associated with sacred ceremonies; it can also refer to land itself). We don't forget about *tywerrenge*. We still keep going, singing, and ceremonies all the time, singing all the time and painting all the time, shield and dancing. What belongs to this country, belongs to the Aboriginal culture, we never lost, keep going ahead. . . . The landscape painting is the country itself, with *tywerrenge* himself. *Tywerrenge* and songs come out of the body of the country. See all this one, this little waterhole. We're not like whitefella who can take a photograph and say what pretty country it is; we've got the song to sing for that country.

Source: Wilkins 1993, 73

commodities that can be bought and sold. Thus, they have started to ask the question of who benefits from the recording of the knowledge, and to investigate how they themselves can control and market their knowledge and products (Posey and Dutfield 1996; Brush and Stabinsky 1996).

Secondly, indigenous knowledge has become a symbol for many groups representing the regaining of control over their cultural information. Reclaiming their indigenous knowledge has become a major strategy in many parts of the world for revitalization movements, defined as "a deliberate, organized, conscious effort by members of a society to construct a more satisfying culture" (Wallace 1956). For example, in Canada, the Berger Commission Inquiry, which helped articulate aboriginal views and lent credibility to local knowledge and management traditions, contributed to the development of a revitalization movement (Zachariah 1984). Some of the major aboriginal cultural groups in

Alaska and Northern Canada, including the Inuit, Dene, and Cree, have been carrying out their own traditional knowledge studies (e.g. Dene Cultural Institute 1993) as part of an effort to strengthen their culture and assert their land rights. Chapter 10 deals with some of the experiences in using traditional knowledge to prepare land and resource claims by aboriginal groups. Such revitalization is not merely a cultural exercise; it is about empowerment and political control.

A case in point comes from Hawaii, where the native revitalization movement has allegedly "re-invented traditional culture" to suit its political needs (Keesing 1989). According to this view, authentic, pre-contact Hawaiian culture is largely irretrievable, having been demolished by colonialism. The new cultural identity being created is "invented" through the use of symbols and values, but the resulting version of Hawaiian culture does not correspond to any specific time period (Linnekin 1983). These views have been challenged by some scholars: "As there are no longer any real Hawaiians, culture specialists are the only possible custodians of their former way of life," retorts Friedman (1992), and he proceeds to point out that the values in question are in the "lived experience" of contemporary rural Hawaii.

QUESTIONS OF OWNERSHIP AND INTELLECTUAL PROPERTY RIGHTS

As pointed out by Posey and Dutfield (1997, 75), indigenous knowledge is treated by most legal systems as part of the "public domain"; it can be used by any person or corporation as soon as it leaves the community. When researchers publish the results of their work, they may place sensitive indigenous knowledge in the public domain, unwittingly passing it to corporations who can use it for financial gain without any obligation to return benefits to the community (Posey and Dutfield 1996, 1997).

Until recent years, the study of traditional knowledge was carried out by Western scientists and social scientists, mostly ethnobiologists and human ecologists (see chapter 3). It is only relatively recently that indigenous peoples have begun to assert their control over their traditional knowledge. It is related to the significance of the information, as well as to a growing sense among these groups that research by outsiders has not served them well over the years. For example, Said (1994) has pointed out that Western values have continued to permeate historical and ethnographic works on non-Western peoples, raising fundamental questions about how we can actually engage with and comprehend other societies and traditions. One way is to listen to indigenous peoples themselves as they intervene and challenge the academic discourse about themselves; but there are at least three other ways.

The use of traditional knowledge projects, community-initiated and carried out by aboriginal groups themselves, is perhaps the most common way in which indigenous voices are being heard. The book by Johnson (1992) is an attempt to capture the experience of a number of community-based and community-sponsored traditional knowledge studies. Examples of such studies are diverse and include the Darién indigenous lands project in Panama (González et al. 1995); the James Bay Cree trappers' traditional knowledge project in Quebec (Bearskin et al. 1989); the Mushkegowuk Cree land and resource use project in Ontario (Berkes et al. 1994, 1995); and the Marovo Project in Solomon Islands (Baines and Hviding 1993). Some of these projects are described in chapter 10 as examples of the contribution of indigenous knowledge to political empowerment.

A second way that indigenous voices are heard involves the development of indigenous scholarship to provide a direct voice, as done for example by Barreiro (1992), Brascoupe (1992), Holmes (1996), Ravuvu (1987), Roberts et al. (1995), Taiepa et al. (1997), Wavey (1993), Cordova (1997), Collier and Vegh (1998), and others. The community-based cultural documentation projects from Alaska and Northern Canada, as reported in *The Northern Review*, provide particularly strong examples of social action combined with indigenous scholarship (Cruikshank 1995). A third way involves the recording of indigenous knowledge, from the holders of such knowledge, without interpretation. These can then be published on their own or together with Western interpretations, as done, for example, by Majnep and Bulmer (1977), Beaucage et al. (1997), McDonald et al. (1997), and Monseau (1998).

Holmes (1996) provides a powerful voice regarding the significance of indigenous peoples researching their own knowledge and communicating it in a culturally appropriate format. She deals with traditional knowledge as "lived knowledge" based on an "ancestry of experience" of the elders *and the researcher*, and she uses stories as an elder does in her teachings, creating relationships and establishing personal meaning. The concept of ancestry of experience is a significant notion especially for a native Hawaiian because of the importance of genealogy in defining who and what a person is.

Holmes's approach to indigenous knowledge is fundamentally different from the research methodologies of most academics. As outsiders, they tend not to deal with indigenous knowledge as lived knowledge, they lack an ancestry of experience, and they often do not establish meaning by creating relationships. Instead, the researcher often "unpacks" the received knowledge, processing and "reformatting" it in accordance with her or his own cosmology, says Holmes, appropriating knowledge, if not appropriating voice. But such research leaves Western scholars unable "to understand indigenous values or cosmologies, except as 'myth' or 'data'" (Holmes 1996, 380). Indigenous knowledge further suffers because of the way it is communicated by the researcher and because the reader/receiver is often ill-equipped to understand it. Holmes (1996, 383) reflects: "when people hear or read voices of Native Peoples, they can't always attach those voices to particular *practices*. These voices most often arrive through text, not experience, and therefore without everyday referents." If indigenous knowledge is lived knowledge, the reader, lacking the ancestry of experience, will for example "read" Black Elk (Neihardt 1932; Brown 1953) but not hear him.

Holmes's challenge to the study of indigenous knowledge touches on fundamental paradoxes. If only indigenous peoples are truly competent to research indigenous knowledge, then most research would cease. This will solve the problem of knowledge and voice appropriation, but it would also eliminate the bridges being built between Western and non-Western knowledge (and among aboriginal groups themselves). Similarly, for most readers written texts necessarily lack everyday referents, that is, lived experience that validates the lived knowledge. But if this means they are devoid of meaning, then all writings on indigenous knowledge are essentially irrelevant or futile.

Perhaps more constructively, one can define three guiding principles as inspired by Holmes's critique. First, the study of indigenous knowledge always needs to be participatory; it cannot be done without the collaboration of indigenous peoples as equals (Holmes 1996, 376). Second, it helps to remember that the written accounts of indigenous knowledge, any indigenous knowledge, will necessarily be incomplete, unless the reader has lived that knowledge and can supply her or his own referents. *The written page will never be an adequate format for the teaching of indigenous knowledge.* It can only be taught properly on the land. Third, not only the researcher but also the reader of indigenous knowledge has to be prepared to question her or his own values, to be reflexive, and to be prepared to "unpack" one's own values before unpacking those of the indigenous culture in question. As such, cross-cultural sensitivity is at the heart of all research and understanding of traditional knowledge.

PRACTICAL SIGNIFICANCE AS COMMON HERITAGE OF HUMANKIND

The need for indigenous groups to control their knowledge has to be balanced against the need to share their insights as part of the common heritage of humankind. There are tangible and practical reasons why traditional ecological knowledge is so important for the rest of the world as well, quite apart from the ethical imperative of conserving cultural diversity. Many of the following points, of course, directly concern local peoples as well. The following list is adapted from various sources (IUCN 1986; Healy 1993; Berkes 1993). The seven areas identified here are not meant to be exclusive categories; they meld into each other. They deal with aspects of ecology and resource management only and exclude other areas of indigenous knowledge, such as pharmacological or medical applications.

Traditional ecological knowledge is critical for:

- Biological information and ecological insights
- Resource management
- Conservation of protected areas
- Biodiversity conservation
- Environmental assessment

- Social development
- Environmental ethics.

We look at each of these areas in detail below.

Traditional Knowledge for Biological Information and Ecological Insights

New scientific knowledge can be derived from perceptive investigations of traditional knowledge, for example, with respect to species identifications and crop varieties, natural history, behavior, and life cycles. Classic examples of biological and ecological insights from traditional knowledge include the "three sisters" agriculture, as it is called by the Iroquois, a sustainable agricultural system of corn, beans, and squash widely practiced from the United States to Chile (Barreiro 1992), and traditional marine lagoon fish polyculture systems (Johannes et al. 1983). A telling example of the level of detail available from indigenous knowledge is provided by Johannes, an expert on tropical reef fish ecology. When Johannes was working with fishers in the tiny archipelago of Palau in the Pacific in the mid-1970s, he obtained from local fishers the months and periods as well as the precise locations of spawning aggregations of some fifty-five species of fish that followed the moon as a cue for spawning. This local knowledge amounted to more than twice as many species of fish exhibiting lunar spawning periodicity as had been described by scientists in the *entire world* at that time (Johannes 1981).

Other examples of traditional ecological insights come from the Canadian North, where local knowledge often far exceeds that of the Western scientist who has a seasonally limited research period. It is common among northern field researchers to draw upon the knowledge of their local assistants. Systematic recording and acknowledging of such knowledge goes back to the work of Freeman (1970), who supplemented his own observations and scientific information with local knowledge from the Inuit of Belcher Islands to summarize the biology of fifty-six species of Hudson Bay birds. In addition to biological information on life cycles and distributions, scientists have also noted Inuit ecological knowledge of predation, competition, and mutualistic interactions among Arctic species. Examples include the Inuit knowledge of the interactions of narwhal (*Monodon monoceros*) and killer whales (*Orcinus orca*), and of eider ducks and great black-backed gulls (Freeman 1993b). Until the 1940s, the world of science did not even know that there was a major population of eider ducks (*Somateria mollissima sedentaria*) that lived year-round in Hudson Bay. Nakashima (1993) pointed out that as late as the 1960s, the standard book on the birds of Labrador stated that "the only authority for the wintering of this eider on the open waters of Hudson Bay" were the Inuit (Eskimo), a situation grudgingly described by the book as "acceptable for the present." The very considerable Inuit knowledge on the eider was finally recorded by Nakashima in what is probably the only Ph.D. thesis in traditional knowledge that concentrates on a single species (Nakashima 1991).

Traditional Knowledge for Resource Management

The current interest in indigenous peoples as resource managers goes back to the early 1980s (Klee 1980; Williams and Hunn 1982), and the use of traditional knowledge for resource management at least to the 1860s (see the example of using Cree hunters' rule of thumb to estimate goose populations by Barnston, 1861, cited in chapter 1). Much of the controversy about the resource management capability (as well as ecological wisdom) of traditional peoples stems from the fact that these societies have been impacted by social and economic changes that have resulted in loss of knowledge and altered practices. For example, the incorporation of practices favoring individual decision-making (as opposed to traditional cooperative hunting) among a group of Kotzebue Sound Inupiat in Alaska has coincided with sharp declines in the numbers of beluga whales (Morseth 1997). As Polunin (1984) puts it, traditional management systems are often overtaken by events.

However, many resource use practices consistent with sustainability do remain and can be used for resource management. For example, Duffield et al. (1998) demonstrate the feasibility of using local knowledge to construct indicators to monitor the sustainability of mountain environments. Another practical application of local knowledge comes from Newfoundland. Hutchings (1998, 1) says, "the collapse of Newfoundland's northern cod fishery may have been predicted by changes in fishing practices and fishing effort by Newfoundland inshore and offshore fishers." Neis et al. (1996) conclude that information from fishers, combined with scientific data, (1) can contribute to knowledge of cod behavior, ecology, and stock structure, (2) help understand trends in catchability, (3) inform future research, (4) increase awareness of stock abundance inshore, and (5) increase awareness of interactions among different fisheries (e.g., juvenile cod by-catch in the capelin fishery).

The complementarity of local knowledge and scientific knowledge is an increasingly important theme in resource management. For example, there is an emerging consensus in Oceania that, given the scarcity of scientific knowledge and research resources, alternative coastal fishery models are needed. These models involve the use of local knowledge to substitute for, or complement, scientific knowledge (Hunt 1997; Johannes 1998). The use of traditional ecological knowledge in an experimental way to learn from management interventions, with subsequent policy changes, makes it a potential tool for Adaptive Management. The similarities between Adaptive Management (a branch of applied ecology) and traditional management are explored in chapters 4, 6, 7, and 9. Both indigenous knowledge and Adaptive Management focus on feedbacks and the maintenance of ecological resilience (Alcorn 1989; Holling et al. 1995). These observations compelled us to ask: How can resource management be improved by supplementing scientific data with local and traditional knowledge? How can information from resource users themselves broaden the base of knowledge necessary for decision-making for sustainable resource use (Berkes and Folke 1998)? The present volume is in part a follow-up to these questions.

Traditional Knowledge for Conservation of Protected Areas

Conservation programs often need to encompass a broader view of the role of local people of the area, their knowledge and interests, and their social and economic needs. The World Conservation Union (IUCN) has been looking into conservation with people at least since the early 1980s (McNeely and Pitt 1985), and protected area management has increasingly become a social science (McNeely 1996). Protected areas may be set up to allow resident communities to continue their traditional lifestyles, with the benefits of conservation accruing to them. Especially where the local community jointly manages such a protected area, the use of traditional knowledge for conservation is likely to be very effective (Berkes et al. 1995). Hence there has been a growing interest in co-management, a partnership between government agencies, local communities, and others, in the sharing of authority and responsibility of management, also called collaborative management or joint management (Borrini-Feyerabend 1996).

Creating stakes in conservation facilitates the use of traditional ecological knowledge for conservation, provided of course that authorities are willing to use local insights in the true spirit of collaboration. For example, in the Keoladeo National Park in India, the local population argued for years that the grazing of water buffalo in the park was consistent with conservation objectives and should be allowed. After many years of strife between park authorities and local people, a long-term study by the Bombay Natural History Society finally corroborated the local view, showing that the grazing of water buffalo helped counter the tendency of the wetland to turn into grassland. The ban on grazing had adversely affected the wetland and the park, which was famous for its bird life, and the solution was to return to water buffalo grazing once again (Kothari 1996; Pimbert and Gujja 1997). Such success stories are not many. In various regions such as Latin America, the presence of indigenous peoples in protected areas is a matter of considerable controversy (see chapter 9).

Traditional Knowledge for Biodiversity Conservation

Some traditional knowledge and resource management systems are of special interest because they seem to allow less intensive use and greater biological diversity. Many of the areas of the world that contain high levels of biodiversity are also the areas in which indigenous peoples are found (Posey and Dutfield 1997). This relationship may not be accidental: many indigenous resource use practices tend to conserve biodiversity, as traditional groups rely on a portfolio of resources for their livelihoods, rather than concentrating on a few species for cash income and exports. This contrast has been observed in the early colonization of the United States (Cronon 1983), and in more recent cases, in the colonization and "modernization" of areas previously controlled by indigenous groups (Oldfield and Alcorn 1991). Due to loss of control of resources, breakdown of land use and knowledge systems, population growth, commercialization, and technology change, many traditional and rural peoples of the world cannot be considered conservationists. However, many of these groups do still retain elements of resource use practices that are consistent with the protection of biodiversity (Berkes et al. 1995). For example, Poffenberger et al. (1996) mapped tribal areas in India and areas of remaining forest cover. With the exception of semiarid lands (where there is no forest anyway), the authors found a close correlation between the two.

The book *Global Biodiversity Assessment* recognizes that "where indigenous peoples have depended on local environments for the provision of resources over long periods of time, they have often developed a stake in conserving biodiversity" (Heywood 1995, 1017). Borrowing from Gadgil et al. (1993), the volume includes examples of traditional practices that conserve biodiversity: maintaining sacred areas and other ecological refugia; protecting selected species through taboos and other social mechanisms; protecting critical life history stages; and using the guidance of local experts as environmental stewards. As well, the volume provides examples from a variety of ecosystem types of multispecies, multiple-use resource systems that protect and enhance local biodiversity at the level of varieties, species, and landscapes.

Indigenous conservation, where it exists, is not based on the same ethic as modern conservation but seems generally consistent with it. For example, Colding and Folke (1997) analyzed available data on specific-species taboos and found that about one-third of the identified taboos prohibited the use of a species listed as threatened. Colding (1998) further explored the adaptiveness of taboo practices by modeling. Remnants of sacred areas are found in many regions of the world, and even at sea (McClanahan et al. 1997). However, there is a great deal of controversy on the questions of whether indigenous peoples' agendas are completely consistent with biodiversity conservation objectives, and whether any human use compromises biodiversity (Redford and Stearman 1993; also see chapter 9 in this volume).

Traditional Knowledge for Environmental Assessment

People who are dependent on local resources for their livelihood are often able to assess the true costs and benefits of development better than any evaluator coming from the outside. As Chief Robert Wavey (1993) of northern Manitoba puts it, "people retain a record of what the land and resources have provided for generations, and the Aboriginal people are the first to see the changes." Their time-tested, in-depth local knowledge can be useful in compiling inventories of elements of local ecosystems. Such knowledge and local conceptions of systems are needed to pinpoint the valued ecosystem components in the assessment of environmental impacts of a proposed development. As well, knowledge of the local social system is essential to any social impact assessment (Sadler and Boothroyd 1994). Given that many development projects push through before there is time for the proper completion of scientific studies, the use of local knowledge becomes even more important (Berkes and Henley 1997).

However, some of this information, such as the details of land use, are considered proprietary knowledge. The last thing an aboriginal group wants to do is advertise to the rest of the world its prime hunting and fishing locations! Reflecting on the Manitoba experience, Wavey (1993) argues that indigenous control of traditional land-use information is fundamental to maintaining the proprietary nature of such information and the way in which it is put to use in environmental assessment. In any case, there is no reason to think that an indigenous group will want to participate in the assessment of a project they consider to be damaging, if they have reason to believe that their participation will not result in any fundamental changes to the project. For example, the Cree refused to participate in the assessment of the James Bay II (Great Whale) hydroelectric development project in the early 1990s as a way of registering their opposition and withholding assent.

Even if they are willing to participate, the limited experience in this area shows that indigenous people may well have very different ideas about what constitutes a proper impact assessment (Sadler and Boothroyd 1994; Stevenson 1996; see also chapter 10, below). A major study carried out by the indigenous peoples of the Hudson Bay bioregion, and involving twenty-seven Inuit and Cree communities around the bay, focussed on the cumulative impacts of a number of development projects (McDonald et al. 1997), impacts that government departments were having difficulty dealing with because of jurisdictional barriers and political sensitivities.

Traditional Knowledge for Social Development

The use of traditional knowledge may benefit development by providing more realistic evaluations of local needs, environmental constraints, and natural resource production systems. Involvement of the local people in the planning process improves the chance of success of development (Warren 1991b; Warren et al. 1995). The use of traditional knowledge in development has a relatively short history (Brokensha et al. 1980; Chambers 1983). Initially, "tradition" was seen by economists and development planners as an impediment, an unwillingness to break with the past to embrace scientifically developed agricultural and other improvements. However, as some of the unforeseen consequences of agricultural modernization (such as loss of crop biodiversity) became clear, interest in traditional knowledge was renewed. For example, Richards (1985) regarded indigenous knowledge as a neglected and marginalized resource that had a legitimate place in development programs. Putting indigenous knowledge to work, Richards argued, could result in a "peoples' science," a decentralized, participatory research and development system that would support rather than displace local initiative. Such populist science could then generate an indigenous agricultural revolution (Richards 1985).

A significant finding was that many rural groups were reluctant to abandon traditional practices because these practices were, in retrospect, more sustainable ecologically, economically, and socially. A case in point is the adoption of monocultures of high-yield crop varieties. They produce well in good years but may completely fail in bad. This is a risk that small farmers are reluctant to take. Such findings have been interpreted in terms of risk-aversion. Many traditional practices were adaptive precisely because they reduced the risk of securing a livelihood. Poor people tended to be risk-averse, especially when the margin of safety was small (Chambers 1983). Traditional knowledge has come to be used as a major tool among practitioners who hold that development must be woven around people and not the other way around. It has been of more interest to those involved in social development and community development (Warren et al. 1995), rather than purely economic development.

The use of traditional knowledge has great potential also in designing strategies for culturally sustainable development (Preston et al. 1995). The work of Butz (1996) identifying symbolic values of herding yaks at Pamir pastures provides an example of sustainability planning that takes into account local worldviews. Yak herding not only carries instrumental values, such as milk and meat production, but also symbolic (or noninstrumental) values, such as those pertaining to self-identity, spiritual renewal, a role in local myth and history, ritual significance, and a sense of place.

Traditional Knowledge for Environmental Ethics

The concept of an external "environment" analytically separate from human society can be traced to post-Enlightenment thought in the West (Glacken 1967). It is the basis of the Cartesian dualism of mind versus matter, and hence humans versus environment (Bateson 1972, 337). "Man's dominion over nature," the official ideology of conventional Western science that aims to control the environment, has its philosophical background in Cartesian dualism. By contrast, traditional belief systems of many indigenous groups incorporate the idea that humans are part of the natural environment. As environmental ethicists discuss the re-establishment of this notion in modern society, it is worth recalling that the idea was once widespread throughout the world, until the period of the Enlightenment.

The wisdom of traditional knowledge is consistent with ecology and environmental ethics on the question of the control of nature. The relationship

---

BOX 2.2
DESIGNING ECONOMIC POLICY CONSISTENT WITH
AMERINDIAN VALUES: THE MENOMINEE

"The Menominee employ principles of forest management that illustrate respect. They have given their forest manager the following management guidelines:

1 Produce trees with both quality and quantity.
2 Don't put all the eggs in one basket.
3 Remember that we are borrowing the forest from our grandchildren.

"The first two principles illustrate community and connectedness. Production of quality and quantity requires growing trees to large size for quality, which compromises quantity production. The large stock of older trees indicates that they are not high-graded, which cuts out all of the high-quality trees at once. All species are supported under the principle of keeping the eggs (forest productivity) in different baskets (species). The idea that the forest is borrowed from future generations, expresses the seventh-generation principle."

Source: Trosper 1995, 84

---

may be characterized in terms of a peaceful coexistence of humans-in-nature, or "flowing with nature," as in Taoist philosophy. Perhaps more to the point, some traditional ecology sees humans and nature in a symbiotic relationship, with mutual obligations (see chapter 5). These mutual obligations may lead to "respect," which is a central idea in the relations of many Amerindian groups with nature (Callicott 1994; Trosper 1995).

The field of environmental ethics has received much inspiration from indigenous societies, but details are subject to much debate (e.g., Cordova 1997). At the level of the individual, Suzuki and McConnell (1997) argue for the need to rediscover and live the spiritual connection to nature. As well, there have been various attempts to incorporate ethical values from traditional systems into policies in contemporary society. In an innovative application, Trosper (1995) attempted to identify economic policies consistent with the values of Menominee Indians, for forestry planning (see box 2.2).

Chapter Three

Intellectual Roots of Traditional Ecological Knowledge

Traditional ecological knowledge arose from two separate approaches, ethnoscience and human ecology. The first deals largely with folk taxonomies, ethnobotanical and ethnozoological classifications, of plants and animals. The second deals with indigenous understandings of natural processes, including the relationships of humans with animals, plants, and various environmental and sometimes supernatural factors. The two approaches have been joined by others emphasizing applications of traditional ecological knowledge to contemporary problems such as conservation, resource management, and sustainable development. The various approaches have intellectually distinct roots but are increasingly used together as traditional ecological knowledge matures as a discipline.

Thomas Huxley (as quoted by Gould 1980), once defined science as "organized common sense." When I started my human ecology and fisheries studies in James Bay in the 1970s, I discovered that Cree fishers and I had a great deal in common in terms of interests and knowledge. I was amazed at the detail of their knowledge of seasonal cycles, distributions, and movements of fish; they were only mildly interested in my scientific bag of tricks, such as reading ages from fish scales. What was science to me regarding the ecology of James Bay fish was common sense to them. The fishers were pleasantly surprised that I could tell apart their species. They had noticed only the year before that the summer student field assistant working for the federal government had been mixing up two of the common species. The problem was that the budding scientist did not have his biology right. Otherwise, there was no difference in the species identifications of the scientist and of the Cree fisher. One of the first things I did was to team up with a linguist to make sure I got the correct names and their acceptable variations in a standard orthography used by linguists (Berkes and MacKenzie 1978).

The study of traditional ecological knowledge, like the study of the Western science of ecology itself, begins with the identification and naming of species, ethnobiology. It proceeds to the study of ecological processes, or functional relationships, and people's perceptions of their own roles within environmental systems. This second area may be called ethnoecology, defined by Toledo (1992) to include four main streams: ethnobiology, agroecology, ethnoscience/anthropology, and environmental geography. More broadly, it may be called human ecology. It is practiced by a diverse group of scholars, dominated in numbers by anthropologists who are well-versed in ecology. Many of them consider themselves to be in the field of ecological anthropology or cultural ecology, which is considered a subfield of cultural anthropology (Netting 1986). Human ecology, however, is not a subfield of anthropology. It is also practiced by interdisciplinary scholars in other social sciences and by those ecologists willing to take a chance with the study of the ecology of the human species. Although Netting considers cultural ecology to be interdisciplinary, I prefer to use *human ecology* as a more inclusive term to account for the contributions of nonanthropologists.

Traditional ecological knowledge, as a field, is interdisciplinary. Using the terminology of Jantsch (1972), the field is more than a "bringing together of disciplines without coordination," which defines a multidisciplinary approach. Ethnobiology and human ecology are not clearly delimited. They meld into one another, and many of their practitioners cross disciplinary boundaries. Thus the field is integrative and involves synthesis and coordination by higher-level concept, which defines an interdisciplinary approach. As traditional ecological knowledge develops into a distinctive field of its own, one may expect that boundaries will become even more blurred in time, and perhaps it will become a transdisciplinary area, one characterized by the multilevel coordination of the system of concepts used. The two intellectual roots of traditional ecological knowledge, ethnobiology and human ecology, are quite distinct with respect to the interests and backgrounds of the scholars who played a role in their development. They have, however, developed in a synergistic relationship with one another. As Cordell (1995) pointed out, there is a need to expose more of the intellectual roots of traditional ecological knowledge in ethnoscience and its relation to biology, especially biosystematics.

ETHNOBIOLOGY AND BIOSYSTEMATICS: A GOOD FIT

The story of ethnobiology is one of the triumph of science as common sense. Ethnologists and linguists started the field as a study of folk classifications to gain insights into different cultures. But the classifications so obtained attracted the attention of biologists who saw ethnoscience as an opportunity to test whether species identifications were "robust," that is, whether species as identified by scientific experts were the same as those identified by local experts in other cultures. The interest of biologists in turn helped infuse biological and ecological thought into the field of ethnoscience.

Before we get into the story of the common sense of species identifications, some background is needed on the development of ethnoscience as practiced by ethnologists and linguists. Ethnoscience has a relatively long history. The earliest reference quoted by Levi-Strauss (1962, 5) is Barrows's work from 1900 on Coahuila Indians of Southern California who made a living in an apparently barren desert environment by harvesting no less than sixty kinds of edible plants and twenty-eight others of medicinal properties. Such early work contributed to the understanding of local knowledge and livelihoods of different cultures, but the development and systematization of ethnoscience is a much later event, which began in the United States in the mid-1950s.

Ethnoscience emerged out of a need to describe cultures from the inside. It made use of the categories operative within those cultures themselves to gain access into their cognitive universes. It was based on the assumption that the existence of a word to name a concept is the most reliable indication that the concept exists in that culture. Thus, ethnoscience became involved at first with the description of systems of terminologies. Linguistic methodologies were used to provide more rigorous methods for gathering and analyzing data, and the field was sometimes referred to as "ethnographic semantics" (Sturtevant 1964; Colby 1966).

As practitioners became more specialized, they limited themselves to describing sets of terms covering specific areas such as kinship, anatomy, color, and fauna, and each became a field in itself. Ethnoscience soon turned almost exclusively into the study of systems of classification (Murray 1982). Comparative studies, which revealed the existence of universal principles in color nomenclatures, stimulated a similar search for principles of folk classification with regard to flora and fauna. In the 1980s, the *Journal of Ethnobiology* and a professional society devoted to the subject were founded in the United States. Many comparative studies were carried out, and an evolving sequence of classification systems of fauna and flora from around the world was constructed (Berlin 1992). Other areas of ethnoscience concerned with environmental phenomena developed in parallel with ethnobiology and shared this focus on classification, for example, with regard to the ethnoscience of ice (Basso 1972), soils (Pawluk et al. 1992), and the prediction of seasonal cycles (Ceci 1978).

A long-standing debate in biosystematics is whether species are "real packages" or objectively recognizable units in nature, or "a fiction, a mental construct without objective existence" (Gould 1980, 206). Advances in ethnobiology provided an opportunity to put the question to the test. Here finally was "a way to obtain valuable information about whether species are mental abstractions embedded in cultural practice or packages in nature. We can study how different peoples, in complete independence, divide the organisms of their local areas into units. We can contrast Western classifications into Linnaean species with the 'folk taxonomies' of non-Western peoples" (Gould 1980, 207).

The idea of accepting the validity of folk science did not come easily to scientists. But some of the leading systematists of the day had firsthand experience with indigenous peoples and their local knowledge, and that helped the process of acceptance. Mayr (1963) wrote of his experiences with folk biology: "Forty years ago, I lived all alone with a tribe of Papuans in the mountains of New Guinea. These superb woodsmen had 136 names for the 137 species of birds I distinguished (confusing only two non-descript species of warblers)." Diamond (1966) published a more extensive study on the Fore people of New Guinea and found that they had names for all the species as identified by the scientific (Linnaean) classification system. Moreover, when Diamond brought Fore hunters into an area that had birds species they had never seen and asked them to give the closest Fore equivalent for each new bird, they placed 91 of 103 species into the "correct" Linnaean group!

Scientists are a skeptical lot, and soon the search was on for exceptions. An anthropologist, Berlin, and two botanists, Breedlove and Raven, published in 1966 their ethnobotany of the Tzeltal Indians of Chiapas, southern Mexico. Their explicit objective was to challenge Diamond's claim for the generality of extensive one-to-one correspondence between folk science and Western science. Their finding was that only 34 percent of the Tzeltal plant species matched the Linnaean list. The mismatches and the misclassifications, they thought, reflected cultural uses and practices. But a few years later after further study, Berlin's team reversed its opinion and affirmed the close correspondence of Tzeltal and Linnaean taxonomies. They had, in the earlier study, not fully understood the Tzeltal system of hierarchical ordering and had mixed names from several levels. Much to his credit, Berlin (1973) could now conclude that, "there is at present a growing body of evidence that suggests that the fundamental taxa recognized in folk systematics correspond fairly closely with scientifically known species."

Subsequently, Berlin et al. (1974) published a comprehensive book on Tzeltal plant taxonomy. Their complete catalogue of species contained 471 Tzeltal names. Of these, 281 or 60 percent were in one-to-one correspondence with Linnaean names. Of the remaining names, 173 (36 percent) were, in the authors' terms, "underdifferentiated." That is, Tzeltal names referred to more than one Linnaean species. However, in more than two-thirds of these cases, there were subsidiary Tzeltal names to make distinctions within the primary groups, and all of these subsidiary names corresponded with Linnaean species. The remaining seventeen names (4 percent) were "overdifferentiated." Seven Linnaean species had two Tzeltal names each. One Linnaean species, a gourd plant, had three Tzeltal names, one for plants with large, round fruits used for tortilla containers, one for plants with long-necked gourds for carrying liquid, and one for plants with small gourds not used for anything.

Other studies exist of comprehensive folk taxonomies. One of the most frequently cited studies in ethnobiology is a book, *Birds of My Kalam Country* (Majnep and Bulmer 1977), prepared cooperatively by an indigenous expert of the Kalam people of New Guinea and an anthropologist/natural historian. Of the entire Kalam catalog of 174 vertebrate (mammals, birds, reptiles, amphibians, and fish) names, more than 70 percent had one-to-one correspondence with Linnaean names. In most of the other cases, Majnep, the Kalam expert, lumped two or more Linnaean species under one Kalam name. In the other cases, Majnep made divisions within a Linnaean species on account of different uses or values. In some birds of paradise, for example, the sexes were named differently because only males carry the prized plumage. After accounting for understandable differences such as the one above, Bulmer, the Western expert, could find only four cases (2 percent) of inconsistency in the Kalam names by the rules of scientific nomenclature.

MORE ON LINGUISTICS AND METHODOLOGY: HOW TO GET THE INFORMATION RIGHT

The Tzeltal story shows, in addition to the tremendous scholarly integrity of Berlin, Breedlove, and Raven, some of the pitfalls in conducting ethnobiological research. Categories operative within a culture may not be so easy to figure out, and linguistic barriers may be very difficult to overcome. Hunn (1993b) provides a particularly telling case of ethnographic error leading to misidentification (see box 3.1). Note that the error occurred in part because the indigenous language name was not recorded correctly in the first place, and in part because the indigenous informants used it in the English vernacular, no doubt for the benefit of a linguistically challenged researcher.

Hunn (1993b, 17) is very clear about the linguistic requirements of a starting ethnobiologist: "The researcher must first be able to ask this fundamental question in the native language: 'What is the name of X?' (while pointing to some individual organism). And he/she must be able to transcribe the answers

---

BOX 3.1
IDENTIFYING SPECIES CORRECTLY: THE PUZZLE OF CAMAS

Hunn tells the story of "camas," a lily of northwestern North America with an edible bulb that was a staple food of local Indian groups. A local ethnographer published an account of the native food plants of one local group, a Salish-speaking group in the northern portion of the Columbia Plateau. He listed five species of "camas" as important in their diet, identifying "black camas" as *Camassia quamash* but also listing several species of "white camas" as *Camassia* species. These latter species were described as being harvested on extensive dry rocky flats south of the Columbia River. A generation of anthropologists searched for these camas digging grounds unsuccessfully.

"Subsequent ethnobotanical research exposed the original ethnographic error: the term 'camas' was borrowed originally from the Nez Perce Indian language (not a Salish language) by the explorers Lewis and Clark. The term was then appropriated by botanists for both the Latinate genus and species names. The term also entered the local English vernacular, but was generalized by English-speaking settlers to refer to most, if not all, Indian root foods. The Salish Indians described these plants to the ethnographer in the local English vernacular, in which 'camas' has a much wider referential range than it had in the original Nez Perce (and related Sahaptin) language. 'White camas' is not camas at all, in the Nez Perce or the botanical sense, but is used to refer to several species of 'desert parsleys,' members of the genus *Lomatium* of the parsley/celery/carrot family. There is no camas in this part of the Columbia Basin, but plenty of desert parsley. The two types of Indian foods are alike only in that the edible part of the plant is underground. They are found in quite different habitats, are harvested at different times, and are cooked and/or dried for storage in quite distinct ways. To confuse them is to miss a large part of the sophistication of local traditional ecological knowledge."

Source: Hunn 1993b, 17

accurately in that language. It is also necessary to know the difference between a name and other possible responses to that key question, e.g., 'I don't know', 'Yankee go home!', or 'The big, black, noisy bird that craps on your head.' "

Learning a foreign language may not be easy for a researcher who may not have the time or resources for such an undertaking. This does not preclude the possibility of carrying out work in ethnobiology, but it makes care and caution in research even more important. Help may be obtained from bilingual members of the cultural group and from linguistic experts. Hunn (1993b) issues a series of precautions. Here is his list, as augmented from other sources:

1. Indigenous classification systems are less comprehensive across taxonomic categories than the Western scientific system. In general, the gap between the two classification systems increases as the cultural and practical significance of a species decreases. Thus, one would anticipate that all the large mammal species will be named in a traditional system, but only a small fraction of the insects and other invertebrates may be recognized. For example, the Tzeltal language underdifferentiates the numerous Linnaean species of bats and lumps them under a single name. Bats are, in fact, culturally significant (they are associated with evil forces in Mayan belief), but they are nocturnal and difficult to observe. Hunn (1993b, 19) argues that the use of lumped categories and residual categories "is in no way an indication of inability to distinguish species on par with that of a Western scientific expert. Rather, it reflects a principle of mental economy" whereby attention is focused on the species that are important for livelihoods.

2. Species of great importance to a culture may be overdifferentiated as compared to the Linnaean classification, as in the example of Tzeltal gourds. The Hanunoo of the Philippines have names for over ninety varieties of rice, and the Quechuan languages of the Peruvian Andes have several hundred named varieties of potatoes. In some cases, the indigenous system may have a series of names for a Linnaean species but no one general term. This is not surprising, Hunn reminds the reader, considering that the English language lacks a general term for the species *Bos taurus*, calling it "cattle," "cow," "bull," "bullock," "steer," "ox," "heifer," or "calf," depending on the sex and age of the animal and where it fits in the economy.

3. Above the taxonomic level of species, the gap between indigenous classification systems and Western science tends to increase. Many biologists argue that only species are real units in nature, and the names at higher levels of taxonomy are to some extent arbitrary (Gould 1980, 210). Higher-level terms in folk systems will not, as a general rule, correspond closely to scientific systems. The Tzeltal, for example, have four named groups of plant species roughly corresponding to trees, vines, grasses, and broad-leafed herbaceous plants. This schema covers some three-quarters of their plant names but leaves the rest unaffiliated. The Kalam of New Guinea divide their nonreptilian four-footed vertebrates into three groups: *kopyak* or rats, *kmn* for a mixed group of larger game mammals, and *as* for a diverse group of frogs and small rodents. The divisions reflect not biological similarities among the animals (which the Kalam acknowledge but dismiss as unimportant) but the gender division of livelihood activities. *As* are collected primarily by women and children, *kmn* are hunted primarily by men, and *kopyak*, associated with unclean environments, are not eaten at all.

4. Basic names in indigenous classification systems may have two senses: a *core* reference, as Hunn calls it, to a particularly important or conspicuous species, and an *extended* reference to one or more similar species of lesser importance. Whether the term is being used to refer to the core species or to the extended group will depend on the context. In particular, binomial names may pose a problem. For example, the Tzeltal call all robins (Linnaean genus *Turdus*) "*toht.*" They distinguish up to five species by modifying the generic name, for example, "*ch'ish toht*" for the rufous-collared robin, *Turdus rufitorques*. Frequently, however, the core species of the folk genus will be referred to by the unmodified generic name. Whether the term is being used to refer to the genus or the species will depend on the context.

5. Names of plants and animals in traditional systems have not been standardized. The terminology may vary by dialect, by village, and even by individual. Thus, the researcher has to cope with numerous cases of synonymy and homonymy, as Hunn calls them. For example, when I began the inventory of Cree fish names in the eastern James Bay area, my more experienced anthropologist colleague, Harvey Feit, warned me to watch out for acceptable equivalent terms in each community, as well as for differences among communities. Sure enough, we found both (see table 3.1). To complicate matters, there also was an idiosyncratic system of "nicknames" for fish. Depending on her mood, a fisher might call northern pike (*Esox lucius*), "the prince of the waters" (a poetic translation) rather than refer to the species by the everyday Cree name of *chinusaw* (Berkes and MacKenzie 1978). Hunn mentions other complications that can further confuse a researcher. For example, some cultures in Australasia and the Pacific substitute alternative names or circumlocutions in referring to animals and plants, in order to avoid words that may call to mind the name of a recently deceased person.

6. Different cultures have developed detailed classifications of those elements of the environment that are important to them. The researcher should be aware that ecologically or socially important ethnoscientific classifications are not limited to plants and animals. For example, northern indigenous peoples have a rich vocabulary of ice- and snow-related terms. Turkic peoples of Central Asia, traditional horsemen and women, have a detailed terminology of horse colors; modern Turkish carries these terms, even though contemporary urban Turks rarely see a horse. A lake is a lake in English. But in Bangladesh, which lies in the floodplain of three great rivers, the Bangla language has several different terms to differentiate between different kinds of lakes, including *boar* (oxbow lake), *beel* and *haor* (two kinds of natural depressions in low-lying topography),

Table 3.1 James Bay Cree Indian fish names in standard orthography used by Cree linguists.

	Great Whale	Fort George	Wemindji	Eastmain	Rupert House	Waswanipi	Nemaska	Mistassini
arctic char	sùsàsù	sùsàsù	—	—	—	—	—	—
landlocked salmon	unàw	unàw	—	—	—	—	—	—
speckled trout	màsimàkus	màsimàkush	màsimàkush	màsimàkush	màsimekush	màsimekush	màsimekw	màsimekw màsimekush
lake trout	kùkamàs kùkamàw	kùkamàsh kùkamàw	kùkamàsh	kùkamesh	kùkamesh	namekush	namekush	namekush
whitefish	atihkamàkw	atihkamàkw	atihkamàkw	atihkamekw	atihkamekw	atihkamekw	atihkamekw	atihkamekw
cisco	nùtimiwàsù	nùtimiwàsù	nùtimiwàsù	nutimiweshish	nùtimiwesù	utùlipi uchùlipish	utùlipish	—
burbot	miy miyàhkatù	miyàhkatù	miyàhkatù	miyàhkatù	miyàhkatù	miyàhkatù	miyàhkatù	miyàhkatù
white sucker	iyichàw	nimàpi	nimàpi	namepi	namepi	namepi	namepi	namepi
red sucker	nimàpi	mihkumàpi	mihkwàshàw mihkuchikàsh	mihkuchikàsh mihkwàshew	mihkuchikàsh mihkwàshew	mihkwàsew	mihkusew	mihkusew
sturgeon	—	nimàw	nimàw	namew	namew	namew	namew	namew
walleye	—	ukàw	ukàw	ukàw	ukàw	ukàsh	ukàsh	ukàsh ukàw
pike	chinusàw	chinushàw	chinushàw	chinushew	chinushew	chinushew	chinushew	chinusew

Great Whale = Poste-de-la-Baleine, Fort George = Chisasibi, Rupert House = Waskaganish
Note: Scientific names of the species and further details of Cree nomenclature in Berkes and MacKenzie (1978).

44

and flood lands that become shallow, seasonal lakes during monsoon months (Ahmed et al. 1997).

7. Traditional knowledge is often gendered. Rocheleau (1991) writes, "half or more of indigenous ecological science has been obscured by the prevailing 'invisibility' of women, their work, their interests and especially their knowledge." Much of this knowledge is crucially important. Shiva (1988) points out that survival is the ultimate criterion for verification of poor rural women's knowledge. A steady stream of field research indicates the gendered nature of traditional work, such as agricultural specialization, and thus of traditional knowledge. This is reflected in some of the above examples, such as the Kalam division of animals. Even where there is no clear gender specialization in ethnoscientific knowledge, the researcher would do well to remember that differences in work and interests will likely translate into gender differences in depth of knowledge and the path of transmission. For example, among the Cree of James Bay, men and women share many items of traditional knowledge and bush skills. Nevertheless, in one community, two-thirds of the instructors of young females in the transmission of bush skills were found to be women. This figure climbed to 80 percent in a smaller and more traditional community (Ohmagari and Berkes 1997).

8. Caution should be exercised regarding culture-specific and referential meanings in ethnoscience. Hunn (1993b, 20) points out that the meanings of plant and animal names, such as those discussed above, are referential meanings, only one aspect of meaning of a term that may also include cultural meanings. For example, *dog* means *Canis familiaris*; but *dog* can also mean "man's best friend" in one culture, "sled-puller" in another, and "dinner" in a third. "Once the referential meaning has been established," says Hunn, "a whole world of other cultural meanings is accessible to the student of that system of traditional ecological knowledge."

EXAGGERATION AND ETHNOSCIENCE: THE ESKIMO SNOW HOAX?

One of the persistent problems in traditional knowledge research is the question of the reliability of information. Can indigenous knowledge be tested? Is it verifiable against scientific knowledge? Experienced researchers know that with some groups, *how* people say things may be more important than *what* they say. As Bielawski (1992) puts it, "Inuit knowledge resides less in what Inuit say than how they say it and what they do." The researcher must be familiar with the mode of communication of a particular group of people. For example, Felt (1994, 259) writes that Newfoundland fishers "communicate their understanding about their world through personal anecdotes and long stories and yarns about community members of yesteryear. Humor is frequently used, as are 'cuffers,' or exaggerated stories told in competition with other fishers." As an example, the author produces the cuffer about setting fish nets anchored to icebergs, an unlikely practice (because of safety concerns—icebergs tend to roll over), yet signaling the phenomenon that a retreating ice edge tends to be a good place to fish because of abundance of fish food (e.g. Berkes 1977).

The controversy over Eskimo (Inuit) snow terminology is a particularly interesting example about how exaggerated information may get perpetuated in the literature, in this case through no fault of the Eskimo themselves. Geoffrey Pullum is a linguist who has written a book about fallacies that the general public commonly believes, despite the best efforts of experts to set the record straight. "In the study of language," he says, "one case surpasses all others in its degree of ubiquity: it is the notion that Eskimos have bucketloads of different words for snow" (Pullum 1991).

Borrowing from Martin (1986), Pullum traces the original source to the distinguished anthropologist Franz Boas, whose commentary about four distinct Eskimo root terms about snow was picked up in the 1940s by an "amateur" (that is, a nonlinguist, nonanthropologist) and embellished to produce seven or more categories. In the course of several successively more careless repetitions over several decades, as traced by Martin, the number of snow terms had been inflated to the order of one to two hundred!

Pullum (1991, 163) not only questions these numbers but also the evidence that the Eskimo terms are more differentiated than those in English. He points out that not only do some groups such as skiers use specialized terms such as *powder* and *crust*, but even among the general population there is a range of terms in common use: "the stuff in question is called *snow* when fluffy and white, *slush* when partially melted, *sleet* when falling in a half-melted state, and a *blizzard* when pelting down hard enough to make driving dangerous."

Pullum's points about scholarly sloppiness and the susceptibility of the public to cling to misinformation are well taken. However, some of his analysis shows a poor reading of ethnoscience: "When you come to think of it, Eskimos aren't really that likely to be interested in snow. Snow in the traditional Eskimo hunter's life must be a kind of constantly assumed background, like sand on the beach. And even beach bums have only one word for sand" (Pullum 1991, 166). And further: "The fact is that the myth of the multiple words for snow is based on almost nothing at all. It is a kind of accidentally developed hoax perpetrated by the anthropological linguistics community on itself" (Pullum 1991, 162).

These conclusions are of course not accurate. In a discourse of traditional ecological knowledge, it is important to point out that there is not only anthropological but also ecological evidence that bears on the question. Arctic ecologist Bill Pruitt has been using Inuktitut (Eskimo language) and other indigenous terminology for types of snow for decades (Pruitt 1960). He says, "Boreal ecologists deal with aspects of nature, particularly snow and ice phenomena, for which there are no precise English words. Consequently, our writings and speech are larded with Inuit, Athapascan, Lappish and Tungus words, not in any attempt to be erudite but to aid in the precision in our speech and thoughts" (Pruitt 1978, 6).

Table 3.2   Some specialized snow terminology.

Term	Source	English equivalent
aŋmaŋa	Inuit	Space formed between drift and obstruction causing it.
api	Inuit	Snow on the ground, forest.
čiegar	Saami	"Feeding trench" through undisturbed api.
čuok'ki	Saami	Layer of solid ice next to the soil.
fies'ki	Saami	"Yard crater" of thin, hard and dense snow caused by reindeer digging.
kaioglaq	Inuit	Large hard sculpturings resulting from erosion of kalutoganiq.
kalutoganiq	Inuit	Arrowhead-shaped drift on top of upsik; moves downwind.
pukak	Inuit	Fragile, columnar base layer of api.
qali	Inuit	Snow on trees.
qamaniq	Inuit	Bowl-shaped depression in api under coniferous tree.
sändjas	Saami	Fragile, columnar basal layer of api (= pukak)
suov'dnji	Saami	"Feeding crater" excavated in the api.
upsik	Inuit	Wind-hardened tundra snow cover.

Source: Adapted and condensed from Pruitt (1984). The Inuit terms are from the Kovakmiut; Saami = Lappish from Northern Scandinavia.

Table 3.2 provides a sampling of some of this specialized snow terminology and illustrates the importance of ecological considerations in the study of languages and ethnoscience. The case illustrates cross-cultural shortsightedness that one has to guard against. It also shows how wrong a narrow disciplinary perspective (in this case linguistics) can be, if the evidence from the broader interdisciplinary view is not consulted.

HUMAN ECOLOGY AND TERRITORIALITY

In chapter 2, we touch upon the social and cultural significance of traditional ecological knowledge with regard to the sometimes sacred dimensions of indigenous knowledge, such as symbolic meanings and their importance for social relationships and values. Linguistics is one key to the understanding of social and ecological relationships in a culture. However, the study of functional relationships between people and the environment, and people's perceptions of how they fit within environmental systems, falls into the area of human ecology, and more specifically cultural ecology.

Cultural ecology is an ethnological approach that sees the modes of production of societies around the world as adaptations to their local environments. The field has its origin in the work of Steward (1936) on the social organization of hunter-gatherer groups. Steward argued against environmental determinism, which regarded specific cultural characteristics as arising from environmental causes. Using band societies as examples, he showed that social organization itself corresponded to a kind of ecological adaptation of a human group to its environment. He defined cultural ecology as the study of *adaptive processes* by which the nature of society and an unpredictable number of features of culture are affected by the basic adjustment through which humans utilize a given environment (Steward 1955).

Subsequent work showed that the study of processes of human adaptation to the environment was a productive line of inquiry in cultural anthropology, and that sound empirical data were available to document wide-ranging and systemic ecological relationships (Lee and Devore 1968; Netting 1986). Even though traditional ecological knowledge is generated locally, comparative analysis has shown the existence of similar ecological adaptations in comparable areas. In some cases, such as in shifting cultivation systems and the use of fire, traditional systems may show functional equivalents in quite different cultural and geographic settings (see chapter 4). All of this makes the study of traditional ecological knowledge more than just locally significant. Because traditional systems often involve long-term adaptations to specific environments and resource management problems, they are of interest to resource managers everywhere. One example of such an adaptation is human territoriality and the use of resources on a territorial basis.

An early practitioner of cultural ecology was the American ethnologist Speck (1915), who saw the system of hunting territories used by the aboriginal people of Labrador as a method of resource conservation. His findings were later attacked on the basis that family-based hunting territories came into being *after* the fur trade and therefore could not have represented an aboriginal land tenure system (Leacock 1954). The latter argument about the origin of the family territory system is probably correct, although the point is still debated (Bishop and Morantz 1986). From a resource management point of view, however, Speck's original point is valid. Community-based (but not family-based) territories were probably the primary practice for resource management at one time in North America. According to Sutton (1975), probably most native peoples in North America had systems of land tenure that involved rules for resource allocation within the group and for control of access to resources, and the prerogative to convey to others certain resource-use rights but not outright alienation. That is, the produce of the land was subject to rules and allocation decisions but the land itself was never "for sale" (see box 3.2). The point is, rights apply to specific resources, not to land as such (Trosper 1998).

Most indigenous land tenure systems in North America have disappeared; the James Bay area is one of the exceptions. Since the 1970s, much detailed work has been carried out to determine how these territorial land tenure systems work (Feit 1991). Forms of territorial systems found among the James Bay Cree, who live in the lands to the west of the Naskapi and Montagnais (Innu) of Labrador, are of the communal property type. Each community (in this case Chisasibi) holds a communal territory that is further subdivided into hunting territories of family groups (Berkes 1989b). A senior hunter leads each group and enforces

---

BOX 3.2
CREE HUMOR: LAND AS "REAL ESTATE"

Cree people use a great deal of humor in their daily interactions, as do many groups of North American aboriginal people. In the contemporary world, much of Cree humor deals with the absurd or inexplicable things that Euro-Canadians (*wapstagushio*, white man) do. Such as regarding God's land as a commodity.

It was spring, just at the end of the goose hunting season. Ice was slowly clearing off James Bay, and a Cree companion and I went down the coast from Chisasibi to check some fish nets. As we took a tea break on a high piece of rock overlooking the bay, we spotted two large canoes approaching. Several families were returning to the village of Chisasibi after a month or so in a goose hunting camp. The Cree are a gregarious people, never missing an opportunity to visit and to catch up on local gossip. So the canoes stopped at our tea-break camp, offering some smoked goose and not refusing some fresh boiled fish. They noticed me, of course; an outsider and a white man in the bush is always a curiosity. Shortly after, my companion was asked about my business in being there. His response, delivered in Cree, left the visitors helpless with laughter—several minutes of prolonged laughter—or so it seemed to me, as I sat feeling uncomfortable but also curious. What *did* he say that was considered so outrageously funny?

My companion explained later that he had merely said, "Oh, yes, this *wapstagushio*. He is here to look over some real estate." I must admit, I did not see the humor at that time. But the Cree had just concluded a land claims case and were negotiating a treaty with a government that was intent on redefining aboriginal rights and asserting its own control over the land to clear the way so that hydroelectric dams could be built. So imagine, hunters go to the peace and quiet of a month-long goose hunt, away from court cases and the threats of the mad industrialized world. When they return at the end of the goose season, the first thing they run into is this *wapstagushio*, drinking tea and snacking on boiled whitefish, sitting on bare rock in the middle of nowhere. He is casting his greedy eyes about, appraising the real estate value of this piece of God's land.

Source: Berkes field notes, Chisasibi, James Bay

---

the community's rules. Only members of the family or people invited by them are permitted to trap furs on this land, but it is generally understood that any community member can hunt or fish to feed his or her family. Within a territory, individual hunters lay claim to beaver houses. Violations of general rules of hunting, fishing, and trapping are dealt with through customary law and enforced by social sanction.

Hunting rights limit the number of hunters who can operate in the family territories and in the communal territory as a whole. This way, high levels of productivity can be obtained with a limited hunting pressure. Where the human population is large and growing, the territory system can have the effect of limiting the number of active hunters and stabilizing the overall hunting pressure. We tested this hypothesis using an eighteen-year data set. Over this time period, the population of the Eastern James Bay Cree nearly doubled and the percentage of participation rate in the traditional land-based economy declined, but the size of the population participating (i.e., the number of active hunters) in fact remained stable, as did the resource base (Berkes and Fast 1996).

Fishing, hunting, and gathering territories also exist in the Pacific Northwest. Their continued use has been well documented from northern British Columbia (Collier and Vegh 1998). The Nass River area near the British Columbia–Alaska border provides an example of the use of territorial systems in the management of Pacific salmon (Berkes 1985). The Nass River watershed is claimed as traditional tribal territory by the Nishga Indians. Within it, each Nishga community used one part of the watershed, within which specific salmon fishing sites were controlled by a chief on behalf of a *house*, a kinship-based social group. Thus, resource territories were organized hierarchically, from the watershed level down to specific fishing sites. In many parts of the Pacific Northwest, rules of sharing and reciprocity ensured that house chiefs took responsibility for allocating resources equitably within the house. Periodic *potlatches*, commonly held by many groups, were a mechanism for sharing the surplus of their fishing activities. Trosper (1998) suggests that potlatches may have served the function of solving the "tragedy of the commons" by creating a disincentive to accumulate individual wealth.

However, to view territoriality merely as a resource management mechanism is to miss half of the story. The potlatch is not only for resource sharing; it is culturally significant in its own right. Land is important for cultural reasons as well. For example, among the James Bay Cree, it is important for the education of the young and for knowledge transmission (Ohmagari and Berkes 1997), the perpetuation of social values such as sharing and reciprocity, and the reproduction of culture, which is unconsciously known and embodied in action (Preston 1975). As Feit (1991, 227) explains, "Hunting territories are both systems of practice and culture, intertwined and closely linked to distinctive social forms and relations. . . . The replication of distinctive ideologies of land and social relations has been central to the ability of Algonquian peoples to maintain distinctive systems of land rights."

Much work in classical human ecology was concerned with territoriality and land tenure systems in a diversity of cultural groups and geographic areas. For example, no less than five of the eleven chapters in the book by Williams and Hunn (1982) deal with territories. Such territories were found in marine coastal as well as in terrestrial environments, for example, in Oceania (Johannes 1978) and among the tribes of the Pacific Northwest. The Kwakiutl had named fishing banks (Boas 1934). Among nonaboriginal groups, Acheson (1975) reported territorial resource use among commercial lobster fishers in Maine. Such findings led various international resource management circles to suggest that land and marine tenure systems should be used as the basis of management. For example, Christy (1982) proposed that governments should consider recognizing local territorial use rights in fisheries (TURFS) toward improving resource management systems.

The basic ecological reasoning behind territoriality is simple. Ecologists consider territories as a mechanism by which population size can be matched to the limits of available resources. Territoriality is considered a behavioral self-regulatory mechanism found among many mammal and bird species, especially the predatory ones such as wolves. The presence or absence of territories and variations in resource control patterns have been explained by the use of economic and ecological models. These models, first developed in animal ecology, were applied to human groups by Dyson-Hudson and Smith (1978), who defined territory as "an area occupied more or less exclusively by an individual or a group by means of repulsion through overt defense or some form of communication." The economic defensibility model predicted territorial behavior when the costs of exclusive use and defense were exceeded by the benefits gained. Dyson-Hudson and Smith (1978) argued that the most important factors in determining the cost-benefit ratio were the predictability and abundance of a resource: "a territorial system is most likely under conditions of high density and predictability of critical resources." If a resource was not critical for the well-being of a group, it was not worth defending. Similarly, if a resource was too rare or too abundant, there was no benefit to be gained from territoriality.

Richardson (1982), among others, applied the economic defensibility model to the data-rich Northwest coast from California to Alaska. He found that the model was generally useful in explaining patterns of resource control; the resources most frequently subject to access restrictions were those that were predictable and abundant, such as salmon. He also found, however, that the Dyson-Hudson and Smith model was inadequate to explain patchiness of resource use and of territories. As well, he suggested that some cases of territoriality may have purely cultural (as opposed to ecological and economic) explanations. In a similar vein, Chapman (1985) pointed out that marine tenure in parts of the South Pacific may be explained more simply in terms of local politics and power relations, rather than in terms of resource management. Yet others noted that traditional management may exist in the *absence* of territories, as in the case of Icelandic inshore fishers (Palsson 1982).

Since the 1980s, the emphasis on territories and economic models seems to have been replaced by a broader view of the social role of territoriality as part of culture, as argued for example by Feit (1991). As well, territoriality-based analysis has been largely replaced by one that emphasizes property rights and institutions. For many, territoriality is important, but it is only one aspect of a larger system of rights, obligations, and rules. As ecologists remind us, all species adapt to the resource limits of their environments. However, behavioral self-regulatory mechanisms among human groups are more complex than those found in other species. Many animal populations have territories; many human groups have common property institutions that are often systems of access rules, sharing rules, and appropriate resource use behavior (Berkes 1989b; Wilson et al. 1994).

INTEGRATION OF SOCIAL SYSTEMS AND NATURAL SYSTEMS: IMPORTANCE OF WORLDVIEWS

One of the major areas of study in human ecology of recent years is the integration of resource management and social systems. The book by Williams and

Hunn (1982), dealing mainly with the indigenous groups of the Pacific North-west and of Australia, is one of the earlier examples of the study of comparative cultural ecology and resource management. A large body of literature on tra-ditional management systems in Oceania, compiled by interdisciplinary groups of marine ecologists, geographers, anthropologists, and others (Johannes 1978; Klee 1980; Ruddle and Johannes 1990; Freeman et al. 1991), has revolutionized management thinking. Similarly, the tropical forest use of traditional cultures of the Amazon region has come under study by interdisciplinary teams, leading to a reconceptualization of tropical forest conservation (Posey and Balee 1989; Redford and Mansour 1996).

These studies have contributed to a search for alternative resource manage-ment systems. They have provided insights for more holistic, systems ecology–based approaches (Regier 1978), and for adaptive systems based on local knowl-edge and practice. The rediscovery of ecosystem-like concepts among traditional cultures in many parts of the world was an important stepping stone in the appreciation by ecologists of traditional holistic understandings of nature (see table 3.3). Basically, two characteristics make these examples ecosystem-like concepts. First, the traditional unit of land or water in each of these cases is defined in terms of a geographical boundary (usually a watershed boundary). Second, the traditional concept considers everything within this environmental unit to be interlinked.

The territories of the Gitksan (Gitxsan) and Wet'sewet'en people of the Pa-cific Northwest provide an example. These territories are closely associated with a specific group of people. They are used for a variety of resource gathering ac-tivities and are controlled by chiefs on behalf of kinship groups. Chiefs describe their territorial boundaries as "from mountain top to mountain top" and orient themselves by two directional axes within this watershed framework: vertically up and down from valley bottom to mountain top, and horizontally, upstream and downstream (Tyler 1993). Detailed land use maps of the kinship-based house groups (*wilps*) of the Gitxsan show that there is a close correspondence be-tween watershed areas and *wilps* or clusters of *wilps* (Collier and Vegh 1998). A close examination of these maps reveals that they are not merely territories but watershed-ecosystems-as-territories.

The examples in table 3.3, compiled by Berkes et al. (1998), provide only a sampling of a wide range of indigenous applications that resemble the ecosystem concept. However, the important point to keep in mind is that there are many differences, as well as similarities, between these traditional and Western con-cepts of ecosystems. It would not be correct to label the examples in table 3.3 simply as prescientific ecosystem concepts because they differ in context and conceptual underpinning. In chapter 1, we consider the Dogrib Dene (Atha-pascan) notion of *ndè*, which could be translated as "ecosystem" except that *ndè* is based on the idea that everything in the environment has life and spirit (Legat et al. 1995)—which makes it considerably different from the mechanistic concept of ecosystem in ecology.

Table 3.3   Examples of traditional applications of the ecosystem view.

System	Country/region	Reference
Watershed management of salmon rivers and associated hunting and gathering areas by tribal groups	Amerindians of the Pacific Northwest	Williams and Hunn (1982); Swezey and Heizer (1993)
Delta and lagoon management for fish culture (*tambak* in Java), and the integrated cultivation of rice and fish	South and Southeast Asia	Johannes et al. (1983)
Vanua (in Fiji), a named area of land and sea, seen as an integrated whole with its human occupants	Oceania, including Fiji, Solomon Islands, ancient Hawaii	Ruddle and Akimichi (1984); Baines (1989)
Family groups claiming individual watersheds (*iwor*) as their domain for hunting, fishing, gathering	The Ainu of northern Japan	Watanabe (1973); Ludwig (1994)
Integrated floodplain management (*dina*) in which resource areas are shared by social groups through reciprocal access arrangements	Mali, Africa	Moorehead (1989)

This brings us to the consideration of these conceptual underpinnings, worldviews, or cosmologies. One of the classical studies of indigenous cosmologies was carried out by Reichel-Dolmatoff (1976) among the Tukano of the Colombian northwest Amazon, showing how the belief in the spirits of game animals restricted overhunting and how shamanism functioned in the management of natural resources. Reichel-Dolmatoff drew attention to Tukano cosmology as representing a blueprint for ecological adaptation, positing worldviews as the organizing concept behind the cultural ecology of a group (box 3.3).

One of the major lines of inquiry in the field of traditional ecological knowledge concerns cosmologies and worldviews. Are traditional worldviews relevant to present-day resource stewardship, and to the reexamination of our current attitudes toward the environment? Our view of the world and the universe and how we relate to them is the *source* of our values, our cosmology (Skolimowski 1981). Our observations of the world around us are invariably structured through the concepts supplied by our cosmology. Modern Westerners have a characteristic worldview regarding the place of humans in nature, one to which Bateson, Capra, and Berry allude, as cited in chapter 1. Evernden (1993) argues that, in

---

BOX 3.3
TUKANO COSMOLOGY

According to Reichel-Dolmatoff, in Tukano culture, the individual person considers himself or herself as part of a complex network of interactions that include not only society but the entire universe. An essential interrelatedness of all things means that a person has to fulfill many functions that go far beyond his or her social roles, and that are extrasocietal extensions of a set of adaptive norms. These norms guide a person's relationships not only with other people but also with animals, plants, and other components of the environment. The rules the individual has to follow, says Reichel-Dolmatoff, "refer, above all, to cooperative behaviour aimed at the conservation of ecological balance as the ultimate desirable quality. Thus the relationship between man and his environment is being formulated not only on a cognitive level, but clearly it also constitutes an effective personal relationship in which individual animals and plants are treated with respect and caution."

The Tukano are aware that, argues Reichel-Dolmatoff, to maintain resources "a number of regulatory mechanisms have to be instituted and, what is more, have to be fully respected by all members of the society. These social controls of necessity possess marked adaptive implications and must be enforced primarily in those aspects of existence which, to a large degree, determine survival. I shall mention here: population growth, the exploitation of the physical environment, and aggression in interpersonal relations. It is quite clear to the Tukano that, in order to ensure individual and collective survival and well-being, adaptive rules have to be established to adjust the birth-rate, the harvest-rate, and to counterbalance all socially disruptive behaviour."

Reichel-Dolmatoff emphasizes the role of the shaman as a healer of illness, not so much at the individual level, but at the level of "supra-individual structures that have been disturbed by the person. To be effective, he has to apply his treatment to the disturbed part of the ecosystem. It might be said then that a Tukano shaman does not have individual patients; his task is to cure a social malfunctioning. The diseased organism of the patient is secondary in importance and will be treated eventually, both empirically and ritually, but what really counts is the reestablishment of the rules that will avoid overhunting, the depletion of certain plant resources, and unchecked population increase. The shaman becomes thus a truly powerful force in the control and management of resources."

Source: Reichel-Dolmatoff 1976, 311, 312, 315

---

the dominant Western society of the post-Enlightenment period, humans are akin to aliens because they have a self-identity distinct from the world around them. The ecologist as a scientist "is forced to treat nature as essentially non-living, a machine to be dissected, interpreted and manipulated" (Evernden 1993, 20). In a similar vein, Skolimowski (1981) argues that our cosmology is based far too heavily on empiricism and scientism and is too mechanistic and analytic; it is insufficiently based on humanistic notions and morality toward nature.

Such generalizations are not universally true for all cultures. Even some Western traditions reject the view of a secularized and depersonalized nature. These include the alternative Christian views of nature, such as those of St. Francis (White 1967) and St. Benedict (Dubos 1972). There has been much discussion, as well, regarding Taoist, Zen Buddhist, and Sufi views on the environment (Pepper 1984; Callicott 1994). Some of these views are consistent with pantheistic traditions of many indigenous peoples. Perhaps the explanation is that both the present-day indigenous groups and some of the spiritual traditions of Eastern and Western mainstream religions have been borrowing from the same wellspring of ancient wisdom of human-environment relationships. The question of worldviews is crucial to the analysis of traditional ecological knowledge. Chapter 5 provides one example of the unique worldviews of indigenous societies.

To summarize, ethnoscience and human ecology are at the intellectual roots of traditional ecological knowledge. The discipline started with the documentation of species lists of different cultures, and it elaborated a science of folk taxonomies of plants and animals and, later, of other environmental variables. It proceeded to the study of functional relationships of the elements of local knowledge so documented, including the study of human perceptions of ecological processes, and the process of human adaptation to the environment (Steward 1955). Some of the work of human ecologists in the 1970s and the 1980s emphasized territoriality (Malmberg 1980; Berkes 1986a). Although this work is important and has continued to date, others have approached traditional resource management systems using a framework that deals with property rights and institutions. In this new emphasis, access rules are only one set of rules within a larger set of rights and obligations. Finally, context and worldviews are of key importance in human ecology. As Reichel-Dolmatoff (1976) pointed out, the researcher needs to study the worldview as the organizing concept behind the cultural ecology of a group, without which the logic of many traditional management systems would be difficult, if not impossible, to access. The next chapter proceeds to examine in more detail a selection of traditional ecological knowledge systems.

Part Two

Practice

Chapter Four

Traditional Knowledge Systems in Practice

Throughout history, all human groups have depended on careful observations of the natural world. If they learned from these observations, they adapted successfully. If they did not, the consequences were probably deadly. Survival is the ultimate criterion for verification of traditional ecological knowledge, and adaptation is key. Thus, the practice of indigenous knowledge is, above all, the story of how social/cultural systems adapt to specific ecosystems.

Traditional knowledge and resource management practice have the potential to contribute to the current understanding and use of a wide variety of ecosystems. Western civilization is largely based in north temperate regions of the world, and it is not surprising that most of Western resource management science has concentrated on temperate ecosystems. This has created some problems for resource management elsewhere. For example, many tropical marine ecologists have pointed out that fishery management designed for the characteristics of the North Atlantic does not at all work in tropical marine ecosystems. The same could be said about a number of other environments that we, as inhabitants of temperate ecosystems, consider "marginal." These include tropical forests, arid lands, mountains, and Arctic ecosystems. Hence, *Our Common Future*, one of the first international documents to raise these issues, drew attention to the relevance of tribal and indigenous peoples' knowledge, with their long-term views and a contextual understanding of the local environment, for lessons in the management of resources in tropical forest, mountain, and arid land ecosystems (WCED 1987, 12; also quoted in chapter 1).

However, the mere possession of knowledge does not guarantee that a given human group will live in harmony with its environment. There are many known cases of environmental mismanagement by traditional societies. We can, however, make an educated guess that, everything else being equal, societies with much environmental knowledge *and* a high capacity to learn are more likely to possess sustainable resource use practices than those without. As we are dealing with a knowledge-practice-belief complex, one can further guess that the possession both of an appropriate social organization to put knowledge into resource management practice and of a worldview consistent with ecological prudence were also adaptive. Here *ecological prudence* is used in the sense of Slobodkin (1968), who observed that many predatory species generally act in a way that prevents the depletion of their food supplies. He found this to be so even with fairly simple organisms, as well as with mammals with their often elaborate systems of social regulation, such as territoriality.

Ecologically speaking, the human species may reasonably be characterized as a K-strategist, that is, a species adapted to maintain populations close to the ecological carrying capacity (Gadgil 1987). Thus, in human groups, one would expect to find social regulation of resource use, including territoriality and a range of other social mechanisms designed to prevent resource depletion, as discussed in chapter 3. After all, basic principles of evolutionary ecology are applicable to the human species, too.

Several chapters in part 2 make reference to two concepts, Adaptive Management and Social Learning. Adaptive Management is an integrated method for natural resource management (Holling 1986; Lee 1993; Gunderson et al. 1995). It is *adaptive* because it acknowledges that environmental conditions will always change, thus requiring management institutions to respond to feedbacks by adjusting and evolving. Adaptive Management, like some traditional knowledge systems, takes a dynamic view of ecosystems, emphasizes processes (including resource use) that are part of ecological cycles of renewal, and stresses the importance of resilience, that is, the buffering ability of the system to absorb change without breaking down or going into another state of equilibrium. As well, Adaptive Management, like many traditional knowledge systems, assumes that nature cannot be controlled and yields predicted; uncertainty and unpredictability are characteristics of all ecosystems, including managed ones. In both cases, feedback learning is the way in which societies deal with uncertainty. Often, this is not learning at the level of the individual, but *social learning* at the level of society or *institutional learning* at the level of institutions (Ostrom 1990).

The objective of this chapter is to describe the workings of a sample of indigenous knowledge and resource management systems in a variety of ecosystem settings. The chapter provides the context and background for the other chapters in part 2. Two themes run through the chapter. The first is about evolutionary ecology and cultural evolution: traditional knowledge represents the summation of millennia of ecological adaptations of human groups to their diverse environments. The second theme concerns the compatibility of traditional wisdom with some current ecological approaches to resource management, specifically Adaptive Management. The chapter begins with examples of resource management from tropical forest ecosystems, and then moves to semiarid lands, island ecosystems, and coastal lagoons and wetlands.

TROPICAL FORESTS: NOT AMENABLE TO MANAGEMENT?

Until the 1970s, our conventional view of tropical forests was that they were biological museums in which a vast inventory of biodiversity had accumulated in part due to the absence of ecological disturbance. Tropical ecosystems were thought to be both stable over time and "mature"; ecosystem complexity was believed to be related to stability, in turn a function of maturity. Tropical forests were thought to be fragile and not amenable to management because they were adapted to constant (or stable) conditions and ill-adapted to withstand the unpredictable effects of human activity and resource exploitation (as summarized by Lugo 1995).

By the late 1970s, many ecologists had abandoned the idea that ecosystem complexity and stability were necessarily related. Moreover, the concept of stability was seen to be problematic because it was used to mean several different things. Holling (1973) proposed instead the concept of ecosystem *resilience* as the ability of a system to absorb change and still persist. The use of this concept has proved useful in many areas. Lugo (1995) suggested that the key to managing the tropical rain forest is to focus on its resilience, rather than on its supposed fragility and unmanageability.

What is the evidence for the resilience of tropical ecosystems? At the theoretical level, ecologists are increasingly recognizing the importance of natural disturbances in maintaining tropical forest ecology (Denslow 1987). At the empirical level, there is an accumulation of evidence that forests once believed to be primary are in fact the products of human disturbance and management dating back perhaps millennia (Sanford et al. 1985; Gómez-Pompa and Kaus 1992a). These findings stimulated research on local traditional systems, not only in the Amazon but also in other tropical forest areas. A number of traditional systems used in the tropics illustrates how human use and disturbance can be made compatible with sustainability. Shifting cultivation or swidden systems are common in all tropical areas of the world—the Amazon, parts of Africa, South and Southeast Asia, and New Guinea (De Schlippe 1956; Spencer 1966; Brookfield and Padoch 1994; Redford and Padoch 1992). Swiddening involves the clearing, planting, harvesting, and fallowing of small areas over a multiyear cycle. Shifting cultivation, sometimes pejoratively called slash-and-burn, has received much attention as one of the major degradative processes in tropical forest areas when population pressures increase and rotation time is shortened. When that happens, land degradation may occur and biodiversity may be reduced as a result of repeated intervention in the regeneration process.

However, many environmentalists have confused indigenous shifting cultivation that is properly carried out, with slash-and-burn as practiced by outsiders for short-term gains, inadvertently exaggerating the role of local people in tropical deforestation (Dove 1993). "Slash-and-burn agriculture accounts for only 30 percent of tropical deforestation in Latin America. . . . Slash-and-burn agriculture by colonists (under government incentives to clear the land) is different from the shifting agriculture practiced over millennia by the indigenous inhabitants" (Gómez-Pompa and Kaus 1992b). Likewise, Brookfield and Padoch (1994) state, "wholesale burning of the Amazon rainforest by settlers has helped stigmatize all burning, including that practiced sustainably by indigenous peoples."

Studies elsewhere also show that traditional shifting cultivation is not a part of the problem of tropical deforestation but rather part of the solution. Ramakrishnan (1992) describes multispecies systems of four to over thirty-five crop types, based on locally adapted native varieties, in the tribal areas of northeastern India. The indigenous system (locally termed *jhum*) requires sophisticated local ecological knowledge. The farmers optimize the use of soil nutrients by appropriate changes in the crop mixture depending on the length of the *jhum* cycle and the consequent high/low soil nutrient levels. On hill slopes, farmers combine r-strategist species (prolific cereals and legumes) with K-strategists with emphasis on vegetative growth, such as leafy vegetables. The aim is to maximize production from the site by mixing these two kinds of species with different reproductive strategies, in imitation of the early stages of plant succession in these forests (Ramakrishnan 1992).

Shifting agriculturalists studied by Ramakrishnan (1992) seem to have an intuitive understanding of the ecological requirements of two groups of plants that biologists call C-3 and C-4 species. The soil on steep hill slopes is highly heterogeneous and the availability of nitrogen uncertain. The C-4 species with high nutrient-use efficiency could grow well in nutrient-poor microsites, whereas C-3 species with low nutrient-use efficiency are suited to nutrient-rich microsites. "Such a C-3/C-4 strategy helps in coexistence of species through mutual avoidance. The positioning of the C-3 and C-4 crop species under *jhum* in northeastern India imitates the local natural communities, with the more nutrient-use efficient species being located in the nutrient-poor upper parts of the slope and less efficient species situated at the base of the slope" (Ramakrishnan 1992, 381).

Some earlier work found that shifting cultivation was conservative of ecological processes but, in general, swiddens did not compare in complexity to the surrounding forest. However, when shifting cultivation was analyzed as an *agroforestry system* and the use of trees was also taken into account, then the overall results of managing forest patches were conservative of biodiversity as well. Such are the findings of Alcorn (1984) with Huastec agroforestry in northeastern Mexico, Posey (1985) with the Kayapo who create "forest islands" at the edge of the Amazon rain forest (the forest-savanna ecotone), and Irvine (1989) who found that the succession management of the Runa of the Ecuadoran Amazon actually enhanced forest biodiversity.

In effect, many of these indigenous systems manage forest succession, as illustrated by the work of Denevan et al. (1984) with the Bora of Peru. The investigators selected fields of different ages to examine vegetation changes in the staged process of abandonment and fallow. The Bora planted a wide variety of crops, the main staple being manioc (a starchy root crop) of which they recognized some twenty-two varieties. Peanuts, another major crop, were grown in second- or third-year fields. The three-year-old field contained at least twenty crop varieties, including fruit trees that were still young. The five-year-old field, with maturing fruit trees, looked more like an orchard than a field, with crops such as manioc almost phased out. The nine-year-old field consisted mainly of bushes and a ten- to fifteen-meter-tall secondary growth; coca was the most valuable crop. The oldest field studied, a nineteen-year-old fallow, contained some twenty-two useful tree species for edible fruit, medicines, construction wood,

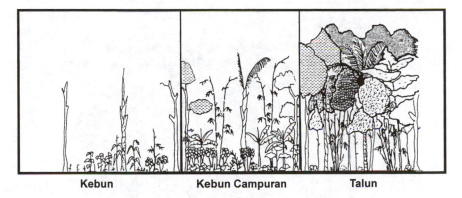

Kebun   Kebun Campuran   Talun

Figure 4.1 Successional stages of the *kebun-talun* system, West Java, Indonesia. *Source:* modified from Christianity (1986).

and other materials. Denevan et al. (1984) found that the most productive fallow stage was at four to twelve years. Before that, the fruit trees had limited production; after that, many of the useful species had been shaded out. Harvesting of some species continued, however, for twenty to thirty or more years.

One of the reasons why such good examples of shifting cultivation come from Latin America is that the Amazon is relatively less densely populated than, for example, South and Southeast Asia. It is in these more densely populated areas of the tropics that one finds more intensive management systems—systems in which the fallow stage has been shortened or bypassed. For example, two of the most common traditional agroforestry systems in West Java, Indonesia, are *kebun-talun* (rotation between mixed garden and tree plantation) and *pekarangan* (home garden intercropping system) (Christianity et al. 1986). *Kebun-talun* is a system that increases overall productivity and serves multiple functions by sequentially combining agricultural crops with tree crops. The system consists of three stages, each serving a different function. The first stage is *kebun*, a planting of a mixture of annual crops, mainly for the market. After two years, *kebun* evolves into *kebun campuran*, a transition stage in which annuals are mixed with half-grown perennials. When the harvesting of annuals is completed, the field is usually abandoned for two or three years and becomes dominated by perennials (*talun* stage) before the cycle starts all over again (see figure 4.1). However, even a short fallow has become difficult to maintain, as Java has turned, due to population increase, into one continuous urban concentration.

Better adapted for higher population densities is *pekarangan* (home garden), which consists of a mixture of annual and perennial crops grown on land surrounding a house. A *kebun-talun* may be converted to a home garden by building a house on it. Instead of clearing the trees to plant field crops as in *kebun-talun*, some of the home garden trees are usually kept as a permanent source of shade for the house and the garden. Field crops are planted continuously under the trees. There is no rotation but year-round harvest at irregular

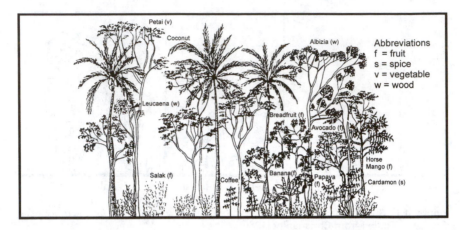

Figure 4.2 A representative home garden (*pekarangan*), West Java, Indonesia. *Source:* modified from Christianity (1986).

intervals. Plant species diversity is higher than in *kebun-talun* and may often be in the hundreds. As well, animals are always an integral part of the home garden. *Pekarangan* may look chaotic, but it makes full use of available space and diversity of resources (see figure 4.2). Both of these above-mentioned systems retain some of the essential elements of the original tropical forest ecosystem, such as relatively high biodiversity. It is also possible in some instances to convert a tropical forest ecosystem into a completely different system of production, such as an irrigated rice system, but that is another story (see chapter 9).

SEMIARID AREAS: KEEPING THE LAND PRODUCTIVE

Much of the traditional ecological knowledge literature on arid and semiarid lands concentrates on soil and water conservation techniques in agriculture (e.g., Bocco 1991; Pawluk et al. 1992; Reij et al. 1996). An example is provided in box 4.1. The material selected here instead considers how traditional management systems can directly alter the habitat and increase the productivity of the environment. Two kinds of active interventions are discussed, one regarding the establishment of forests at the edge of semiarid lands, and the other, the use of fire for habitat management.

A striking example of traditional ecological knowledge systems helping forest growth in semiarid lands comes from northwestern Kenya. For over half a century, African pastoralists and their livestock have been blamed for overgrazing and desertification. The assumption of negative pastoralist impact on rangelands continues to shape resource management policy (Niamir-Fuller 1998). It is true that cattle concentrations near villages and towns can pose sustainability

---

BOX 4.1
WATER HARVESTING IN SEMIARID ENVIRONMENTS: THE ZUNI

"In many cases, soil and water conservation is the principle underlying indigenous farming methods. A common technique used by traditional peoples from Mesoamerica to the Sahel includes the use of weirs, dams, or terrace walls to slow runoff and foster the deposition of upland sediments. In this way, eroded slopes are rehabilitated as topsoil builds up behind structures. . . .

"Native Americans in the southwestern United States have farmed successfully in a precarious arid and semiarid environment for over a millennium. Some of the methods used by the Zuni include the careful placement of fields on alluvial fans, complex manipulation of runoff, and management of gully formation. It appears that harvesting water and sediment from drainages has allowed the Zuni to favorably influence soil moisture, nutrient status, and texture of soils within their fields."

Source: Pawluk et al. 1992, 300

---

problems, especially if cattle owners remain in one spot. Traditionally, however, African pastoral systems were characterized by large-scale movements and the rotation of grazing areas. The large-scale movements of pastoralists and their cattle mimicked the migrations of wild ungulates. Like wild herbivores, domestic herds followed the annual cycle of rainfall and new grass growth, moving to seasonally productive lands to take advantage of the new growth of high-protein grasses, followed by a return migration after the food supply was exhausted.

Smaller-scale movements (micro-mobility) and the rotation of grazing lands were also important for sustainability (Niamir 1990). Carrying capacity and stocking rate calculations, both equilibrium-based concepts of primary importance to Western range managers, were of no meaning in the Sahel, where rainfall varied unpredictably from year to year as well as from season to season. Instead, traditional herders had rules that tracked ecological conditions of the range and controlled micro-mobility, resulting in the flexible management of the actual stocking rate. These rules acted through four main variables: the length of grazing on a patch by a herd; the frequency with which the same patch is visited; rotation time (rest interval) between each visit; and the distance between grazed sites (Niamir-Fuller 1998).

The Ngisonyoka Turkana of Kenya are nomadic pastoralists, still engaged in a relatively traditional lifestyle at the time of the study by Reid and Ellis (1995). They kept their sheep, goats, and camels in circular enclosures, moving them with the seasons, about once a month on the average. The researchers had observed that seedlings of *Acacia tortilis*, the dominant tree species in the dry woodlands of the region, often appeared during the first rainy season after pastoralists abandoned their corrals. The entire area of the old corrals was often covered with dense circular patches of seedlings and young trees, corresponding to cycles of movement (Reid and Ellis 1995).

Acacia seedpods made up an important part of livestock diets. The goats and sheep digested many of the seeds they ate. Some, however, were not digested and were scarified. These germinated at higher rates than did noningested seeds. The researchers compared *Acacia* growth in abandoned corrals with that in control plots and found that seed density was eighty-five times higher in corrals than in controls. Corral soils were enriched with organic matter (ninefold higher carbon than controls), nitrogen (threefold), and phosphorus (sixfold), and they retained more moisture. Successful germination and survival of *Acacia* in noncorral sites were restricted to the occasional year with high rainfall, but Acacia in corral sites found a highly favorable microhabitat—the abandoned corral provided an environment in which seeds ready to germinate were deposited in nutrient- and moisture-rich patches of dung and soil.

The memory of Turkana herders for both location and time is excellent. Using "Turkana event calendars" previously developed by anthropologists, Reid and Ellis (1995) relied on local traditional knowledge to age *Acacia* stands, and they considered this technique more reliable than tree-ring counts. Using this approach, they were able to reconstruct the history of development of fourteen *Acacia* forest patches in the area, ranging in age from one to thirty-nine years.

"Contrary to conventional wisdom," Reid and Ellis (1995, 978) point out, "pastorals may be improving rangelands in South Turkana by enhancing recruitment reliability in this important tree species." The Turkana case is probably not an exception. Similar pastoralist-livestock-*Acacia* interactions may be found in South Ethiopia and South Kenya. A similar mechanism may explain the presence of *Acacia* stands in nutrient-enriched patches in the middle of nutrient-poor savanna in South Africa near Iron Age Tswana settlements. "If so," Reid and Ellis (1995, 990) conclude, "this suggests that livestock may have affected tree recruitment in some African environments, not just for the past few decades, but for hundreds of years."

Traditional practices help create forest islands in some semiarid areas of South America as well (Posey 1985). In the savanna landscape at the southern fringe of the Amazon, the Kayapo people plant small mounds of useful plants. They tend these mounds casually and add to them over time, planting and harvesting a succession of plants from annuals eventually to trees, in some ways similar to the management of swidden plots. A new planted mound, *apete*, peaks in crop production in about three years; sweet potatoes continue for five years, yams and taro for six, and papaya and banana for longer. Old *apete* are not abandoned but continue to be managed for fruit and nut trees and other products. The resulting forest islands are difficult to identify as human-made (see box 4.2).

Fire has been used by traditional peoples, not only by horticulturalists but also by hunter-gatherers for habitat management in a variety of geographic areas (Turner 1994; Barsh 1997). This is well documented now, but for a long time conventional wisdom held that hunter-gatherers did not modify their habitat, much less use fire to do it. There was a romanticized belief, as Lewis (1993b, 395) put it, "that 'primitive people' live, or at least once lived, in some undefined

---

BOX 4.2
THE KAYAPO OF BRAZIL: MANAGERS OF THE FOREST EDGE

The Kayapo Indians of central Brazil live in the watershed of the Xingu River, which is near the southern limit of the tropical forests of Amazonia and includes *terra firme* and gallery forests interspersed with areas of more or less open *cerrado* (similar to savanna). Their knowledge, management, and use of the floral and faunal resources of the forests in their territory are astonishingly subtle and complex. It is unlikely that the Kayapo are unique—they are simply, and by far, the best studied of the many Indian groups of Amazonia.

"Like almost all the Indian groups in Amazonia, the Kayapo hunt, fish, and gather a great many species of the fauna and flora of the forests and practice shifting cultivation. They also concentrate native plants by growing them in resource islands, forest fields, forest openings, tuber gardens, agricultural plots, and old fields, and beside their trails through the forest. . . . Forest patches (*apete*) are created from open *cerrado* in areas prepared with crumbled termite and ant nests and mulch. . . .

"Perhaps the most surprising and significant of their many resource management techniques is the creation of the *apete* forest patches. Posey became aware that these isolated patches of forest were man-made only in the seventh year of his research among the Kayapo. As he pointed out, 'Perhaps the most exciting aspect of these new data is the implication for reforestation. The Indian example not only provides new ideas about how to build forests from scratch, but also how to successfully manage what has been considered to be infertile *campo/cerrado*.'"

Source: Taylor 1988, in reference to Posey 1985

---

condition of 'harmony with nature,' engaged in environmentally benign ways of exploiting resources which either could not or would not have allowed people to alter 'what nature provides.' "

There were many fragmentary anthropological references to the use of fire by the aboriginal people of California, but the systematic study of the evidence did not start until the 1960s (Lewis 1973). Lewis was a young student when he first saw the effects of fire in a chaparral-dominated area and became receptive to the idea that fire may be used to make the environment more productive (see box 4.3). Indeed, until the late 1880s, Kumeyaay bands of Southern California cultivated a kind of grain, since extinct, by harvesting, burning the stubble, and broadcasting seeds (Shipek 1993). Broadcast with the grain were seeds of leafy vegetables and other annuals; this produced an interplanted field not recognized by Europeans accustomed to plough-cleared monocultures. On steeper slopes, the Kumeyaay planted shrubs that produced food and medicine and broadcast seeds of annuals and perennials following controlled burns. Below-ground parts of chaparral survived the burning and resprouted. As the chaparral vegetation increased in size, the grains disappeared first, followed gradually by the other annuals and perennials. It was then considered time to reburn the slope (Shipek 1993).

Fire management was used for different purposes in different areas, but Lewis's cross-cultural comparative studies show that there are remarkable similarities as well. These similarities occur through functionally parallel strategies employed by hunter-gatherers to maintain "fire yards" and "fire corridors" in

BOX 4.3
REDISCOVERING THE WISDOM OF CHAPARRAL
BURNING IN CALIFORNIA

Lewis writes that in 1960 he was involved "in the essentially futile effort of trying to stop a large, extremely intense brush fire in Sequoia Park, a fire which was only extinguished when it ran out of fuel along the crest of a mountain ridge. Ignited near the bottom of a canyon, ten thousand acres of dense chaparral erupted in what was described as a 'fire storm,' in an area which had not been burned for 70 or more years."

As a part of their efforts to contain the conflagration, a firebreak was cut from two directions across a drainage. Very near to where the fire lines were linked, Lewis and colleagues stumbled upon a long-abandoned Indian campsite that was probably used by the Western Mono in the trans-Sierran trade of obsidian and salt. All indications were that it had been regularly used over a long period of time; but in 1960, it was almost completely overgrown by dense brush and a large number of oaks, which were undoubtedly a source of acorns. The site was situated just a few yards from a ravine that, except for spring runoff, was apparently dry for most of the year.

Given the fact that the "natural growth" in the burn area consisted of an impenetrable thicket of chaparral, Lewis was puzzled: what made it a desirable campsite for the aboriginals? With instructions to get out as quickly as possible, he did not give the question of the site's unlikely location much further thought, until a year later when he revisited the area to locate it for the park historian.

"Twelve months after what had been described in the newspapers as the 'total destruction' of brush and trees," Lewis writes, "a new and profuse growth of grasses, herbs, and sprouts of various chaparral species had emerged from the ashes. Most impressive was the number of deer observed browsing and grazing on the burn site.... At the same time—and during the same month as that of the previous summer—water was still running in the ravine, and the 'unlikely place' for a campsite offered views up and down the drainage. It was at this point that I began asking myself serious questions about why Indians would have set fires in chaparral stands—and, conversely, why we did not."

Source: Lewis 1993b, 390, 391

northwest California, western Washington, northwestern Alberta (Canada), Tasmania, New South Wales, western Australia, and Australia's Northern Territory (Lewis and Ferguson 1988). Thus, traditional knowledge lends support to fire ecologists and advocates of prescribed burning who emphasize the role of fire in the renewal cycle of ecosystems and who have been challenging the official dogma that all fires should be suppressed.

However, this is not to say that fire ecologists are necessarily comfortable with traditional practices. In the Kakadu National Park, Australia's Northern Territory, where both sides agree that fire is a natural feature of ecosystems and a key to maintaining habitat diversity, great differences in opinion separate park managers from Aborigines. The managers want "controlled burns," planned in advance and based on the calendar and scientific criteria, and they believe that "fire is basically bad but *can be used* to good purpose," whereas the Aborigines' notions of the need to burn rest on many rules of thumb and a basic belief that "fire is good and *must be used*" (Lewis 1989).

ISLAND ECOSYSTEMS—PERSONAL ECOSYSTEMS

It is said that island peoples see the limitations of their environment more readily than do those who live on continents. Thus, it is probably not a coincidence that the Asia Pacific region is particularly rich in traditional knowledge and management systems, and many of these have been documented in detail, especially from Japan and parts of Oceania, that is, Melanesia, Micronesia, and Polynesia (Klee 1980; Johannes 1981; Ruddle and Akimichi 1984; Ruddle and Johannes 1985, 1990; Freeman et al. 1991). The most widespread single marine conservation measure employed in Oceania was reef and lagoon tenure. The basic idea behind reef and lagoon tenure has to do with self-interest. The right to harvest the resources of a particular area was controlled by a social group, such as a family or clan (or a chief acting on behalf of the group), which thus regulated the exploitation of its own marine resources. As Johannes (1978, 267) explained, "it was in the best interest of those who controlled a given area to harvest in moderation. By doing so they could maintain high sustained yields, all the benefits of which would accrue directly to them." A wide range of traditional regulations and restrictions applied to resource use. Some of these could be attributed to religious or superstitious beliefs (Johannes 1978) and some to power relationships in general (Chapman 1985) and regional differences in systems of political authority (Chapman 1987). But, by and large, reef and lagoon tenure rules operated as institutions for the management of common property resources.

Some authors think that various cultural beliefs and rituals inadvertently served to conserve resources. For example, Polunin (1984, 267) argues that "exclusive areas became established not because people wished to conserve resources, but rather because they tended to exploit more and eventually came up against neighboring people doing the same sorts of things." Johannes (1978, 352), however, holds that many restrictions were clearly intended to conserve fish: "almost every basic fisheries conservation measure devised in the West was in use in the tropical Pacific centuries ago." Table 4.1 lists some examples. Many of these locally devised regulations no longer exist, and reef and lagoon tenure systems themselves have been degraded through various episodes of colonization. However, they are being revitalized in some of the Pacific island nation states (Baines 1989; Ruddle 1994b).

Environmental management in the Pacific goes beyond fisheries regulations. Chapter 3 points out that ancient conceptualizations of ecosystems exist in several Amerindian, European, and Asian cultures, especially as watershed-based units (see table 3.3, above). It appears that the richest set of examples was found in Oceania. Examples include the ancient Hawaiian *ahupua'a* (Lind 1938; Costa-Pierce 1987), wedge-shaped land units granted by the king to lesser chiefs, the *konohiki*. They encompassed entire valleys and stretched from the top of mountains to the coast and shallow waters. Figure 4.3 shows an idealized *ahupua'a*, with a forested mountain zone (functioning as a watershed conser-

Table 4.1 Traditional marine conservation measures of tropical Pacific islanders.

Method or regulation	Examples
Closed fishing areas	Pukapuka; Marquesas; Truk; Tahiti; Satawal
Closed seasons	Hawaii; Tahiti; Palau; Tonga; Tokelaus
Allowing a portion of the catch to escape	Tonga; Micronesia; Hawaii; Enewetak
Holding excess catch in enclosures	Pukapuka; Tuamotus; Marshall Islands; Palau
Ban on taking small individuals	Pukapuka (crabs); Palau (giant clams)
Restricting some fisheries for emergency	Nauru; Palau; Gilbert Islands; Pukapuka
Restricting harvest of seabirds and/or eggs	Tobi; Pukapuka; Enewetak
Restricting number of fish traps	Woleai
Ban on taking nesting turtles and/or eggs	Tobi; New Hebrides; Gilbert Islands
Ban on disturbing turtle nesting habitat	Samoa

Source: Adapted and summarized from Johannes (1978).

vation area protected by taboo), integrated farming zones in upland and coastal areas, a fringe of coconut palms along the coastline (storm and wind protection), and brackish water and seawater fish ponds (Costa-Pierce 1987). Such land use would be called integrated watershed planning in the contemporary terminology, and the land unit in question is clearly an ecosystem unit, with its biophysical boundaries. The Hawaiian *ahupua'a* disappeared with colonization, but similar systems exist in other Pacific islands and some are considered still functional in the contemporary world.

The variations of the Hawaiian system may be found in the Yap *tabinau*, the Fijian *vanua*, and the Solomon Islands *puava* (Ruddle et al. 1992). In each, the term refers to an intimate association of a group of people with land, reef, and lagoon, and all that grows on or in them. This "integrated corporate estate" concept is effectively the "personal ecosystem" of the group in question: "*puava* is a defined, named area of land and, in most cases, sea. A *puava* in the widest sense includes all areas and resources associated with a *butubutu* (descent group) through ancestral rights, from the top of the mainland mountains to the open sea outside the barrier reef" (Hviding 1990, 23). The Fijian *vanua* is conceptualized in similar terms (Ravuvu 1987; Ruddle 1994b). *Vanua* describes the totality of a Fijian community. Depending on the context, it may be used to refer either to a social group (*vanua* = tribe, descent group, lineage) or the territory it occupies (*vanua* = tribal estate), thereby expressing the inseparability of land and people in the Fijian ethos. Fijian spiritual affinity with land is illustrated in expressions such as *ne qau vanua* ("the land which supports me and to which I belong"), and *na vanua na tamatu* ("the people are the land") (Ravuvu 1987; Ruddle 1994b).

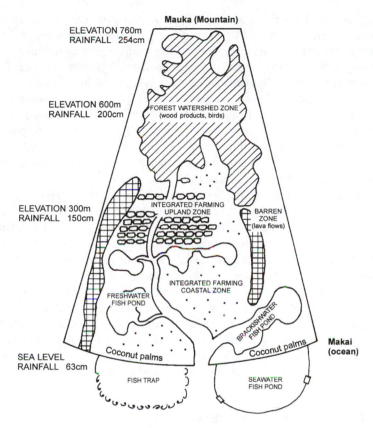

Figure 4.3 The *ahupua'a* system of ancient Hawaii. *Source:* modified from Costa-Pierce (1987).

One important and interesting feature of these ecosystem concepts, as pointed out by a number of researchers (e.g., Ruddle et al. 1992), is that land and sea space exist as a continuum, and that indigenous categories do not dichotomize resources into "ownable land" and "unownable sea" as do Westerners. Using the example of Roviana lagoon, New Georgia, in the Solomon Islands, Aswani (1997) challenges this view. He pointed out that the territorial unit (*pepeso*) is conceptually a single property domain that extends from the top of the mountains to the midpoint between South New Georgia and the next island. However, the people make a clear economic distinction between land and sea. Most significantly, Aswani (1997) argues, the sea cannot be claimed through its physical modification as can land. For example, the establishment of a small coconut plantation can be used as the pretext for privatizing land, but the sea remains an "untamed" domain in which communal tenure and access rules are strongly guarded by the chiefs. Examples such as these illustrate the difficulty in making geographical generalizations, and the difficulty in assessing the extent to which traditional systems are shaped by contemporary economic pressures.

Economic pressures influence not only the performance of traditional management systems but also the ethics of management. Johannes, who has extensive experience with traditional management systems in the Pacific, has been intrigued by the fact that some Pacific island peoples clearly possess a traditional conservation ethic, whereas other traditional peoples do not (Johannes and MacFarlane 1991; Johannes 1994). A group of people is said to possess a traditional conservation ethic if they have an "awareness that they can deplete or otherwise damage their natural resources, coupled with a commitment to reduce or eliminate the problem" (Johannes 1994, 85).

It has been noted, for example, that among the people of the Torres Strait area between New Guinea and Australia, which has an abundance of marine resources, a traditional conservation ethic is lacking (Johannes and MacFarlane 1991). This contrasts with an often well-developed conservation ethic among people who live on the smaller Pacific islands such as Palau (Johannes 1981 and personal communication). Johannes has not attempted to provide a conclusive answer to this paradox. It seems possible that some of the differences may be related to the fact that people of small islands receive faster and clearer feedback on their resource exploitation strategies than do others, and these feedbacks increase their ability to learn and to revise not only their management systems but also their environmental ethics and worldviews, a point revisited in chapters 6 and 9 under the discussion of social learning and conservation.

COASTAL LAGOONS AND WETLANDS

One of the first international organizations to express interest in traditional management systems was UNESCO. In 1982, through its Division of Marine Sciences, UNESCO asked the International Association of Biological Oceanography to help organize a steering group to initiate work in this area. The group got going in 1983 at the UNESCO headquarters in Paris and quickly issued a report (Johannes et al. 1983) describing a range of traditional coastal management systems from around the world, pointing out the variations and similarities in the methods devised by peoples of very different areas and cultures. Their examples included

- the *valli* (or *vallicoltura*) of the Venice region, Adriatic Sea, starting in the 15th–16th centuries, designed so that young fish enter the pools with the tide but cannot get out; continued today as complex systems of dikes, gates and ponds;
- the *cherfia* of North Africa, installed at the mouth of lagoons, with openings equipped with concave basketwork that admits fish but prevents large fish from escaping, similar to the *lavoriero* of the Italian coast;

- the *acadja* of West Africa, which combines fishing with fish farming, and consists of immersing piles of branches in the shallow parts of the lagoon (serving to increase fish habitat);
- the Indonesian *tambak*, brackish water (mixed freshwater and seawater) fish ponds, dating back to the fifteenth century, usually installed in delta systems and associated lagoons;
- and, in the inland extensions of the coastal zone, variations of rice-field fishery techniques, such as the Indonesian *minepadi* and *surjan* systems.

The above examples should be considered only a small sample of such systems. In fact, *cherfia* and *lavoriero* type of systems are also found in Greece and Turkey (Berkes 1992); *acadja*-like brush-pile fisheries are found in Bangladesh and Sri Lanka (Amarasinghe et al. 1997); and various kinds of rice-field fisheries are found in India, the Philippines, Indochina, and China as well.

Some of these systems furnish excellent examples of the application of prescientific ecosystem views. One relevant example is from Indonesia, where traditional systems combined rice and fish culture, and nutrient-rich wastes from the rice-field fishery system often flowed downstream into brackish water aquaculture systems (*tambak*) and then into the coastal area enriching the coastal fishery (Costa-Pierce 1988). The *tambaks* themselves were polyculture ponds, often combining fish, vegetables, and tree crops (figure 4.4).

Indonesia has many kinds of rice-field fishery and water management systems. Some of the more sophisticated kinds, such as the *subak* system in Bali for the management of irrigation water resources, were managed not locally but regionally. The *subak* was part of a water temple system, and the entire regional rice terrace irrigation was often managed as a system by resource managers–priests (Lansing 1987, 1991). The integration of rice-field fishery–*tambak* systems for combined production of rice, fish, and downstream products is an ecologically sophisticated application by scientific standards as well. These systems remained sustainable for several centuries, combined livelihood activities with good conservation practice (note the integration of mangroves into the *tambak* in figure 4.4) but declined with increases in population pressure and the wholesale conversion of coastal wetlands and lagoons into modern shrimp farms for the international trade.

Coastal lagoons, especially in tropical areas, are very productive environments that support a multitude of often conflicting human activities. Not surprisingly, sophisticated local governance systems and allocation rules for lagoon resources have developed in a number of different geographical regions. Amarasinghe et al. (1997) describe one such contemporary lagoon management system from the Negombo estuary in western Sri Lanka. The case study illustrates the sophisticated level of governance that can be achieved by traditional systems and the key role of local institutions.

Of several kinds of fishing operations carried out in the Negombo lagoon, the one known as the *kattudel* or the "stake-seine" fishery (which uses a kind of

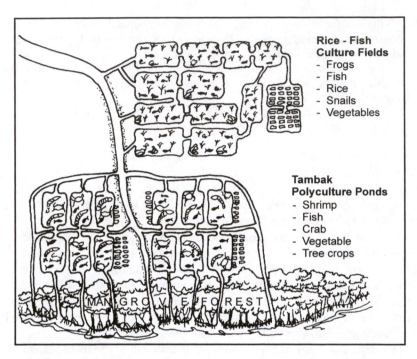

Figure 4.4 Traditional Indonesian coastal zone management. *Source:* modified from Costa-Pierce (1988).

trapnet) targeted high-value shrimp, *Metapaneus dobsoni*, as the shrimp migrated out to the sea. At the mouth of the lagoon, there were twenty-two named fishing sites at which sixty-five nets could be used at any one time. The sites were exclusive. The traditional fishing rights to the sites went back at least to the eighteenth century (and possibly to the fifteenth century) and were controlled by members of four Rural Fisheries Societies (RFS) based in the villages around the lagoon. Elaborate rules governed eligibility and membership in the RFS, the obligations of the fishers, the system by which the four RFS cooperatives shared the resource, and the allocation rules within each RFS. There were 306 members in the *kattudel* fishery out of some 3,000 fishers using the lagoon. The members took turns at the twenty-two fishing sites. A lottery system was used to allocate turns (one night of fishing at a time) for the members, and the turns rotated through the twenty-two sites to give each fisher a chance at the better sites (Amarasinghe et al. 1997).

An important feature of the *kattudel* fishery is that the rules of the fishery, most recently reorganized in 1958, have legal status under Sri Lanka's *Fisheries Ordinance* as "Negombo (Kattudel) Fishing Regulations." This is significant because only through legal enforcement can the strict limits on membership, and hence the limited-access nature of the fishery, be maintained. Closing access to a common property resource is important for its biological and economic sustainability (Amarasinghe et al. 1997).

The *kattudel* case shows that lagoon fisheries and associated traditional management systems can be sustainable over long periods, but this does not mean that such systems are stable throughout long periods. Rather, crises often punctuate relatively uneventful times. The real test of the management system in question is whether it can adapt (or be successfully redesigned) to respond to these crises. The *kattudel* fishery in the case study has been through turbulent times, most recently in the 1940s and the 1950s, and has evidently survived the various crises. Some other systems in the South Asia region, for example a *kattudel*-type trap-net fishery near Madras, India, have not survived well the intense conflicts brought about by caste group competition, apparently in this case because traditional resource use rights were not protected by government law (Mathew 1991), as they were in the case of the Sri Lankan *kattudel* fishery.

As recognized by the UNESCO working group (Johannes et al. 1983), traditional coastal and lagoon fisheries around the world provide a rich set of local adaptations from which modern management systems can learn. These systems are found not only in isolated parts of the world but also in industrialized areas. Examples include "fisheries brotherhood" systems that act to regulate resource use and manage resource conflicts, the guild-like *prud'homie* system of the French Mediterranean, and the *confreries* of Catalonia, Spain (Alegret 1995). It is true that many of these systems have declined over the years. On the other hand, many new systems have in the meantime evolved in various parts of the world. Examples include the lobster territory system practiced among the commercial lobster fishers of Maine in the United States (Acheson 1975), and a system of managing net fishing sites, with remarkable parallels to the Sri Lankan *kattudel* fishery with its rotation of lottery-allocated fishing rights, that evolved in the 1980s in Alanya on the Turkish Mediterranean coast (Berkes 1992).

CONCLUSIONS

The theme of development-stability-crisis-adaptation appears over and over in many types of coastal and lagoon fisheries, and no doubt in other resource types as well. The findings in a variety of traditional resource management systems are in agreement with the central thesis of a remarkable book on Adaptive Management, *Barriers and Bridges to the Renewal of Ecosystems and Institutions* (Gunderson et al. 1995). *Barriers and Bridges* holds that resource crises are important for the renewal of management institutions (because the crisis forces social learning by the institution), just as dynamic ecosystem processes (including such "crises" as fire) are important for the renewal of ecosystems. The California fire management case lends support to Adaptive Management analysis. This case sees ecosystems in dynamic change and holds that it is ecologically more sensible to let small, frequent fires burn to clear leaf litter ("fuel load") in forests before it accumulates, than to suppress all fires—which only sets the stage for fires of disastrous proportions when they finally do occur (Holling 1986). These ideas challenge conventional resource management science with its equilibrium-centered emphasis on keeping resource yields constant, as in maximum sustained yields of timber or fish.

There is another challenge posed by traditional management systems, supported by the dynamic view of ecosystem renewal in Adaptive Management, and it pertains to the role of resource use in maintaining healthy and productive ecosystems. The lesson from tropical forest management systems such as shifting cultivation, *kebun-talun*, and *pekarangan* is that it is feasible to sustain a productive landscape and a high degree of biodiversity by maintaining a variety of uses. These productive uses are compatible with the tropical forest ecosystem, without losing the resilience of the system. The tropical forest ecosystem can absorb the perturbation of long-fallow shifting cultivation, and in fact flourishes with it. Thus, if the objective is to conserve tropical forests, a strategy of focusing on resilience, through a knowledge of regeneration cycles and ecological processes, such as plant succession, may be the key to tropical forest sustainability (Lugo 1995; Holling et al. 1995).

Seven principles that Alcorn (1990) derived from the indigenous agroforestry strategies of the Huastec and the Bora of tropical Mexico incorporate this kind of resilience thinking. These traditional strategies (1) take advantage of native trees and native tree communities; (2) rely on native successional processes; (3) use natural environmental variation; (4) incorporate numerous crops and native species; (5) are flexible; (6) spread risks by retaining diversity; and (7) maintain reliable backup resources to meet needs should the regular livelihood sources fail. Strategies such as these may be of value for creating better management practices in tropical forest ecosystems. In fact, practical applications of traditional knowledge in coffee agroforestry show that it is feasible to use ancient wisdom to create resilient modern cropping systems without destroying the essence of the tropical forest (Brookfield and Padoch 1994; more in chapter 9, below).

Thus, Adaptive Management focusing on resilience does not require that all uses of the tropical forest be eliminated. Nor does management require a precise capability to predict quantitative yields (such as food or timber), but only a qualitative capacity to devise systems that can absorb and accommodate future events in whatever unexpected form they may take. To do so necessitates greater attention to ecosystem processes rather than ecosystem products, as McNeely (1994) puts it. The evidence from traditional knowledge systems, including that discussed in this chapter, is that such qualitative management capacity and attention to ecological processes were in fact developed by cultural evolution in many groups and ecosystems. The intuitive ecological sense of traditional knowledge is often consistent with dynamic, multi-equilibrium, ecosystem-based analyses in contemporary ecology (Berkes et al. 1997).

However, traditional knowledge and practice are often inconsistent with the kind of conventional resource management science that takes poor account of ecosystem dynamics and focuses on quantitative yields. Given this inconsistency, it is not surprising that many Western-trained resource management professionals take a dim view of traditional resource use. For example, Leach (1994), writing about Sierra Leone, West Africa, points out that many professional foresters see any conversion of the closed-canopy forest as degradation. Yet such conversion may be viewed positively by the local people, for whom the resulting bush-fallow vegetation provides a greater range of products than does the closed-canopy forest. A similar situation is seen in the Asian and American examples discussed in this chapter. At the same time, the conversion is consistent with forest renewal cycles.

Many of these conclusions seem to apply to a number of different areas in the tropical forest zones of the world. As well, the conclusions from the Kayapo case apply to savanna–tropical forest ecotone areas in other parts of the world. Fairhead and Leach (1996) argue that the mixed forest savanna is the outcome of forest expansion into the savanna, resulting from the deliberate management of the soil, trees, and fire by peasant farmers of West Africa. The farmers' oral history indicates that the increase in forest area is due to their management interventions; time-series aerial photo comparisons support farmers' oral history.

Similarly, in the case of herders and semiarid lands, resource management professionals often blame pastoralists for overgrazing and desertification (Niamir-Fuller 1998). However, the Turkana example shows that pastoralists' activities can improve the vegetation cover. More generally, Leach and Mearns (1996) argue that pastoralists' herd management and land management strategies often make the most of productive opportunities in a dryland ecosystem—an ecosystem characterized by variability and nonequilibrium conditions that preclude the application of such conventional Western resource management tools as carrying capacity analysis and animal stocking densities (Behnke et al. 1993). Thus, traditional pastoralists "may have long been practicing resource management attuned to non-equilibrium ecological conditions," and hence the task in designing new and more appropriate resource management in savanna ecosystems would do well to build on the traditional skills of Africa's herders, rather than to replace them (Leach and Mearns 1996, 29).

Our Common Future drew attention to the relevance of indigenous knowledge for the sustainable use of three kinds of ecosystems—tropical forests, mountains, and arid lands (WCED 1987). This chapter deals with two of these, plus the use of traditional ecological knowledge for the management of two other kinds of ecosystems, islands and coastal lagoons. The subject of another type of ecosystem, the subarctic, is taken up in the next three chapters. Any detailed study of traditional knowledge needs to account for the worldview of the group in question. Thus, chapter 5 starts out by providing an *emic* account of the local worldview, that is, as seen by the local people themselves. Chapter 6 is the story of one major resource, the caribou, and crisis-forced learning and adaptation by the traditional management institution, paralleling cases in *Barriers and Bridges*

(Gunderson et al. 1995). Chapter 7 is a detailed human ecological analysis of one resource system in one area; it is an outsider's academic interpretation, an *etic* view, using the Cree Indian fishery management system as the illustration. Taken together, these three chapters provide one case study that uses three different approaches to illustrate some of the principles and issues introduced here in chapter 4.

Chapter Five

Cree Worldview "from the Inside"

According to the beliefs of the Cree of eastern James Bay, it is animals, not people, who control the success of the hunt. Hunters have certain obligations to fulfill toward the animals, maintaining a respectful relationship. A continued, proper use of resources is important for sustainability. Cree social values such as reciprocity apply to human-animal as well as to social relationships. These beliefs indicate a cosmology in which humans are part of a "community of beings" within the ecological system.

Not all cultures in the world share the dominant Western view of a secularized, utilitarian, depersonalized nature. The existence of alternative views of the natural environment is important as part of the cultural heritage of humankind. This cultural diversity is akin to biodiversity as the raw material for evolutionarily adaptive responses (Gadgil 1987). Indigenous worldviews are both diverse and different from the dominant Western worldview. This chapter provides a look into the worldview of one North American aboriginal group from the Canadian subarctic.

The Cree people of Chisasibi survived three centuries of fur trade as essentially hunter-gatherers. After settling into permanent communities in the 1960s and coming into close contact with the industrial society in the 1970s (due to the construction of the James Bay hydroelectric project), their lifestyle came to maintain an uneasy balance between being independent hunter-trapper-fishers and being rural North Americans at the margin of the dominant society. Although their philosophy of the natural environment was changing rapidly, in pace with their integration into the dominant society, they still professed and practiced a distinctly different view of the world as of the 1980s.

The material presented in this chapter is based on focus group discussions with a volunteer, self-selected working group of senior hunters from the local Cree Trappers Association (CTA). The work was initiated by the CTA to provide educational material on Cree culture for youth, to record and strengthen traditional practice, and to educate the outside world in defense of Cree culture and subsistence economy. The report of the project was published by the Cree themselves (Bearskin et al. 1989); parts of it were published by the researcher as well (Berkes 1988b). The quotations are from the original report prepared for the Cree. Brackets are used as asides to the reader.

The report was prepared through five sets of meetings and five drafts over a year and a half, and it was corrected by members of the group through revisions at each step. Hunters' statements were written in standard English, as requested by them, and the text modified by them as necessary. The text of the chapter preserves the Cree narrative form and contains direct quotes. The researcher/compiler comes in merely to provide context, mostly at the beginning and the end of the chapter. The material is based on the then-current practice of mature hunters in Chisasibi; it is not an elders' account of past practice.

In the belief system or religious ideology of the Cree, the living environment is a community of beings that are supernatural as well as natural, as previously noted by other researchers working with Cree groups elsewhere (Preston 1975; Tanner 1979; Feit 1986; Scott 1989; Brightman 1993). These beings possess what Westerners might consider extranormal powers. They have spirits that are sentient; they are watchful and aware of people's behavior. This belief in animal spirits persists among the Chisasibi Cree despite the best efforts of missionaries to eradicate it (Berkes 1986b), and it shapes their worldview.

The chapter focuses on a selection of three Cree beliefs to illustrate their unique worldview: (a) it is the animals, not people, who control the success of the hunt, (b) hunters and fishers have obligations to show respect to the animals to ensure a productive hunt, and (c) a continued, proper use is necessary for maintaining production of animals. The hunter's obligations toward animals are intertwined with social obligations, so that the environmental ethic of the Chisasibi Cree is an integral part of a comprehensive philosophy of life.

ANIMALS CONTROL THE HUNT

In Western science and its applications to fish and wildlife management, it is assumed that humans can control animal populations. In Cree worldview, by contrast, "human management" of animals and environment is not possible. Rather, it is animals who control the success of the hunt. The Cree believe that animals know everything humans do; they are aware of hunters' activities. In the past all living things talked, communicated with humans. Many Cree legends carry this theme, and the idea is alive among contemporary hunters as well:

> I had a fish net out in a lake and at first I was getting quite a few fish in it. But there was an otter in the lake and he was eating the fish in the net. After a while, fish stopped coming into the net. They knew there was a predator there. So similarly game know about the presence of hunters as well. The Cree say, "all creatures are watching you. They know everything you are doing. Animals are aware of your activities." In the past, animals talked to people. In a sense, there is still communication between animals and hunters. You can predict where the black bear is likely to den. Even though the black bear zigzags before retreating into his den to hibernate, tries to shake you off his trail, you can still predict where he is likely to go to. When he approaches his den entrance, he makes tracks backwards, loses his tracks in the bush, and makes a long detour before coming into the den. The hunter tries to think what the bear is thinking. The hunter and the bear have parallel knowledge, and they share that knowledge. So in a sense they communicate.

The hunter always speaks as if the human is the passive partner in this relationship. The hunter is successful if the animal decides to make himself available. The hunter has no power over the game; animals have the last say as to whether they will be caught. The hunter has to show respect to the animals because the hunter is dependent on game. The game is not there for the taking. There is no guarantee of a kill; the game has to be pursued. The increase in the hunter's success, as he reaches his prime, goes hand in hand with the increase of his respect for the animals. Another way of putting this would be that he develops respect for game as he becomes a better hunter. The two factors are mutually related. The Cree notion of "success" or being a "good hunter" is not measured by the size of the hunter's kill; it is measured by the ability of the hunter to "get what he/she needs."

Young people are taught early on to show respect to the animals. If a hunter does not follow the expected practices of respect, it happens very easily that the disrespectful individual will kill nothing. For such a person, game would be scarce. Even if he sees game in the bush, the Cree believe, something happens, something prevents him from getting the game. This includes all animals, not just big game and fur animals, but also small game and fish. This is a fundamental belief shared by almost all hunters. A hunter never gets angry at game. If a hunter has no luck, he looks at himself to blame, not the animals. When the animals are not making themselves available, quite often, they are only "returning the discourtesy," as the Cree see it. Sometimes a hunter may be unlucky for no reason, but this is rare. In a community of hunters, it is an obligation of the more successful hunters to share their catch with the unlucky hunter. Sometimes a hunter is disrespectful to animals without intending to be.

> My brother was trapping otter. He had left his trap in the water a bit too long. Normally, one checks traps quite often. There was an otter in the trap, but it has been in the water too long. The fur was coming off. My brother was really worried: he had caused the fur to spoil, and knew that this was a crime against the animals. He said the otter would retaliate for this by not being caught. He thought it would take perhaps three years before the otter will decide to come back to his traps again.

Since hunting success ultimately depends on the willingness of animals to be caught, a hunter familiar with an area will often have the best success. Conversely, a stranger in an area will have poor hunting success, for, as the Cree say, "the land is unfamiliar with him."

> I once invited a coaster [someone who has a hunting territory on the James Bay coast], a good hunter, to my trapline north of the Chisasibi [La Grande] River. He was a stranger there. Even though he was a good hunter and had done nothing wrong to the animals, he did not have much luck. There is a saying, "the land and game would feel unfamiliar or uneasy with you if you are a stranger there." Such a person may have poor luck at first, but later on game will get to know him.

According to Cree beliefs, the success of a hunter peaks with age, up to a point. After this peak, a hunter's success would be expected to decline, and his sons or other hunters in the group are thought to inherit part of an older hunter's success. When an old man passes away, some younger people will inherit his animals. The whole process may be considered a cycle, from child, to hunter at his peak, to old man. During this cycle, the amount of animals available remains constant, but the distribution of success varies.

> As a hunter gains experience, he becomes better and better in hunting. He reaches a peak and after that his hunting success goes down. An old man would not be expected to hunt as well as he did when he was at his peak. It is common knowledge that an old man's hunt declines. This often happens after a man reaches 50 or 60. But an old hunter does not worry about his hunting success because he knows he has had his day, that he used to kill many. My uncle was a good trapper, but in his old age he did not catch many. He used to say jokingly that "the game were letting go of him." He would say that he was being ignored by game: the game were leaving him alone. He did not care to kill any. But he set traps anyway. For him, it was a way of life.
>
> When an old man dies, another person takes on from him. It is almost as if that the old man's game is now passed on to a younger person in that group. It is a fundamental belief of the Cree people that a young man would inherit an old man's game.
>
> My father used to catch lots of game. He used to say that once his sons started to hunt, his own hunting success would go down. And in fact, so it happened. My brother, who was an exceptionally successful goose hunter when he was young, now hunts fewer geese. But his sons make up for his losses. It can be said that his four sons inherited part of his catch.

The cycle of hunting success is one of many cyclic phenomena in the Cree worldview. Another one concerns cycles of animal abundance. The cyclic disappearance and reappearance of game animals is thought to be related to the willingness of animals to be hunted. The Cree believe that almost all animals go up and down in abundance, some in shorter cycles and some in longer cycles. For Chisasibi hunters, animals known to disappear and reappear include:

- Caribou, which disappeared around the turn of the century and reappeared in the 1980s;
- Beaver, which were scarce in the area between about 1930 and 1950 and increased thereafter;
- Marten, which declined twice since the turn of the century. In the 1980s it was very scarce in the inland traplines. However, in the coastal traplines it began to reappear in 1982–83;
- Porcupine, which were last plentiful in 1960–70 and declined in the 1970s; and
- Small game animals—snowshoe hare, rock and willow ptarmigan, spruce and sharp-tailed grouse, which are known to have eight- to ten-year cycles, from one peak of abundance to the next.

While the shorter of these cycles (e.g., hare and ptarmigan) are recognized by Western science, longer cycles such as those of the caribou are not. Many biologists believe that management or lack thereof is responsible for the increase or decrease of caribou. By contrast, the Cree believe that animals who disappear for a time sooner or later come back by themselves, not as a consequence of management by humans. Disappearing animals such as caribou and marten are said to go under the water or underground. This is thought to be something similar to the disappearance of animals such as ptarmigan, fox, lynx, and snowshoe hares in very cold weather. The belief in the eventual return of disappearing animals is very strong.

> My uncle who would have been about 90 [in 1984] missed the caribou. By the time he was old enough to hunt, caribou had already declined. An old man told him not to worry, the caribou would be back some day. And they are back now. Sometimes my uncle did not believe the old men. He asked them, "Where do they go when they disappear?" They answered that it has been known in the past that caribou disappear under the water. There would come a time when they would reappear later. He was at first amazed to hear this, but believed it later on. He came to know that all the animals you see, porcupine, fur animals and others, disappeared from time to time. In his early hunting days, marten were plentiful. He saw them decline and later come back again, all in his lifetime.
>
> He was hunting. He came to a little pond. There were fresh caribou tracks on the new snow. The tracks were leading into the lake. He walked across to the other side of the lake; he thought caribou had swum across. But here were no caribou tracks on the other side. Caribou had submerged. When he went back to the camp, the older men said, "Yes this is how big game and fur animals disappear. But they will someday come back again."
>
> A young trapper was checking his muskrat traps in the Sakami River area. He found one of his traps had sprung underwater. He thought it was a muskrat because there was a muskrat den nearby. But instead, he found a marten in his trap. There were no marten tracks in the area; he must have come up under the water. The young trapper was scared. He thought it was unnatural, a bad omen. He returned to the camp [to consult the elders]. The old men reassured him. They said it was not a bad sign, but marten lived under the water, too. I have seen marten tracks coming out of a fishing hole in the ice. The tracks went out of the lake, around a clump of trees, as if the marten was looking for other martens, and back to the lake and into the hole again.

OBLIGATIONS OF HUNTERS TO SHOW RESPECT

Since animals control the hunt, lack of respect for the animals will affect hunting success because animals can retaliate by "returning the discourtesy." The Cree say that the main reason for showing respect to animals is that humans and animals are related, they share the same Creator. Just as one respects other persons, one respects animals. Cree culture is rich with rituals related to respect (see Tanner 1979). Among the Chisasibi Cree, respect for the animal is shown in several ways:

- The hunter maintains an attitude of humility when going hunting;
- The animal is approached and killed with respect;
- The animal is carried respectfully to camp;
- Offerings are made to the animal;
- The meat is butchered according to rules signifying respect;
- The meat is consumed according to rules signifying respect; and
- The remains of the animal are disposed of properly.

The rule about an attitude of humility is both important and universal. Hunters should not boast about their abilities. Otherwise, they risk catching nothing because they are being disrespectful of game.

> While fishing with a group of people to the south of my area on the James Bay coast, I once boasted that I could catch as many trout as anyone else. It was a good area for speckled trout, and the fishermen were pulling out some 50–60 fish in each of their nets. My net was in the middle of all the other nets. But when I pulled it out, there was only one trout in it! In similar ways, many people have experienced a loss of hunting success after boasting.

> The hunter had a cord which he used for carrying black bear. But on this one hunt, he left his cord behind in the camp, laughing and boasting that he could carry any black bear without the cord. He did in fact kill a black bear on that trip. But he found out that he was not able to carry it. [The speaker is saying that this bear was too big for the hunter to carry without the benefit of a rope to tie its limbs over his chest and hips]. The moral of the story is that whatever fun you make of a black bear, this will backfire on you.

The hunter should also maintain an attitude of respect when approaching game. The killing will be done quickly and simply, without mess. The hunter should use a gun appropriate for the size of the animal. For example, a small-bore gun is used for the smaller animals. A hunter wants an animal to look its best. One does not want blood all over the place. If a hunter used an oversized gun, for example, on a beaver, this would be a transgression.

The Cree see similarity between social relations among humans and those among humans and animals, especially those animals considered particularly powerful and worthy of respect.

> When a hunter visits a camp, he lets it be known that he is a visitor (*maantaau*), a person from another camp. He approaches respectfully and modestly; he announces himself simply, (*nitikushin*) [I am here]. People in the camp come out to greet him as soon as they hear him. When they come out, he has already taken his snowshoes off and put them upright in the snow. People in the camp admire his snowshoes. They say, "These are beautiful snowshoes," they admire the craftsmanship, the good material and design. They note that he is a successful, able hunter.

> When a hunter approaches a black bear den in winter, he does not make an exhibition of himself. He announces himself simply and with humility: "I am here." ... There is similarity between the hunter announcing himself at the camp, and the hunter announcing himself at the bear's den. The hunter shows as much respect to the bear as he shows to people. It is almost as if he is arriving at the den as a visitor, hoping that the bear will accept him.

After every successful hunt, the first thing that the Cree hunter does with the animal is to check the fat content. This is a hunter's "quality control" of the game: the more fat the better, for it shows a healthy animal. With a goose, one pinches the fat layer under the skin [the subcutaneous fat] after removing a handful of feathers from the belly. With a black bear, one cuts the skin in front of the chest, just over the breast bone, to check the fat. This done, the animal is ready to be carried to the camp, and there are rules of respect at this stage as well.

There are proper ways of carrying game. For example, a beaver is normally pulled on its back in the snow. A stick is placed through the nose and a cord is attached to it. However, if there is ice stuck on the back fur, then the hands would be tied, and the animal flipped over and dragged on its front side. Similarly, there are proper ways to carry geese (tied by the necks and draped over the shoulders of the hunter). With black bears, two people can carry a bear with a pole, with the bear's limbs tied. Or a hunter can carry a bear on his back, paws over the shoulder, legs held under the hunter's arms, like a child, and the limbs tied in front over the hunter's chest.

> Carrying a bear has symbolic significance for the hunter. My friend and I killed a black bear. My friend gave me the bear [that is, a gift of respect]. I tried to carry the bear but it was very heavy. I tried to lift it, but I tumbled and fell down, time and again. My friend said, "Now it is *really* yours." The point is that the human hunter is not all-powerful. Even though I tried hard, the bear prevailed over me. This way, I really earned the bear. It was now truly mine.

Once carried to the camp, offerings may be made to the animal as a show of respect. In the past, offerings were made to all animals, even including fish. In the 1980s, offerings were being made only to the more powerful animals such as the black bear. When a hunter makes an offering to animals and to old men, he is, in effect, entering a reciprocal relationship, asking them to give him game. In the practice of Cree hunters of Chisasibi, offerings can be made with tobacco [not indigenous to the subarctic] and with pieces of meat or skin thrown into the fire.

> Offerings made to an animal indicates respect. It also means that the hunters are asking the animal to provide game for them. Similarly, offerings can be made to dead men [that is, respected elders]. Offerings to old men in their graves are fairly common, sometimes even to not very old men, and occasionally to women, too.

There was a respected old man who died on the point of a particular lake. He was buried there. When people went by his grave, they would make an offering to him. They rolled tobacco in tree bark and left it there. They were asking the old man to provide game for them in return for the tobacco.

A black bear is brought into camp. Hunters sit in a circle, with the bear in the middle. Someone smokes a pipe beside the bear and makes a gesture of offering the pipe to the bear. Or a piece of tobacco is placed in the bear's mouth as an offering. Once the bear is skinned, a piece of the meat is thrown into the fire. These offerings mean that the hunters are thanking the Provider.

Respect for animals is shown also in the way meat is butchered and distributed. There are special ways to cut every kind of animal, and for different uses of the animal's meat. For example, a loon is butchered differently from a goose. The pattern of cut will be different if a whitefish is going to be smoked as opposed to one that is going to be fresh-boiled. Some of the methods of cutting and preparation are related to showing respect for the animals. For example, when dismembering a goose, women are supposed to cut the wing off the body [and not to break it off]. Otherwise, it is said, the husband's luck in the goose hunt will be affected. In butchering a black bear, first the men cut the patterns on the bear. After that, the women skin the bear, and finally the men cut the limbs. There are special cutting patterns especially for the big game.

The owner of the game, say a black bear, decides as he starts to cut it on how to distribute the meat among the families sharing the camp. [In the case of a group hunt for a large animal, the general rule is that the "owner" is the person who has made the "crippling shot."] He may keep the skin for the fur and may give portions of the meat to others to distribute further. The first hunter may give the bear to a second hunter, and the second hunter may decide to pass the meat to a third. This kind of ritual sharing is considered important for social relations. Commonly, a young hunter would give the meat to one of the old men or old women in the camp, who would then do the honors in distributing it. This signifies deference and respect for the elders. Especially with big game animals, the custom is that an elder would distribute the food, thus showing respect for the animal.

Respect is also shown with the consumption of the game. The major principle is that everything is consumed and there is no waste. It is important that everything that is killed is eaten. Killing for fun [or for "recreation" or "sport" without eating it] is a transgression. What one kills, one keeps for eating. Young boys who kill small animals, when they are learning to hunt, make a gift of these animals to an old woman who prepares them. The food will then be consumed by the old woman and the boy and symbolically by the whole family. One elder says, "We are done for as a hunting society if we ever reach the point of taking only the haunch of a moose or caribou, as white hunters do."

Traditional Cree cooking uses all parts of the animals. For example, goose feet, necks, and head are eaten; goose fat is rendered or boiled down for later use. Seal intestines stuffed with seal blubber are a delicacy for some coastal people.

Fish heads are boiled, fish internal organs including liver, eggs, and intestines (but excluding stomach contents and gall bladder) are stir-fried; fish bones are sometimes eaten, pounded into *pimihkaan* (fish pemmican). Blood is used in blood pudding and stews; this is a delicacy. However, there are certain parts of animals that are *not* eaten. For example, caribou brains are not consumed but used in tanning skins. Polar bear liver is not consumed because it is poisonous [due to the extremely high content of vitamin A].

It is said that the whiskey jack, or gray jay, hovers about hunting camps, checking to see that nothing is wasted. In the case of some animals, respect is shown by consuming the meat only in the camp [presumably because it is a sacred place]. For example, black bear meat is eaten only in the camp; one is not allowed to take bear meat as lunch when checking traps [and one does not usually take it to the village, not a sacred place]. Similarly, lynx is shown respect by consuming the meat within the camp.

Proper disposal is the final stage in showing respect. After the edible parts have been consumed, hunters take proper care of the bones and other remains. The following are hung on trees or placed on top of wooden platforms: all black bear bones, and all skulls (including beaver, lynx, porcupine, muskrat, marten, otter, and mink). The following are returned to water because they are water animals: bones of beaver, otter, mink. There are no general rules for the disposal of the bones of waterfowl species, but some hunters hang the throats [trachea] of geese on trees or camp posts. Dogs are not allowed to eat black bear, beaver, and porcupine meat or bones. Other animal remains, including fish remains, would be buried. Another recommended way of disposing of fish remains is to collect them and place them where scavenger birds can feed on them.

Campsites are to be left tidy and clean. All garbage would be cleaned up and burned before breaking camp. [Some of these rules seem to be recent adaptations. Traditionally, the only waste in the camp consisted of animal remains, bones, and wood, which are natural materials that easily go back to nature. In modern life, however, there is also plastic, metal cans, glass, and paper which create a disposal problem in campsites.] Good hunters take special care to burn and/or bury these materials also, so that the young generations will inherit a clean environment.

IMPORTANCE OF CONTINUED USE FOR SUSTAINABILITY

It is the animals who control the success of the hunt, and hunters have obligations to show respect to the animals. Another important principle that characterizes Cree worldview is the belief that the continued use of resources is important to achieve a sustainable, productive harvest.

The tallyman [a senior hunter in charge of a territory, a steward] takes care of a trapline so that the beaver continue to be productive. Taking care of a trapline means

not killing too many. A trapper paces himself, killing what he needs, and what can
be prepared by the women, so that there is no wastage of meat and fur, and respect
for the animals is maintained. He should also make sure that the area is rested [by
rotating the sectors of the hunted area]. Normally a trapper should rest parts of his
trapline for two or three years but no longer than four years. If he leaves it, say, six
or ten years, he is not properly using his area, and the beaver will not be plentiful.

The concept of resting the hunting area is fairly well known. Many (but not
all) Cree trappers divide their territory into three or four sectors. They hunt and
trap only in one sector at a time, and "rest" the others. [Rotation of the hunting
territory resembles fallowing in agriculture. Feit (1973; 1986) has shown with
another James Bay Cree group that the beaver harvest from a sector rested for
two years or more is significantly greater than that from a sector harvested with
no rest.] The trapper continually observes the environment and monitors the
health of the beaver-vegetation system. He observes vegetation changes, beaver
tooth marks on cut wood to estimate the age composition of beaver in lodges, and
looks for other evidence of overcrowding, such as fighting among the beaver.
The Cree see the interaction between beaver and vegetation as a relationship
of balance. It is a balance that can flip if the beaver overharvest their food
supply. The Cree practice of resting an area, followed by heavy harvesting of
beaver, keeps the system from reaching the critical point at which food would
be depleted and the balance will be lost. Thus, not only overuse can lead to a
drop in productivity, but in the Cree worldview, so does underuse.

> In an area which has not been trapped for a long time, there will be many empty
> beaver lodges. This may be due to disease because of overcrowding, or it may be
> due to beavers depleting their food supplies. The trapper knows that in an area
> which has not been trapped for a long time, various types of beaver food such as
> aspen would be in low supply. If there has been a fire, this also affects the beaver.
> Trappers know that three or four years after a fire the beaver will again begin to
> inhabit the area. At first, however, they would be eating more of the root foods. The
> trapper may resume trapping again when the willows are half-grown. This may be
> some eight to ten years after a fire.

The hunter is always watching the environment, monitoring it for signs and
signals. Rotation and resting the land is good practice. [The Cree notion of the
importance of continued use is superficially similar to that in Western resource
management science but probably has different philosophical roots. "Continued
use" is not an obligation, in the sense of rules of respect; it is simply good
"management" consistent with the ideas of renewability and animal cycles.]
The principle that animals control the hunt takes precedence over the principle
of continued use:

> From the new camp, the hunter set out the next day with his traps. He was lucky
> to find beaver lodges, four or five of them, and he was quite happy about that. He
> sent his son to go even further east the next day. The son checked the traps set the

previous day and brought in the beaver. The next day after that, the son checked the last set of traps but had no luck. They waited several days and checked again: still no beaver. He took the traps out, "let them be, they will increase for the next time," he said. He was not catching anything, and there was a meaning to that. The beaver did not want to be caught yet. Next fall, he would come back to this area, and maybe then the beaver would be ready to be caught.

The principle of continued use has to be tempered also with common sense and good management. The "manager," in the Cree system, is the senior hunter, called the tallyman. [In Feit's (1986) terminology, the steward.] The senior hunter is the observer of nature, the interpreter of observations, the decision-maker in resource management, and the enforcer of rules of proper hunting conduct. He is also the political leader, ensuring for example that no one goes hungry in the group. There is little doubt that in the old days, the steward was a spiritual leader as well (see box 5.1, which is about the Innu who are close relatives of the Cree).

BOX 5.1
SHAMANISM AMONG THE INNU (MONTAGNAIS) OF LABRADOR

In Innu culture, what is the shaman (kakushapitak)?

Kakushapitak means a person who can see through, who can foretell, who has authority, power. His power lies in using the "shaking tent" (*kushapitakan*) to foretell events, locate animals and travel through time to learn about families. The shaman masters other techniques to foretell the future such as the chant and drum, the dream, scapulomancy. The shaman is said to be powerful if his predictions, advice or news are correct. The most powerful shaman is the one who always tells the truth. Some shamans were strong, others weak. The strong shaman was always a great hunter, while the weak ones did not have this skill.

How were shamans considered in everyday life?

The shaman was a person like anybody else. No particular deference was paid to him. He was respected because he was a great hunter. He played a leadership role like that of a chief today. He knew where to hunt and the group trusted him.

How does the shaman transmit his power?

Ussitshimiush, the sack [medicine pouch] which contains the power, is passed on from generation to generation. For instance, had my great grandfather Toby been a shaman, he would have passed it on to my father who would in turn have passed it to me, Mathieu André. I then could have passed it either to my eldest son or my youngest. If a shaman did not have a son, he would pass it on to his grandson.

How is it that Innu shamanism has died out?

Once the priests arrived, they fought against the ritual. They also prohibited the shaking tent, saying the shaman was helped by the devil, that it was diabolic. The Innu believed that, but I think a superior spirit gave the Innu knowledge of everything that concerns the environment and enables him to act. The old people were afraid of the priests. People say that when old Pukue, one of the great shamans of Sheshatshit, died (and my grandmother witnessed this), his *ussitshimiush*, his sack, was burned. And I think that is one of the reasons why shamanism has disappeared among us.

Source: Nuk André in conversation with his father, Mathieu André, an Innu author and elder (André 1989, 5, 6)

It is the steward's obligation to follow up on the activities of a group that had violated the rules of proper hunting behavior by engaging in unrestrained exploitation.

> The tallyman went to trap a part of his trapline. He had not been there for several years, but he had given permission to another group to trap it a few years previously. These people had reported plenty of beaver at that time. But the trapper knew that there would not be many beaver in that area because these other people had killed too many. He knew this because when these people returned to the village that year, their furs had not been prepared properly. Many of the furs had to be thrown out. They had killed indiscriminately—young, old, every animal. Some of the beaver may even have been trapped out of season. The trapper visited, one after another, lakes and ponds which he knew to be good beaver lakes. There were beaver signs, but these were old signs from before that group's visit. Beaver had declined, had not produced because those trappers had not taken care of that spot. They had done wrong to the game. In such cases, game retaliates. Leave nothing behind—and it affects the later hunt. Bad practice has repercussions for later years.

As the enforcer of community norms, it becomes the steward's obligation to expose "doing wrong to the game." In the process, the steward can initiate social sanction on the guilty parties, shaming them publicly [usually done by the use of humor] and using the example to remind everyone else of the rules.

CONCLUSIONS

The general principle that "animals are killed but not diminished" has also been noted by other researchers elsewhere in Cree lands (Tanner 1979; Feit 1986; Brightman 1993). Is this concept in the sense of "ecologically sustainable use," or is it in the sense of a reincarnation of a "constant supply," so to speak, of animals? In contrast to some other groups of Cree hunters—for example, those in Northern Manitoba (Brightman 1993) and the Waswanipi Cree of Quebec (Feit 1986)—the Chisasibi Cree did not articulate the notion of reincarnation of animals.

Historically, the Cree believed that "the numbers of animals available to hunters in the future could be influenced by ceremonial regeneration; the numbers killed or the parts utilized were irrelevant" (Brightman 1993, 289). If Brightman is correct, and the historian Ray's (1975) work also supports that conclusion, the Cree of the 1700s did not associate hunting with depletion. Cree traditional ecological knowledge did not include the consideration of population dynamics of game, and in fact still does not. Brightman (1993) has argued further that the concept of game depletion by overhunting is not aboriginal but represents the influence of Western game management practice. Chapter 6 on caribou examines how the hunting ethic of an aboriginal group itself may change, and chapter 7 on fisheries analyzes how the Cree seem to be able to manage resources sustainably, given that their management system presumably did not include any accounting by numbers.

Another major difference between Cree views and Western views concerns the nature of "killing." The Cree do not consider the killing of game as an act of violence. The hunter loves the animals he kills (Preston 1975); after all, the animals can only be hunted if they agree to be hunted. Similarly, the Cree have difficulty with the Western notions that hunting involves suffering on the part of the animals, and that the best conservation (as some argue) would mean not hunting the animals at all. To the Cree, if the game want to be left alone, they would let the hunters know. Otherwise, the proper conservation of game does include the hunting and eating of animals. The preservationist ethic is not compatible with Cree conservation: "When you don't use a resource, you lose respect for it."

The Chisasibi Cree view of the living environment as a "community of beings" is not a particularly unusual view. Other eastern James Bay Cree groups such as the Mistassini (Tanner 1979) and the Waswanipi (Feit 1973; 1986) have similar views, as do some of the more distant Cree groups in northern Manitoba and Saskatchewan (Brightman 1993). Many other aboriginal groups of North America have similar beliefs as well. For example, writing of the Koyukon of Alaska, a Dene (Athapaskan) group culturally unrelated to the Cree, Nelson (1982, 218) states that they regard the environment "as a community of entities that are intrinsically supernatural as well as natural. In fact, the strict western conceptual distinction between natural and supernatural would probably make little sense to the Koyukon."

The James Bay Cree worldview, as emerging from this chapter, is consistent with Colorado's (1988) characterization of native science as a holistic and religious perspective grounded in empirical observation. The cosmos has a unity and integrity that is Creator-given, and it is the task of humans to discipline their minds and actions to recognize and understand its workings. The Cree worldview is also consistent with Trosper's (1995) analysis of commonly shared Amerindian attitudes of respect toward nature. Trosper argues that there are four commonly (but not universally) held values that are components of *respect*: community (including the "community of beings" view with social obligations and reciprocity); connectedness; concern for future generations (as exemplified by the Iroquois notion of responsibility for the "seventh generation"); and humility (see box 5.2).

Trosper (1995) observes that many of these values are also found in some Western environmental philosophies; for example, in Leopold's (1949) land ethics, as also noted by Callicott (1989). However, in Leopold's thought there is no human-nature reciprocity. Rather, it is a one-way street in which it is the humans who are to extend their ethics to include nature; animals have no obligations to nourish humans. Also poorly represented in Western environmental ethics is one of the four components of respect, and one that is of great importance to the Cree: humility. Leopold comes close to the notion of humility

---

BOX 5.2
EXPRESSING HUMILITY: THE KOYUKON OF ALASKA

"When the river ice breaks up each spring, people speak to it, respectfully and acknowledging its power. Elders make short prayers, both Christian and traditional Koyukon, asking the ice to drift downstream without jamming and causing floods. By contrast, some years ago, the U.S. Air Force bombed an ice jam on the Yukon River to prevent inundation of communities. Far from approving, some villagers blamed subsequent floods on this arrogant use of physical force. In the end, nature will assert the greater power. The proper role for humans is to move gently, humbly, pleading or coercing, but always avoiding belligerence."

Source: Nelson 1993, 217

---

by promoting an ethic that reduces humans from superiority to equality ("from conqueror of the land-community to plain member and citizen of it," Leopold 1949, 240).

Traditional worldviews of nature are diverse, but many share the belief in a sacred, personal relationship between humans and other living beings. To quote Callicott (1982, 306), "The implicit overall metaphysic of American Indian cultures locates human beings in a larger *social*, as well as physical, environment. People belong not only to a human community, but to a community of all nature as well." This community-of-beings worldview is common not only among Amerindians but other hunter-gatherer and horticultural peoples as well (Gadgil and Berkes 1991). In general, these beliefs probably go back to the dominant pantheistic tradition before the rise of monotheistic religions (see box 5.3).

BOX 5.3
IROQUOIS PANTHEISM

"Animism, which permeates pantheism, involves the theory of the existence of immaterial principle, inseparable from matter, to which all life and action are attributable. In the pantheist view the entire phenomenal world contains godlike attributes: the relations of man to this world are sacramental. It is believed that the actions of man in nature can affect his own fate, that these actions are consequential, immediate and relevant to life. There is, in this relationship, no non-nature category—nor is there either romanticism or sentimentality.

"The Iroquois view is typical of Indian pantheism. The Iroquois cosmography begins with a perfect sky world from which falls the earth mother, arrested by the birds, landing upon the back of a turtle, the earth. Her grandchildren are twins, one good and the other evil. . . . The opposition of these two forces is the arena of life; they can be affected by man's acts in the world of actuality. Consequently all acts—birth and growth, procreating, eating and evacuating, hunting and gathering, making voyages and journeys—are sacramental."

Source: McHarg 1969, 68

Pantheistic traditions still exist in some contemporary groups such as the James Bay Cree (even though they are now formally Christians), as they once existed in pre-Christian Europe and survived for a time in the Christian mysticism of St. Francis (White 1967). The culture and traditional ethics of the Cree are thus significant not only for their own sake but for linking us with a millennia-old human heritage. A community-of-beings worldview is particularly meaningful today, as it signifies a cosmology in which humans are part of the ecological system. The next two chapters explore in some detail how Chisasibi Cree views of the environment translate into actual human-animal relationships in resource use.

Chapter Six

A Story of Caribou and
Social Learning

This chapter chronicles how the Cree learned to deal with the variability in caribou numbers and the fact that caribou are depletable. It uses historical evidence and contemporary observations of cultural evolution in action and builds a picture of social learning in which elders manage cross-generational information feedbacks to make sense of resource intervention outcomes. Elders and stewards provide leadership, carry and transmit knowledge, and sometimes reinterpret new information to help redesign management systems.

Practice is not always true to belief. Philosophers point out that "ethics bear a normative relation to behavior; they do not describe how people actually behave, but rather set out how people ought to behave" (Callicott 1982, 311). For example, the Koyukon people of Alaska often violate their own rules on limiting harvests when they hunt caribou (Nelson 1982). Anyone who has worked with hunting peoples knows that rules of ethics are sometimes suspended. But one can say that about any culture or any group of people; there is always a gap between the ideal practice and the actual. The story of caribou is important in this regard. Cree elders in Chisasibi readily admit that they once overhunted the caribou. However, the events that took place in the community in the mid-1980s indicate that the Cree hunters as a group learned from that experience. The caribou story illustrates how traditional beliefs, such as those described in chapter 5 about cycles and the return of animals, play out in the real world, and how community-based systems can learn and evolve. It also illustrates the role that traditional stewards and elders play in providing leadership for collective decision-making. It shows why almost all traditional cultures consider elders so important. Elders provide corporate memory for the group, the wisdom to interpret uncommon or unusual events, and they help enforce the rules and ethical norms of the community.

The main issue here is the development and application of a conservation ethic in a social group, an issue first raised in chapter 4. *Conservation ethic*, defined here after Johannes (1994), is the "awareness of one's ability to deplete or otherwise damage natural resources, coupled with a commitment to reduce or eliminate the problem." We hypothesize that a conservation ethic can develop if a resource is *important or limiting, predictable and depletable*, and if it is effectively under the control of the social group in question so that the group can reap the benefits of its conservation (Berkes 1989a). We explain each point of the hypothesis in turn.

If a resource is superabundant there is no adaptive advantage in developing a conservation ethic for it, nor a territorial system for its defense. The resource has to be predictable and abundant, and important for the group, if not outright limiting (see chapter 3 on territoriality; Dyson-Hudson and Smith 1978; Richardson 1982; Nelson 1982; Berkes 1986a). If the resource is not depletable, it is perfectly logical (and, one may argue, ecologically adaptive) to kill excess numbers in hunts that are sporadic in space and time. The perturbation of the system can then provide feedback to the resource manager, as well as a store of food. As Nelson (1982, 223) points out in his discussion of Alaska caribou hunting, "a natural response is not to limit harvests intentionally, but the precise opposite—take as much as possible, whenever possible, and store the proceeds for later use."

Finally, there is the question of the control of the resource. Societies do not establish conservation rules and ethics for the benefit of outsiders. The evidence on this question shows that the incursion of outsiders, and the inability of the group to defend an important resource, causes the lifting of rules and conservation ethic (Feit 1986; Berkes 1986a). Once open-access conditions are created, perfectly conservation-minded stewards may well become participants themselves in a "tragedy of the commons" rather than allow the outsiders to take the remaining resource. Such free-for-all depletions of resources seem to have happened in the case of beaver in James Bay in the 1920s, and the overkill of North American bison at the turn of the century (Berkes et al. 1989). In some cases, the condition is reversible: if local controls can be reestablished, the group can again reap the benefits of its own restraint, and conservation rules and ethics become operative once more (Feit 1986; Berkes 1989b).

The significance of the caribou case is that the nature of the resource does *not* lend itself well to the development of a conservation ethic. To be sure, caribou is one of the most important species of the North American subarctic and Arctic, just as its close relative, reindeer, is important in Northern Scandinavia and Siberia. But they come in very large numbers when they come, and they are unpredictable. As one Dene Indian saying goes, "no one knows the way of the winds and the caribou" (Munsterhjelm 1953, 97). To aboriginal hunters once upon a time, caribou must have seemed superabundant and undepletable. Furthermore, large herds of caribou migrate long distances and are hunted by different groups of people, making local control, and thus local conservation, all but impossible, except in the cases of small herds of woodland caribou. It is relatively easy to envision the conditions under which a conservation ethic can develop for a range of species important for traditional Amerindians, for example, Pacific salmon (Swezey and Heizer 1993; Gottesfeld 1994), black bear and beaver (Nelson 1982), beaver and moose (Feit 1973; 1986), and Canada goose (Berkes 1982). All of them are predictable resources, or at least their harvest areas are predictable from year to year, and they are depletable over a cycle of relatively few years. Not so in the case of caribou.

"NO ONE KNOWS THE WAY OF THE WINDS AND THE CARIBOU"

As the most abundant large mammal of Arctic and subarctic North America, caribou (*Rangifer tarandus*) has a special importance in the traditional economy of the aboriginal peoples of tundra and the lichen-woodland zone. Charles Elton, one of the founders of modern ecology, was interested in caribou population dynamics as an illustration of population cycles in subarctic ecosystems. In his classic 1942 book, Elton used the records of missionaries and fur traders to document the decline of the George River caribou herd of the Quebec-Labrador Peninsula at the turn of the century. When abundant, animals of this herd migrate in large numbers, as do barren-ground caribou, but they show physical characteristics that are intermediate between woodland and barren-ground caribou, considered by some biologists as two distinct subspecies.

Elton's (1942) reconstruction indicated that there was a general population decrease after about 1905. The most westerly of the three subpopulations of the George River herd occupied the James Bay and Hudson Bay coast. This subpopulation had started declining earlier, through the 1880s and the 1890s. As the population decreased, the range of the George River herd contracted, and the peripheral range was presumably the first to be abandoned. Sources consulted by Elton mentioned one final large kill in 1914 at the crossing of the Caniapiscau River, which runs north-south and bisects the Quebec-Labrador Peninsula. By 1916, the herd was so reduced that, for the first time in living memory, the caribou did not migrate across the George River, which also runs north-south but is closer to the Atlantic on the Labrador side of the Peninsula.

The George River herd stayed as a small population nestled in the hills of northeastern Labrador, still hunted by the Innu of Labrador. Population surveys as late as the 1950s showed a small herd, perhaps as few as 5,000, and biologists speculated on the reasons for the decline of the herd, citing a variety of possible explanations, including extensive fires in Labrador and climate change, but often emphasizing the key role of aboriginal hunters and the repeating rifle, which had become extensively used in the area at the turn of the century (Banfield and Tener 1958). Then the herd started a rapid increase in the 1960s, with a noticeable expansion of range in the 1970s and the 1980s (see figure 6.1). Piecing together information from aerial surveys, tagging studies with radio collars, observation of tracks, hunters' observations, and kill locations, one could assemble the larger picture of the return of the caribou. The migrations penetrated further and further west and south, in larger and larger numbers, and the caribou started to linger in the more distant areas. The recovery of the George River herd has been dramatic and well documented. The caribou reached a population of some 600–700,000 animals, one of the largest *Rangifer* herds in the world by the end of the 1980s, and reoccupied the old range of the herd all the way to the coast of James Bay and Hudson Bay (Jackson 1986; Messier et al. 1988; Couturier et al. 1990).

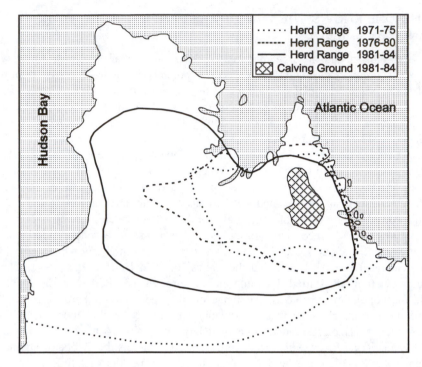

Figure 6.1   Range expansion of the George River caribou herd, 1971–84 (Messier et al. 1988), and after 1984 (Couturier et al. 1990).

Juniper (1979) referred to the George River herd as an "irrupting" population. But was the population change a real cycle? Was it a real recolonization of the former range? Perhaps even more interesting, if the dramatic decline of the caribou at the turn of the century was due to the aboriginal hunter and the improved hunting technology, how then was it possible that the caribou population was increasing with such force in the 1970s and the 1980s, in the presence of vastly greater numbers of aboriginal hunters with even better guns and transportation technology, including snowmobiles?

The fact of the matter is, caribou population increases and decreases are a scientific problem yet unresolved. The conventional biological view of caribou does not include population cycles, simply because no one has a sufficiently long data set. Ten-year cycles of snowshoe hares and lynx lend themselves to scientific analysis, but the multigenerational caribou cycle (if it is a cycle) does not.

Suffice to say that some ecologists think that the fluctuations of caribou numbers are the result of complex and interrelated processes, including the slow growth (50–100 year) of lichens, the winter food of caribou. If conditions are favorable, individual caribou are healthy and have extra energy reserves (fat); the reproduction rate is high and calf mortality low. Under such conditions, caribou numbers can build up quickly by exponential growth. By the time predator numbers catch up, the range may be overgrazed and the caribou not so healthy. The double effect of poor range and high predation may result in a depression of caribou population to very low levels. The population remains depressed for a long time, before lichens slowly recover and conditions become favorable to the increase of caribou once more.

The effects of other factors such as hunting pressure, climate change, and fires can add complexity to this general pattern. For example, the effect of heavy hunting during the decline phase can knock down the population size even lower, while the same thing during the increase phase merely dampens the fluctuation. Calf survival is an important factor and can be affected by weather (wind and temperature) as well as by predator mortality. In a way, biologists do have an overall model of caribou population changes, based on population surveys, computer simulation studies, and knowledge of other cycling species, but the science of caribou is still uncertain. Many ecologists are reluctant to refer to caribou as a cycling species for the lack of hard data. Western science has simply not recorded a full cycle of increase-decline-increase.

ABORIGINAL HUNTERS AND TRADITIONAL KNOWLEDGE OF CARIBOU

By contrast, aboriginal hunting peoples of Alaska and Northern Canada have experienced many full cycles. For example, the Inuit, who live to the north of the Cree above the tree line, believe that there is a natural population cycle in caribou (Milton Freeman, pers. comm.). To the Cree also, caribou population fluctuations are cyclical, but these are not predictable, periodic cycles. Cree elders' wisdom predicts the return of the caribou but says nothing about its timing, consistent with the Dene notion about the unpredictability of the ways of the caribou. To the Cree, caribou declines and increases are mysterious—but only in part. They are partially explainable in terms of hunter-animal relationships. Declines are related to the ethical transgressions of hunters, as explained in the last chapter. Whereas Elton's (1942) data come from biological science and from the records of missionaries and traders, the "data" of the Cree hunter come from culturally transmitted traditional knowledge, stories told by elders, and from the hunter's own day-to-day observations. The caribou are part of the living landscape shared by the Cree and other beings.

However, Cree caribou knowledge is not likely to be as rich as that of the Dene (Northern Athapascans) who occupy the broad swath of the subarctic from Manitoba to Alaska, and who are among the great experts on caribou. According to Smith (1978), the very social organization of the Dene groups of the central Canadian subarctic can be explained in terms of adaptation to caribou movements. Rules regarding kinship and marriage favored the formation of social links across a broad front.

Hunting groups were strategically situated in a long narrow front (of some 1000 km), with relatively shallow depth, near the treeline, from a point west of Hudson Bay to Great Slave Lake.... They were thus potentially in contact with all the constituent herds of the Kaminuriak, Beverly and Bathurst populations of caribou. The hunting groups may be viewed as strategically situated reconnaissance patrols for collecting information on caribou movements and intentions.... Survival resulted from the spatial placement of regional and local bands and hunting groups, bound to one another by complex ties of kinship and marriage, which provided a communications network extending through those bands dependent on the caribou. (Smith 1978, 75, 83)

The spatial arrangement of the bands followed the transition zone from forest to tundra, making it possible for the hunters to exploit either zone. Local band centers were located at fishing lakes to provide a reliable food supply. Summer excursions to the north of the tree line kept the Dene well-informed of caribou distributions. According to the archaeological record, this spatial arrangement had considerable time depth, allowing hunters to accumulate a great many generations of data (Smith 1978). The reconnaissance system of the central subarctic Dene is unusual among traditional knowledge and management systems because of its ability to collect synchronic data (short time-series over a large area) as well as diachronic data (long time-series). It shows that under certain circumstances, synoptic systems of data collection characteristic of Western scientific systems can also develop among traditional peoples. It is the capability of collecting such traditional ecological knowledge that made the Dene the experts on the caribou.

By contrast, anthropologists and other Western scholars do not associate eastern James Bay Cree with caribou. Many of their neighbors, the Inuit of Northern Quebec and the Innu (Naskapi and Montagnais) of the eastern part of the Quebec-Labrador Peninsula, are all well-known caribou specialists, although probably not to the same degree as some of the Dene groups. By contrast, the eastern James Bay Cree have seen and hunted the occasional small groups of caribou over the past century, but certainly not the great migrations of caribou. Thus, the notion of "Cree traditional knowledge of caribou" is at odds with the fact that most Chisasibi Cree had never seen a caribou until the 1980s. Caribou herds were last present in the area in the 1910s (Speck 1935, 81; Elton 1942). Records of the Hudson's Bay Company (HBC) from the 1600s to the 1800s indicate that caribou were periodically abundant in the area. It was one of the major food resources of the James Bay Cree in the area north of Eastmain, and a source of irritation to HBC traders because Cree hunters would periodically take off after the caribou instead of concentrating on trapping furs for the HBC (Francis and Morantz 1983, 7).

Hunting grounds of the Chisasibi Cree people are rich in caribou-related place names. Examples include Point Attiquane (Caribou Point) where caribou antlers from ancient hunts may still be found, and Maanikin Lake, *maanikin* being a caribou aggregating device, a corral. The official name of the lake on the map is Lake Darontal, near the much larger Lac Julian. Caribou-related expressions are found in Cree language as well. For example, a late spring snowfall is called *attiksthaw*, newborn-caribou-footprint-snow. Chisasibi hunting lore is likewise rich with caribou natural history. Examples include, "How do you tell the sex of animals in the herd you are following?" (From the shape of digging marks in snow, "feeding craters" to reach lichens; males and females dig differently.) "How do you tell if there is a really big bull in the group?" (His tracks in the snow would go wide around trees because the big bull takes care not to entangle his large antlers. This is important to know for safety reasons: caribou are not usually dangerous, but Cree hunters are wary of big bulls.)

A traditional winter caribou hunt was a communal affair and targeted not individual animals but groups of caribou. A *maanikin* would be constructed with posts placed like a fence. The fence would get narrower and narrower and force the caribou into a single file. Snares would then be used to tangle up and stop them, and the animals would be dispatched with bows and arrows and spears. To lead the caribou into the corral, the ancient hunters used trees in the general shape of human figures, dotting the land to deflect caribou into the area toward the *maanikin*. The Cree technique is similar to the traditional practices of the Dene of the central subarctic. The Dene used what Smith (1978) calls "chute and pound," made of cut trees with a maze within the pound in which the caribou were caught in snares or speared. A variant was a drift fence that directed caribou along certain paths. The *inukshuk* of the Inuit, built of stone in the shape of human figures, served a similar purpose to the Cree and Dene drift fences, showing that these ethnically distinct groups shared certain traditional practices.

CARIBOU RETURN TO THE LAND OF THE CHISASIBI CREE

Chisasibi hunters saw their first large caribou hunt of this century in the winter of 1982–83. According to information from hunters, most of the kills occurred in the far eastern portion of the community hunting area and amounted to some one hundred animals. The following winter, large numbers of caribou appeared further west, in an area accessible by road. In fact, many were right on the road serving a newly constructed hydroelectric dam in the eastern part of the community area. Hunters said "large numbers" were taken, probably several hundreds but the actual kill was unknown, and the hunt was a frenzied affair. The caribou stayed in the area only for a month or so. Chisasibi hunters used the road, bringing back truckloads of caribou. There was so much meat that, as one hunter put it, "people overdosed on caribou." Some people even allowed meat to spoil.

People were excited about the return of the caribou. However, community leaders were concerned, not because of large numbers killed, but because some hunters had been shooting wildly, letting wounded animals get away, killing more than they could carry, wasting meat, not disposing of wastes properly. Chisasibi Cree hunters' code speaks strongly about wastage and calls for burning or burying of animal remains. The leaders were worried that hunters' attitudes and behaviors signaled a lack of respect for the caribou, a serious transgression of the traditional code in which ritual respect ensures that animals will continue to make themselves available. It is a system of mutual obligations: "show no respect and the game will retaliate" (see chapter 5).

In the winter of 1984–85, there were almost no caribou on the road. Hunters in trucks waited and waited and many left empty-handed. Those who had the skills to go into the bush and hunt without causing disturbance nevertheless came back with reasonable kills. According to information from hunters, about three hundred caribou were taken, only a fraction of the hunt in the previous year. Back in town, many people were now worried: Had the caribou decided not to come to the Chisasibi hunting grounds after all? The time was right for elders and leaders to do something about their concerns and to draw some lessons from the apparent reluctance of the caribou to come back.

A community meeting was called. Two of the most respected elders stepped forward. Among the Chisasibi Cree, there is no one traditional chief. The elected chief occupies a political position and may change from election to election. The real leadership is a corporate leadership provided by a group of senior hunters and respected elders, as represented in this case by the two elders who came forward. The elders did not voice their concerns and neither did they criticize the hunters who had been breaking the code of ethics. Instead they told a story.

It was the story of the disappearance of the caribou shortly after the turn of the century. Caribou had been declining on the James Bay coast in the latter decades of the century but continued to be plentiful in the Caniapiscau area, near the center of the Labrador Peninsula. This was a great caribou hunting area and a culturally important region where neighboring groups mixed. The Cree of Chisasibi came from the southwest, the Cree of Mistassini came from the south, the Cree of Great Whale came from the northwest, the Naskapi and Montagnais (Innu) of Labrador came from the east, and the Inuit of Ungava Bay came from the north to hunt the great migrating herds of caribou as they crossed the Caniapiscau River.

It was here, in the 1910s, that a disaster occurred, the elders told. Hungry for caribou and equipped with repeating rifles, which had just become widely available, previously respectful hunters became dizzy with newfound power over animals, lost all self-control, and slaughtered the caribou at the crossing points on the Caniapiscau, in an area known as Limestone Falls. Instead of "taking care of the caribou," the hunters killed too many and wasted so much food that the river was polluted with rotten carcasses, the elders told. The following year, the hunters waited and waited, and there was no caribou. None at all. The caribou had disappeared and they were not to be seen for generations.

The elders were now coming to the point of the teaching. The story they were telling was in fact familiar to most, if not all, of the hunters. The slaughter and the subsequent disappearance of the caribou were etched in the collective memory of Chisasibi Cree and had became part of their oral history. But the disappearance of the caribou was not permanent, the elders reminded the hunters. All changes occurred in cycles, and all was not lost. Subsequent to the disaster, the elders continued their story, the wise men had made a prediction: the caribou would once again become plentiful. The caribou would return one day, but the hunters had to take good care of them if the caribou were to stay. It was this prediction that the elders were now retelling, some seventy years later, in Chisasibi in the winter of 1984–85.

By all accounts, the elders' words had a profound effect on the younger hunters. The caribou had indeed come back, true to the old peoples' prediction, validating oral history. However, by violating traditional ethics, were they about to lose the caribou once again?

In the winter of 1985–86, the hunt was carried out very differently. It was a productive hunt and 867 caribou were taken, about two per household, according to the survey done by the Chisasibi Cree Trappers Association (CTA). The CTA had now taken upon itself the responsibility of monitoring the hunt. Overseen by the elders, hunting leaders, and other hunters who make up the membership of the CTA, the hunt was conducted in a controlled and responsible manner, in accordance with traditional standards. There was little wastage, no wild shooting. The harvest was transported efficiently, and wastes from butchering were cleaned up promptly. The Cree exercised their self-management rights under the James Bay Agreement that had been signed ten years previously. The Cree hunters devised the solutions themselves, and government resource managers were not even involved (Drolet et al. 1987).

The caribou kept coming. To the Cree it seemed that the caribou were responding to the restoration of proper hunting ethics and respect. They were moving much deeper into the Chisasibi area. Some of the largest numbers were seen halfway between the coast and the eastern limit of the Chisasibi community hunting area. Hunters were ecstatic. In the spring of 1986, caribou were seen right on the James Bay coast for the first time in living memory. Some hunters were passing up the chance to hunt the small, scattered groups of caribou near the coast, until the caribou reestablished themselves; instead, the hunters concentrated on the larger aggregations of caribou to the east. By 1990, hunters' observations of tracks showed that caribou had reached the sea all along the James Bay coast, reestablishing the former range of the 1900s. Their observations were consistent with the results of surveys carried out by government biologists (see figure 6.1).

How did these remarkable changes come about? What was going through the minds of the people? My own field notes from Chisasibi summarize the events of the three years after the restoration of hunting ethics and provide a closer look at the dynamics of traditional knowledge and ethics in action.

A GATHERING OF THE HUNTERS

The scene: a small meeting room that doubles as the office of the Cree Trappers Association (CTA) in the large building that functions as Chisasibi's administrative center and shopping mall. Topographic maps cover the walls, with the boundaries of Chisasibi's family hunting/trapping territories shown in black lines and the location of last winter's bush radio locations marked with red pins (radios rented from the CTA, one per territory, for safety and communication). Other maps mark the floodlines from the James Bay hydroelectric project and the location of the gravel roads, and the extra-wide (three meter) winter trails being built for the hunters for winter travel. An old man sits in the far corner, playing with what seems to be the pieces of an old bush radio.

The meeting of the Chisasibi CTA does not quite start at the announced hour, but no one seems to mind. We are on "Indian time"; even the band meeting earlier that week had started an hour late. People are dribbling into the meeting room until all the chairs are full (about twenty) and there is little room to sit on the floor (another twenty or so). A couple of more chairs are brought in as a few particularly respected elders enter the room. The head of the CTA does have an agenda for the meeting but the speakers often digress. There are no knee-slapping jokes but much good-humored banter and a great deal of laughter, as members discuss a variety of issues, from the price of beaver pelts to the upcoming spring goose hunt.

A few remain serious. There is a list of topics to be discussed and decided upon and someone has to make sure that the agenda is covered. Discussion is democratic and freewheeling. Experts and the elders speak relatively little. Some of the younger hunters tend to speak more. All speakers receive a respectful hearing. No one interrupts the speaker, and no one is cut short, not even those who are off-topic. Halfway though the meeting, a smiling man brings a large bag of pop drinks and chocolate bars for all to share. A stack of checks is distributed from the last fur auction. Someone brings a photocopy of an anti-trapping letter to the editor of the Montreal *Gazette*. This generates some heated discussion. The topic soon shifts to something more cheerful: increasing caribou numbers. By now, caribou have become just another discussion item for the hunters. The people of Chisasibi have adjusted to a new life with caribou, as my field notes tell the rest of the story.

Winter of 1985–86

The most celebrated issue is the continuing increase in caribou numbers. This winter Chisasibi hunters obtained far more caribou than moose and black bear, the other big game animals of the area. Caribou tracks are running east-west. Two years ago, the herds were still far inland. This year, big hunts are taking place halfway to the coast. For the first time, north coast (north of Chisasibi on the James Bay coast) hunters are reporting that, not only are the caribou coming, but they are staying longer, right into the spring. Not so yet on the south coast. But SH [initials of a person] reports large numbers southeast of Eastmain, the Cree village at the mouth of Eastmain River. Somehow the caribou must have crossed southward across the chain of hydroelectric reservoirs on La Grande River. Old GB jokes that he shot his "first caribou" at age seventy-two, three years ago. [The irony is that "the first hunt" for various species is a rite of passage normally enjoyed by an adolescent hunter.] GL mentions that some of the hunters in the Cape Jones area are refraining from hunting, so that the herds would not be disturbed and scared off. He himself shot two caribou last winter near the coast, at the "Old-Man-with-the-Knife" Lake, just north of the Roggan River, which is an old caribou site according to elders. Elders' information is reliable, he chuckles with satisfaction.

A visit with DS brings out an engrossing tale. DS's father, seventy-seven years old, had never seen a caribou in his hunting area on the north coast of James Bay. The caribou had disappeared in DS's grandfather's time, when his grandfather was in "his prime," in his thirties or forties. The grandfather had been a real caribou expert and had had a great deal of knowledge about the caribou, which he passed on to DS's father, and his father unto him. (GL adds an aside, oral history easily reaches back one hundred years, he says.) DS continues. This winter for the first time, a large group of caribou, about fifty, was seen in his territory. They made a lazy circle, first swinging east, then south, and then clockwise back to the coast. They looked like they were checking out the territory. Not feeding very much. Just looking like they were getting to know the land. They were in precisely the area where his grandfather said caribou were last seen before they disappeared. I finally ask: were you hunting or just watching? DS looks serious and lost in his thoughts. He shakes his head, no, he did not shoot any, just followed them and watched them. The previous year he saw just a few, did not kill any then, either. Now this year they have doubled. Maybe next year they will increase again and get settled into the area.

Winter of 1986–87

Caribou numbers keep on increasing. There are more now on the James Bay coast. They come with the first snow. In November, they appear in the area north of Chisasibi. In December, there is a large migration northward, through Cape Jones and Long Island, where James Bay meets Hudson Bay. They are pursued by wolves. According to the hunters' informal monitoring network, this is the first report of large wolf numbers. One caribou GL got this week had a gash on his leg. The Cree do not normally see many wolves. When they do, they consider it an omen and consult the elders for an interpretation.

Among the north coast families, the SN are still not hunting the caribou on their territory; they are hunting the wolves, though, plenty of them. Some of the other families are hunting the caribou. GL's group got thirteen on a weekend hunt. Many of the hunters went for the large ones, with big antlers. He got two himself, selected them carefully, one medium-sized female and a smaller one for home. He presented the first one to an old man [to honor him, to signify respect]. Hunters noted large fat deposits on the caribou, indicating healthy animals and good feeding conditions. After all, the lichen in that area has been growing undisturbed for almost a century now.

I find SB and his dad with rolled-up sleeves, processing caribou skins. First, they scrape off the inner skin and fat, then they shave off the hair using the blade of an old hockey skate! Then they soak the skin, then they wash it in a solution of brains, a widely used Cree recipe for tanning. SB took five caribou this winter, gave one away. He is feeding two families, and experimenting with the skins. His brother JB smiles; they are experiencing full use, he says, from the hunt to skin processing—the full life cycle of caribou tradition.

In January, the northward migrating herd appeared right at the Hudson Bay town of Great Whale (Poste de la Baleine) for the first time. This is a mixed town of Cree and Inuit, and everyone was surprised to see caribou so close—eye to eye, as one puts it. They get up one morning and see caribou just outside their windows. Only last year, they had to go all the way to Lake Minto for their caribou, an air charter distance. But now the caribou are here and you can approach them. The people maintain self-control, however, and every household takes two but there is no wild shooting and no waste. The chief of Great Whale reports that they had to chase the caribou off the town dump, and off the town's airstrip! He is proud that the people kept their composure. Someone in Chisasibi relates a Great Whale Inuit belief: Never take the first three caribou in the lead. They lead the pack. Instead, you take the ones at the end. If you leave the ones in the front, they will bring the caribou back the next year.

Winter of 1987–88

Now all family groups on the coast are hunting. The caribou are so abundant this spring that they scared off the geese and disrupted the spring goose hunt. Many caribou stay near the coast over the winter. There are some even on Fort George Island, the former village site of Chisasibi. However, there are also signs for the first time that not all is well. Quite a few caribou are found dead in the eastern part of the community territory. Government biologists on the co-management board (the Hunting, Fishing, and Trapping Coordinating Committee established under the James Bay Agreement) ask the Cree representatives for their opinion. Some of the dead caribou seem to have been killed by wolves. The Cree think the wolves do not always eat what they kill. Hunters also notice that fat deposits in the caribou are less than what they were in the previous years. The Cree request though the co-management board that the government start taking measures to control the access of nonnatives into the area and to tighten the regulation of sport hunters. In the meantime, both the government of Quebec and the government of Newfoundland and Labrador are entertaining proposals for a commercial caribou hunt of the George River herd.

CONCLUSIONS

No doubt the caribou will decline again some day, and the eternal cycle will continue. The story told in this chapter unfolded over a six-year period. I was not a participant in the development of the hunt and the redesign of the caribou management system but merely a bystander and a witness who happened to be present at the right time and the right place. I was, after all, studying the Cree fishery, not wildlife management. But I was engaged in participatory research, living and eating with the people of Chisasibi, socializing in the community, going on fishing and hunting trips, and learning about traditional knowledge and practice by doing as well as listening.

Nevertheless, this chapter does not claim to provide a detailed analysis of the events around the caribou case. It merely tells a story and suggests a likely way in which a conservation ethic may have developed or changed on the basis of historical experience and social learning. As far as the Crees were concerned, the disappearance of the caribou in the 1910s was unambiguously linked to the last, big, wasteful hunt. The slaughter was not merely an aboriginal myth; it can be located in historical time through the records that Elton (1942) used. The lesson of the transgression, once learned, survived for seventy years in Cree oral history, and it was revived precisely in time to redesign the hunting system when the caribou returned. Had there been government intervention to regulate the Chisasibi caribou hunt, it could not possibly have had as much impact on the hunters as did the teachings of the elders (Drolet et al. 1987). The lesson delivered (not to kill too many and not to waste) came right at the heels of the validation of the elders' prediction that the caribou would return one day, and it was too powerful to take lightly, even for the most skeptical young hunter.

The caribou story debunks the "noble savage" myth. The ethics described in chapter 5 represent the ideal. The Cree hunter's actual behavior can and does deviate from the ideal and the ethical. However, self-control is a strong social value among the Cree (Preston 1979), and the community provides the support, and the necessary social coercion, to help the hunter remain ethical. The key role in this dynamic is played by the holders of the knowledge and the values: the elders. Cree society relies on oral history, and the elders span the generations to provide information feedbacks. What makes elders "wise"? Certainly, not all old people have wisdom. In my opinion, the "wisdom" in the present case is in the elders' timing (they waited for a whole year after the transgression until people were likely to be receptive to their message), their choice of message (the well-known story of the caribou overkill at Limestone Falls), and their effective use of myth (the ancient prophecy that the caribou will return).

The starting hypothesis in this chapter was that a conservation ethic can develop if a resource is *important* or limiting, *predictable* and *depletable*, and if it is effectively under the *control* of the social group in question so that the group can reap the benefits of conservation. Choosing caribou as the example made the task challenging. The caribou are important, but the remaining prerequisites (predictability, depletability, control) for the development of a conservation ethic are not easily met. The caribou are certainly not predictable, but once they return, certain distributional and behavioral aspects of caribou become predictable, as discovered by the hunter who verifies for his own satisfaction that the caribou were in precisely the area where his grandfather said they were last seen. On the question of depletability, however, information is still missing until it is supplied by historical experience and social learning, so there is now a compelling reason to limit harvests. Note that the Cree are not unusual in this regard (Nelson 1982). The Chipewyan (Dene) also did not have a prohibition against waste when caribou were abundant (Heffley 1981; Nelson 1982).

Finally, the question of control comes up explicitly in 1987–88 when there is a threat that the caribou resource will be opened up to uncontrolled numbers of outsiders. It is interesting to note that the Chisasibi Cree do not see other aboriginal groups as a problem; in fact, they are constantly exchanging information with them (Eastmain, Great Whale) to keep track of large-scale caribou movements. Sport hunters, however, are not part of this network and are not in the sphere of a conservation ethic that is recognizable to the Cree. Hence, starting in 1988, the Cree take political steps to safeguard "their" resources.

Consistent with the findings of other studies on large mammal management of northern indigenous hunters (Winterhalder 1983; Feit 1987), the story in this chapter suggests that the Cree management system for caribou monitors much the same information base as does Western science—geographic distributions, migration patterns and their change, individual behavior, sex and age composition of the herd, fat deposits in caribou, and the presence/absence and effect of predators. Of these indicators, the fat content of the caribou seems to receive relatively more attention by the Cree than by biologists.

This finding may be significant because there is evidence that other traditional peoples and their management systems may also be monitoring fat content. According to discussions in a September 1997 traditional knowledge workshop in Labrador, examples include the Inuit of Northern Quebec, Inuit of Labrador, and the Innu of Labrador. It is commonly known by resource managers (Anne Gunn, pers. comm.) that indigenous hunters belonging to a number of different groups in the Northwest Territories of Canada also monitor caribou fat content. As documented in some detail by Kofinas (1998), three indicators based on the monitoring of body fat (back fat, stomach fat, and marrow) top the list of some nine indicators of a healthy caribou, as used by the aboriginal hunters of the Porcupine Caribou Herd at the Alaska-Yukon border. Nicholas Flanders (pers. comm.) reports that the recording of the fat content will be a major study method in a project in Alaska to integrate Inupiat traditional knowledge and Western science about the Western Arctic caribou herd.

As a rule of thumb, the monitoring of fat content for caribou management makes a great deal of sense because it provides an index of health of both the individual animal and the herd. Fat as indicator of population health integrates the combined effects of a number of environmental factors, such as the condition of the feeding range, acting on the caribou population. It is therefore not surprising that the monitoring of caribou fat content is not merely an area-specific bit of local knowledge but rather a *principle of traditional ecological knowledge* widely applicable across the full range of caribou distribution from Labrador to Alaska.

The Cree system has many similarities to the Western science of caribou management. At the same time, it is fundamentally different from Western science, which often gives priority to quantitative population models for management decision-making. The Cree system, by contrast, neither produces nor uses estimates of the population size. Rather, it uses a qualitative mental model, which provides hunters with an indication of the *population trend over time*. This qualitative model reveals the direction (increasing/decreasing) in which the population is headed; it does not require the quantitative estimation of the population size itself for making management decisions.

Such traditional knowledge is complementary to Western scientific knowledge, and not a replacement for it. Monitoring fat content alone will not lead to good management decisions, for example, in the case of predator-limited (as opposed to range-limited) caribou populations, and in the case of a caribou population affected, say, by two or three successive bad winters (Anne Gunn, pers. comm.). On the other hand, exclusive reliance on biological population survey data will not lead to good management decisions either. There are several cases in the Canadian North and Alaska, with caribou and other wildlife, in which the results of biological censuses misled management decisions and were subsequently corrected by the use of other biological perspectives *and* traditional knowledge of indigenous groups (Freeman 1989, 1992). Such cases illustrate the complementarity of traditional and Western knowledge at a practical level and highlight the need for conceptual pluralism in resource and ecosystem management.

The definitive study of Chisasibi Cree caribou management has yet to be done: How does the hunter make decisions about hunting? How does the practice of the hunt and the overall hunting system actually work? To address such questions requires field observations and data actually based on a series of hunts, documented over several annual cycles. In subarctic North America, few investigations have ever used this approach. Exceptions include the work of Winterhalder (1983) on moose hunting strategies of northern Ontario Ojibwa, and Feit (1987) on the Waswanipi Cree. In the absence of a detailed study of the Cree caribou management system, the analysis in this chapter remains speculative but can be used as a hypothesis. Such a hypothesis can be tested against the findings of a detailed study of a different resource system, the fishery, which is the subject of the next chapter. Are quantitative population models necessary to manage fisheries? Or are there alternative ways of managing fisheries that rely mainly on contextual information and qualitative models that provide information on trends over time and the direction of abundance and availability?

Chapter Seven

Cree Fishing Practices as Adaptive Management

The Cree Indian fishery in James Bay is an example of a traditional system that can provide ecological and resource management insights. This chapter describes the unique characteristics of the fishery: its adaptability, flexibility, use of environmental signals or feedbacks, and its ability to conserve ecological resilience. These characteristics suggest that traditional systems may in some ways be analogous to Adaptive Management with its nonlinear, multi-equilibrium concept of ecosystem processes and its emphasis on uncertainty, resilience, and feedback learning.

When I started working with the Chisasibi fishery in 1974, my original intent was to study the impacts of the giant James Bay hydroelectric project on the Cree fishery. (Impacts included the destruction of the fishery but for different reasons than experts initially thought, but that is another story; see Berkes 1981a, 1988a.) As time went by, I became more and more interested in traditional knowledge and Cree fishing practices. I found that extensive local knowledge existed on distributions, behavior, and life cycles of fish simply because such information was essential for productive fishing, as any fisher knows, and was at one time essential to survival. Chisasibi fishers knew, for example, that in spring the best catches of whitefish were obtained following the melting ice edge in bays; fishers knew where the pre-spawning aggregations were in August, and they knew that in September whitefish was best harvested over a sand-gravel bottom at certain depths of water. While most ethnobiologists busied themselves with the identification of species and the recording of aboriginal classification systems, this was only a minor concern for me. The subarctic was, in any case, a species-poor environment. Thus, my initial traditional knowledge emphasis was on the natural history of fish and fishing. But as I started to gain an understanding of the local system, my interests quickly turned to resource management.

As with many northern aboriginal groups, fish are a staple resource for the Cree of James Bay. They say one can rely on fish even when other resources fail or become unavailable. Unlike many of the other animal resources, the Cree take their fish almost for granted, and no rituals and ceremonies involving fish are found in contemporary Chisasibi (formerly known as Fort George). Nevertheless, there is respect for the fish. The principle that animals are in control of the hunt (see chapter 5) holds also for fish. A fisher does not boast about his or her fishing. It is believed that boasting brings retaliation from the fish—they stop making themselves available. As well, one does not waste fish; one does not abuse fish by swearing at them or by "playing" with them; and one eats what one catches. The Cree are horrified at the thought of catch-and-release fishing practices commonly used in sport fisheries elsewhere in North America.

Most of the Chisasibi Cree fishery takes place in medium and large-sized lakes, in the estuaries of rivers, and on the James Bay coast. The major fishing technique used in the estuary and on the coast involves setting short (50 meter) gill nets of various mesh sizes from 7-meter, outboard equipped canoes. Smaller paddle canoes, sometimes outboard equipped, are used in lakes and rivers. Other fishing techniques include hand-drawn seines at the base of rapids on the La Grande River, rod and reel, and traditional baited set lines for the larger predatory fish. Fishing seasons are part of the seasonal cycle of harvesting activities, and they are signaled by biophysical events in the landscape such as the spring ice breakup in the river and change of color of the vegetation in September. Fishers know how to recognize and respond to a variety of environmental feedbacks that signal what can be fished where and when. Master fishers or stewards provide leadership.

The Chisasibi fishery in 1974 was a subsistence fishery in which people fished for their own needs. There was no competition from commercial fisheries (Chisasibi was too far from markets and there never had been a commercial fishery), and there was minimal competition from sport fisheries. In isolated areas of Canada, subsistence fisheries are not regulated by government, unlike commercial fisheries, which do come under government regulation. The conventional scientific management systems for subarctic commercial fisheries in Canada have employed some combinations of the following tools: the type of fishing gear used, restrictions on gill net mesh size, minimum fish size, season closures, and the prohibition of fishing at times and places when fish are spawning. Catch quotas are common, and maximum sustainable yield calculations based on population dynamics of the stock have also been used in the larger fisheries. The Chisasibi fishery being a subsistence fishery, I knew at the time I started my work that none of the above measures would be in effect. What I did not know was that the Cree had a system of their own.

THE CHISASIBI CREE SYSTEM OF FISHING

At first, the ways of the Chisasibi fishery seemed fairly simple. There were two basic strategies: small-mesh gill nets were used within commuting distance of the village (about a 15-kilometer radius) and a mix of larger-mesh gill nets were used further away. The most distant locations were visited rarely, perhaps once every five to ten years, and were fished mainly with larger mesh sizes (Berkes 1981b; Berkes and Gonenc 1982). Hunters following the traditional rule of thumb of rotating beaver trapping areas over a cycle of four years would also rotate their fishing areas, fishing a lake for some weeks in one year and then resting it for three years before they went back to it.

Table 7.1 Selectivity of different mesh sizes of gill nets for whitefish and cisco.

Net, in.	No. of net sets	Whitefish		Cisco		Ratio of whitefish to cisco
		No.	Avg. wt., g	No.	Avg. wt., g	
2 1/2	219	273	250	2,536	250	1:9.3
3	86	130	563	192	378	1:1.5
3 1/2 and 4	30	102	694	22	552	4.6:1

Source: Berkes (1977)

Table 7.2 Chisasibi, August, catch per life with paired 2 1/2 and 3 inch gill nets.

	Catch per net set, g	
	2 1/2 inch	3 inch
Whitefish	110	227
Cisco	1,211	649
Total fish	3,164	1,439
No. of net sets	18	18

Source: Berkes (1977)

Most of my fishery research took place near the village, where small-mesh (2 1/2 inch or 63.5 millimeter) gill nets caught mostly the smaller-sized cisco (*Coregonus artedii*) and the larger-mesh ones (3 1/2 inch or 88.9 millimeter and larger) mostly the larger-sized whitefish (*C. clupeaformis*). All of this was relatively easy to document after I had accumulated about two years of catch data based on the Cree fishery, traveling with the fishers to their customary locations and recording their catches. Selectivity of the smaller gill net was striking: it caught almost ten times more cisco than whitefish, while the larger gill nets caught five times more whitefish than cisco (see table 7.1). I was unable to establish, however, if the fishers caught more cisco near the village because they used small nets or because there were more cisco than whitefish in the area.

As I got ready to use my own experimental nets, the accompanying Cree fisher who knew my concern but whom I had not asked for help, provided on his own initiative the perfect design for a field experiment. He fished two replicates of two paired nets, one 2 1/2 inch and the other 3 inch, side by side for nine consecutive days just across the river from the village (see table 7.2). The experiment settled the question: there were very few whitefish at that location at that season. Even though the 3-inch net caught relatively more whitefish than did

Table 7.3   Catch per net set (kg) for the four mesh sizes of gill nets in the near-village fishery vs. away.

		Near village	Away from village
2 1/2 nets:	Whitefish	0.3	1.6
	Cisco	2.9	1.4
	Total catch	4.8	6.6
3 nets:	Whitefish	0.7	2.2
	Cisco	0.9	0.7
	Total catch	2.6	5.5
3 1/2 and 4 nets:	Whitefish	1.0	2.9
	Cisco	0.1	0.6
	Total catch	2.1	7.8

Source: Berkes (1977)

the 2 1/2-inch net, the smaller net provided a higher catch per unit of effort, by a factor of two. There was no sense in using 3-inch or larger nets at that *particular* location and season, although the 3-inch net caught equal numbers of cisco and whitefish when all areas and seasons were averaged out (see table 7.3). To make sure that my generalization held, I had to check and account for seasonal and for year-to-year variations in the catch per unit of effort (Berkes 1981b).

I still was not sure, however, if the 2 1/2-inch net actually *maximized* the catch per unit of effort in the area near the village. Could one use an even smaller net and get an even higher catch, even though the individual fish would be rather small? Just where were the limits of the system? Since the accompanying Cree fisher seemed to have no interest in carrying out *that* field experiment, I ended up using my own nets. The experiment did not last very long. With a 2-inch net, I found myself catching immature cisco, good numbers perhaps but definitely immature fish of the 20–25 centimeter size group. By contrast, the 2 1/2-inch net had been catching 25–30 centimeter fish, four to five years old and mostly mature. My catches with the 2-inch net did not escape the attention of other fishers. Over the course of a day, several canoes drifted over to my nets, fishers looked at the size of the fish, measured the mesh with two fingers thrust in, muttered and shook their heads in disapproval. I had been in the village less than a year and already I was finding out what social sanctions were like. At first I defended my experiment as "science," but by the end of the second day, I had pulled out all the nets. (I discovered some months later that Cree had some stock phrases to ridicule fishers who used smaller nets than those dictated by custom: for example, one would say, "his nets are so small, he cannot put his penis through it.")

However, the system of socially enforced minimum mesh size for cisco did not conserve whitefish, a larger species. A mesh size of 2 1/2 inches was taking immature whitefish; this was perhaps an explanation for the scarcity of whitefish in the waters near the village. Paradoxically, however, the apparent depletion of whitefish in that area but not elsewhere suggested an indigenous solution to the classical dilemma of a multispecies fishery. In Western resource management theory and practice, the curves of yield against fishing effort and against mesh size are different for each species. That is, it is always difficult to choose a mesh size because different species of fish grow and mature at different sizes. It is therefore impossible to harvest more than one species at the optimum level for each (e.g., Gulland 1974). In commercial fisheries, the choice of mesh size and other harvesting strategies often represents a compromise, and the overall results are rarely ideal.

What I was observing in the Chisasibi Cree traditional fishery was a management solution with a clear choice: away from the village, the effort was primarily directed at one larger-sized, highly desirable species, whitefish. Near the village, however, the effort was primarily directed against another, cisco, which was also a desirable species but matured at a smaller size and was probably able to withstand a higher fishing pressure. I still had to check whether this strategy *worked* and that the harvest was sustainable over a period of time.

I found that the productivity (measured as the catch per unit of effort) of the Chisasibi fishery as a whole compared favorably with other whitefish fisheries in the Canadian North (Berkes 1977). I also documented the number of reproductive year-classes in the near-village fishery based on essentially one population (or unit stock) of each of the two major species that lived in the lower La Grande River and its estuary. The cisco had four reproductive year-classes, 4, 5, 6, 7, and a few of 8 year-old fish; the whitefish had three year-classes, 6, 7, 8, and a few of 9 year-olds (Berkes 1979). This many year-classes signaled a healthy cisco population and a somewhat overfished whitefish population, consistent with the earlier analysis. But what really made a convincing argument for sustainability was the comparison of my Chisasibi data with the results of a long-forgotten survey from the 1920s (Dymond 1933). Sampled fifty years apart in the same waters, Dymond's whitefish and cisco had exactly the same number of age-classes as mine, and the age-specific sizes were similar (Berkes 1979). Just to make sure, I checked my age and growth data with the data of government researchers working on the impact study and satisfied myself that my biological data were reliable (Berkes 1981b).

By now, I was beginning to get a sense of the Chisasibi fishery as a managed system. The fishers used recognizable management strategies; the harvest was productive and sustainable. By knowing when and where to set the nets, the fishers exercised considerable selectivity over their harvest. In the near-village fishery, the fishers selected for cisco and against suckers (fish that people did not like to eat but used as dog food and trapping bait), and the selectivity could be documented by comparing the subsistence catch against biological samples, year after year (see figure 7.1) (Berkes 1987a).

As well, I was beginning to understand the fundamental ways in which a subsistence fishery differed from a commercial fishery. People fished for their

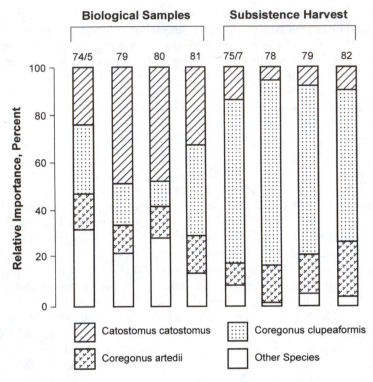

Figure 7.1 Fish species selectivity of the Chisasibi Cree fisher. Compare the biological samples against the subsistence fishery composition, showing selectivity for cisco (*C. artedii*) and whitefish (*C. clupeaformis*) and against suckers (*C. catostomus*). *Source:* modified from Berkes (1987).

needs and there was no incentive to create a surplus. During the seasons when the fish were abundant, as in spring and fall in the La Grande estuary, two small nets were sufficient to catch enough for the needs of an average extended family. But in midsummer, the mean catch per net set decreased to about half of that in the spring months. Fishers compensated for this by setting about twice as many nets so that the daily harvest remained constant (see table 7.4). The marginal effort required to manage an extra net was relatively low. One extra net took only about half an hour to set and minutes to check. In fact, people could set many more nets if they wanted to, but they did not. Their objective was to catch what they needed, about 10 kilograms per day in the case of the extended family (three nuclear families), documented in table 7.4. The narrow range in the table indicates that "getting what you need" is indeed a fine art. Ten kilograms of fish was enough food for the family, and they could still provide smoked fish to their exchange network of relatives and friends. To harvest more would have meant to give away more. But since there was no lack of fish in the community, fish would likely be wasted, a transgression.

Table 7.4 Relationship between fishing effort and catch per net set for one fishing group setting nets near village.

	June	August	October	November
Total fish catch, kg	140	84	60	44
Number of net sets	32	39	14	8
Catch per net set, kg	4.9	2.2	4.3	5.5
Number of days	12	9	7	4
Net sets per day	2.67	4.33	2.00	2.00
Catch per day, kg	11.7	9.4	8.6	11.0

Source: Berkes (1977)

Being a product of Western scientific training, I was for a long time reluctant to refer to the Cree fishery as a "management system." The conventional wisdom is that if a group of traditional people *seemed* to be managing their resources sustainably, this can probably be explained on the basis of too few people and too "primitive" a technology to do damage to the resource. Well, the apparent productivity and sustainability of the Chisasibi fishery *could not* be explained simply on the basis of small population and inefficient technology. If fisheries management is defined as controlling how much fish is harvested, where, when, of what species, and of what sizes (Gulland 1974, 1), then the Chisasibi fishers were managing their fishery. Gulland commented that fisheries rarely achieved all of the above management objectives. It seemed therefore that Chisasibi fishers did better than most fishery managers by the very criteria of Western fishery management science.

SUBARCTIC ECOSYSTEMS: SCIENTIFIC UNDERSTANDING AND CREE PRACTICE

Part of the reason many scientists have difficulty with the notion of traditional management concerns the question of information needs for resource management. The conventional wisdom in fish and wildlife management is that detailed population data are needed for management. According to this view, natural history type of information, including species identifications, life cycles, distributions, habits, and behavior—the kinds of information at which traditional peoples are experts—are important but insufficient for the needs of management. Indeed, Chisasibi Cree fishers lacked quantitative information, that is, they did not have data on the population dynamics of the harvested species. Not only that, the fishers openly disapproved of the kind of research biologists did to gather population information: sampling immature fish, and tagging fish to determine the range of the stock and to obtain population estimates by marking and recapturing.

To the Cree, these practices were disrespectful of the animals; they violated rules regarding wastage and about playing with fish. As for the biologists' objectives of "controlling" fish populations and "predicting" sustainable yields, the Cree thought that these were immodest aims of apparently immature people playing god, given that the success of fishing depended on the fish and the respectful attitude of the fisher. All of this highlights a paradox in the research of traditional management systems: how do some of these societies do such a good job of managing resources, given that the very notion of management is inconsistent with their worldviews? In the case of the Chisasibi fishery, part of the answer lies with the traditional Cree understanding of the subarctic aquatic ecosystem. But Cree understanding of ecosystems is not articulated in the abstract; it is only reachable through their practices in the concrete (Levi-Strauss 1962; Preston 1975). We will therefore switch to a Western ecological discourse on subarctic ecosystems before going back to describing the practice of the Cree fishery.

It is well known that subarctic ecosystems are characterized by low species diversity, high year-to-year variability in the biophysical environment, large population fluctuations or cycles, and generally low biological productivity. However, it is also known that fish population assemblages in unfished or lightly fished subarctic lakes are characterized by a large biomass of old (as much as fifty- to sixty-year-old) and large-sized fish, analogous, as Johnson (1976) pointed out, to the large biomass of trees in moist tropical ecosystems. The biological reason for the high biomass of such species as whitefish and lake trout (*Salvelinus namaycush*) is a matter of some scientific controversy, but the simplest explanation seems to be that proposed by Power (1978). Growth rates of individual fish in the subarctic are relatively rapid until maturity, but after maturity growth rates gradually slow down. Mortality rates decline rapidly through early life and stabilize at a low level once the fish has reached a large size. The combination of this growth and mortality pattern produces a population with many small, few intermediate-sized, and many large fish, hence the unusual bimodal (two-peaked) population length-frequency distribution often observed.

The presence of many large fish in an unfished or lightly fished northern lake gives the misleading impression of high ecosystem productivity. Since primary productivity (plant productivity) is low in the subarctic, fish productivity is low as well. Actual fish production in the estuaries in James Bay (the most productive part of the aquatic ecosystem) was calculated to be 0.3 to 1.3 kg/ha/yr; in the lakes it was even lower (Berkes 1981b). By contrast, in temperate coastal areas, lagoons, and lakes, common values are in the order of 50–100 kg/ha/yr. Those large, old subarctic lake fish only seem to be abundant; in fact, they take a very long time to renew themselves. A trophy-sized lake trout, likely to be over fifty years of age, is almost a nonrenewable resource! According to some studies in lakes of Canada's Northwest Territories, the production-to-biomass ratio of species such as whitefish is about 1:10. That is, as a rule of thumb, only about one-tenth (or less) of the fish biomass can be harvested each year on a sustainable basis for a given body of water.

However, even a fishing intensity that low could result in the removal of many of the old and large fish. This is not necessarily a bad thing, since the removal of such fish (and lowered competition for food) would result in higher survivorship, increased growth rates, and earlier maturation of the younger individuals of the same species. Analogous to harvesting a forest, such thinning of fish populations triggers increased productivity. This phenomenon is known to scientists and managers as "population compensatory responses" (e.g., Healey 1975) and occurs with all living resources. This is the Western scientific counterpart of the Cree notion that continued proper use of resources is essential for sustainability (see chapter 5).

As the rate of exploitation of such a fish population increases, at a certain point the population is not going to be able to compensate for the loss of individuals and will eventually decline. Species will differ with respect to when this point is reached. For example, lake trout has a limited biological ability to respond to exploitation. Whitefish seem to have relatively greater ability but species such as cisco, which mature at a smaller size, are better adapted to withstand high exploitation rates. These differences among species have been used to explain, for example, how the fish species composition of the Great Lakes has historically changed from one dominated by large, old, slow-growing, and late-maturing species like sturgeon (*Acipenser fulvescens*) to one dominated by small, fast-growing, and early maturing fish like yellow perch (*Perca flavescens*) (Regier and Baskerville 1986).

The two basic fishing strategies of the Chisasibi Cree could be interpreted in this light. Small-mesh gill nets used near the village are consistent with the relative abundance of cisco, a smaller species that matures earlier than does whitefish. The use of larger-mesh nets further away in water bodies exploited intermittently is consistent with the maintenance of populations of older and larger fish. Since the Cree do not use ecological formulations to articulate management choices, their system can only be inferred through their practices.

THREE CREE PRACTICES: READING ENVIRONMENTAL SIGNALS FOR MANAGEMENT

Three readily observed sets of management practices provide insights into the "secrets" of the Cree system. The first is about concentrating fishing effort on aggregations of fish. The second concerns rotational or pulse-fishing. The third involves the use of a mix of gill net mesh sizes. All three practices are unusual by the standards of commercial, nontraditional fisheries, although a number of fisheries ecologists have pointed out the merits and potential benefits of pulse-fishing in northern commercial fisheries (Johnson 1976).

The concentration of effort is probably typical of many subsistence systems. Subsistence fishers cannot afford to waste time and effort if they are not catching many. If the return from fishing is poor as compared to that from other subsistence activities, the Chisasibi Cree fisher will very quickly leave his nets and pick up his gun. Because they need to feed their families and because they have limited amounts of equipment, fishers select settings in which fish are easy to catch. Thus, groups of fishers will concentrate, year after year, on the same spawning or pre-spawning aggregations, and on feeding, migrating, and overwintering concentrations of fish, at specific times and places. An example of such a site is the First Rapids of La Grande River where (until dams were built), large numbers of cisco in pre-spawning aggregations could be obtained in August at the foot of the rapids (Berkes 1987a). There is a high premium on fishers' knowledge about the timing and locations of fish concentrations where the catch per unit of effort is known from experience to be high. Fishers of the more traditional families who spend part of the year on the land know the most suitable fishing areas in every bay or lake within the family territory. Given long travel distances, extensive knowledge of the terrain is also essential. This is particularly true on the shallow and indented James Bay coast where the navigator of the canoe needs to know the configuration of the shoreline at different phases of the tide.

The second management practice, pulse fishing, involves fishing a productive area intensively for a short length of time, and then relocating somewhere else. For example, I recorded the activities of one family fishing group that concentrated its effort in a small inlet, perhaps 100 meters by 400 meters at low tide, on the James Bay coast not far from the village. They removed a total of 34 kilograms of fish between June 7 and 12. The initial catch per net set was 6.4 kilograms, and the final, 2.2. kilograms, suggesting that a large part of the fishable stock had been removed over that brief period. The group then located their nets elsewhere but indicated that the inlet was a traditional site for the family and that they would be back the following year. Fishing areas may be recognized as traditional but this does not imply that other community members cannot fish there. Stewards do regulate access and effort through their leadership but do not normally limit the access of others into fishing areas. Fishing effort is deployed flexibly and opportunistically, and the initial success of one group seems to encourage others to converge upon an area. For example, on 24 May, right after ice breakup in another inlet on the James Bay coast, a fishing group set five nets and obtained 40.8 kilograms of fish. By 27 May, there were about twenty nets in the inlet, but as the catch per net declined to about 2.8 kilograms, they were relocated somewhere else (Berkes 1977).

Pulse fishing and fishing area rotation seemed to be taking place over two different time scales. In the intensively fished area near the village, a good spot would be fished at least once a year. Further away from the village, in areas that are hunted and fished extensively (as opposed to intensively), a hunter/fisher may use a particular lake once or so every few years. Since fishing is often coupled with hunting and trapping activities, the ideal practice is a four-year rotation, both among the Chisasibi Cree (see chapter 5) and among other James Bay Cree communities such as Waswanipi (Feit 1973, 1986). Why do people use pulse fishing and rotation? Clearly, the practice optimizes the catch per unit of effort. In the case of extensively used lakes, the practice also helps maintain a population of large-sized fish in the system. The samples available from the more remote fishing locations showed good catches of whitefish of 50–55 centimeters. Since my samples were not many, however, I wanted to make sure that my findings were not due to chance. Checking unpublished length-frequency data of fish harvested by two other Cree groups, the Mistassini and Waswanipi, I could ascertain that whitefish were indeed at about 50–55 centimeters and the lake trout 50–60 centimeters in the more distant, extensively fished lakes, with 40–50-centimeter whitefish in lakes closer to the communities (Berkes 1981b). Each of the data sets showed a scatter of sizes; it seemed that the Cree fisheries took a range of sizes (and ages) and that there were clearly many big ones, especially in the more remote areas.

The third Cree management practice, the use of a mix of gill net mesh sizes, was responsible for the harvest of a range of whitefish sizes in the Chisasibi fishery and, one can assume, in Mistassini and Waswanipi as well. The range of sizes was initially puzzling: if large fish were available, why not take the largest only? After all, that is what commercial fisheries did in the North. Large fish were what the market wanted and there was pressure on the fisher to produce a standard product. Working and living with Cree subsistence fishers revealed a different set of values and priorities. First of all, fishers would say they "used whatever nets they had," denying any conceptual design in management but affirming practice. Second, large fish and small fish (even of the same species) tasted different and were used for different purposes. For example, a cisco or a small whitefish could be cooked on a stick over open fire. Large whitefish could be boiled, smoked (traditional), or fried (nontraditional). A large white sucker (*Catostomus commersoni*) would be smoked; a small one would merely be trap bait. There was a need for a variety of things and certainly no pressure to produce a standard commodity.

The primary mechanism that drove all three management practices (effort concentration, pulse-fishing, and the use of a mix of gill net mesh sizes) was the fishers' reading of the catch per unit of effort. It was the key environmental signal monitored by the Cree; it shaped the decisions regarding what nets to use, how long to keep fishing, and when to relocate. But the Chisasibi fishers monitored other environmental signals as well. They noted and took into account the species composition of the fish coming out of their nets, the size, the condition or fatness (considered very important as a signal of health), and the sex and reproductive condition of the fish. As well, they observed the fish and noted any unusual patterns in behavior and distributions. The conduct of the fishery was guided by the need for different food products, social obligations to contribute to community exchange networks, and the conservation imperatives of "getting what you need" and minimizing waste.

A COMPUTER EXPERIMENT ON CREE PRACTICE
AND FISH POPULATION RESILIENCE

Fishery biologists and managers have for years observed a troubling trend in Northern Canadian commercial lake fisheries for whitefish and lake trout. A lightly fished lake seemingly full of large-sized fish would be selected for commercial fishery development. Exploitation would start with large-mesh gill nets but productivity would soon decline. Healey (1975) has argued, for example, that the use of large gill net mesh sizes (5 1/2 inch, or 139.7 millimeter) in the Great Slave Lake has led to the selective removal of older year-classes of whitefish, thus reducing population resilience but without triggering population compensatory responses such as increased growth rates and earlier maturity. His argument, therefore, suggested the use of smaller mesh sizes. However, in several cases in which smaller mesh nets have been used, populations have inexplicably collapsed (Healey 1975).

After several experiences of this kind, biologists came up with the explanation that in many cases the collapse was related to a combination of two things: (a) because of the removal of the largest fish, population coming to depend on a small number of reproductive year-classes, and (b) poor spawning for two or more years in a row. That is, the simplification of the age-class structure left populations predisposed or vulnerable to collapse if reproduction was poor. Alternatively, one might say that the presence of many reproductive year-classes in the population was an insurance against the variability of the physical environment, which in some years results in complete reproductive failure.

I have been using the example of whitefish in subarctic lakes, but the underlying ecological principle has wider applicability. Ecologists interested in evolution start with the assumption that life cycle characteristics of a species must reflect adaptations for improving the chances of survival of that species in its particular environment. The presence of many year-classes of large and slow-growing fish presumably represents a life-cycle adaptation to fluctuations in the ecosystem. In fact, multiple spawning in fish populations elsewhere has been shown to be of adaptive value in dampening the effects of environmental variability, especially those effects leading to poor reproductive success for two or more years in a row (Murphy 1968). Some authors have questioned the supposed fragility of northern ecosystems, pointing out that these ecosystems have a high degree of ecological resilience (Dunbar 1973), defined here as the ability of an ecosystem to absorb perturbations and yet retain its structure and function (Holling et al. 1995). Multiple reproductive year-classes is likely to be a major mechanism for ecological resilience, especially for long-lived fish species.

Intuitively it seemed to me that the Cree practice of using a mix of mesh sizes was a potential solution to the management dilemma of conserving resilience. Hence I proposed a testable hypothesis based on Chisasibi Cree traditional ecological knowledge and management: *Harvest more year-classes at a lower rate by the use of a mix of different mesh sizes* (as opposed to the selective

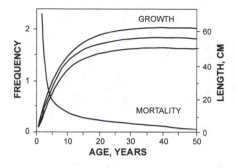

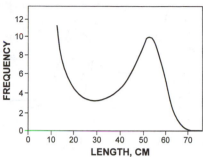

Figure 7.2 Growth and mortality curves of a model lake whitefish population. Intervals on the growth curve indicate ±1 SD. Equations for curves in Berkes and Gonenc (1982).

Figure 7.3 Length-frequency structure of the model whitefish population, as calculated from the growth and mortality curves in figure 7.2. *Source:* Berkes and Gonenc (1982).

harvest of the oldest year-classes at a higher rate by the use of a single large mesh size); *this would stimulate population compensatory responses without reducing the reproductive resilience of the population* (Berkes 1979). The problem with the hypothesis was that it was all but impossible to test with a field experiment, given the fifty-year life span of the northern whitefish. Many descriptive mathematical models in ecology develop and test hypotheses by quantifying processes intuitively known to practitioners. Thus a logical alternative to a fifty-year field experiment was a computer experiment (Berkes and Gonenc 1982).

First, we modeled mortality and growth rates in a hypothetical whitefish population. We showed that under certain assumptions, a characteristic bimodal length-frequency distribution is obtained. How such a peculiar distribution comes about can be shown mathematically through the summation of overlapping size-classes of older fish, using any long-lived species that has low growth rates and low mortality rates after first maturity (see figures 7.2 and 7.3). The population modeled in figure 7.3 postulates relatively few intermediate-sized (20–40 centimeters) fish, and an abundance of big fish with a mode at about 50–55 centimeters representing an accumulation of many old and slow-growing year-classes. The figure also helps illustrate that the fish in these northern lakes are available as easily harvestable large units, not because the populations are highly productive but because they consist of many years of accumulated production. It is a useful way to visualize the appropriateness of a fishing strategy in which one can bank one's food supply by not fishing any one lake year after year but pulse-fishing as needed. Fish as staple is not a matter of faith; those fishers *know* that the large fish are in the bank for tomorrow's needs.

Second, we modeled the effect of a single large mesh size on this hypothetical unfished population (see figure 7.4). Using the known coefficients of selectivity of gill nets for whitefish, it can be shown that the use of a single large mesh size is indeed efficient in maximizing short-term yields because a

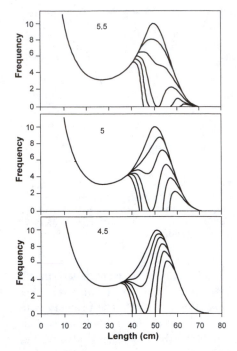

Figure 7.4 The change in length-frequency structure of a model whitefish population when fished with single mesh sizes. Contour lines represent different fishing intensities. *Source:* Berkes and Gonenc (1982).

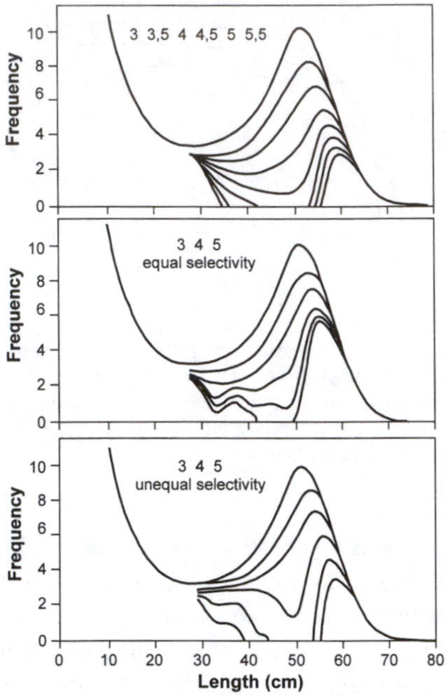

Figure 7.5 The change in length-frequency structure of a model whitefish population when fished with a mix of mesh sizes. Contour lines represent different fishing intensities. *Source:* Berkes and Gonenc (1982).

large biomass is initially available to 5 1/2- and 5-inch nets, which are the mesh sizes actually used in newly developing northern commercial fisheries. However, a 5 1/2-inch net can result in the depletion of fish over 50–55 centimeters, depending on the intensity of fishing. Figure 7.4 can also be used to visualize the results of liberalizing mesh size regulations in a hypothetical commercial fishery from 5 1/2 inches (moderate intensity resulting in the depletion of fish over 55 centimeters), to 5 inches (depletion of fish over 50 centimeters), and to 4 1/2 inches (depletion of fish over 45 centimeters).

Third, we modeled the effect of a mixed mesh size strategy to illustrate what population thinning as practiced by Chisasibi fishers may actually look like (figure 7.5). If the fishery used 3, 3 1/2, 4, 4 1/2, 5, and 5 1/2 inch nets simultaneously, and if the heights of selectivity curves were similar, the length-frequency distribution of the residual population was very similar in shape to that of the original unfished population (see figure 7.5). This conclusion holds for low and intermediate levels of fishing intensity. We also tried out a number of other combinations of mesh sizes and different assumptions of selectivity and found the outcomes to be basically similar (Berkes and Gonenc 1982).

To summarize, the computer experiment illustrates that the thinning of populations by the use of a mix of mesh sizes conserves population resilience, as compared to the wholesale removal of the older age groups by a single large mesh size. Hence the use of a mix of mesh sizes is more compatible with the natural population structure than the use of a single large mesh size alone. Using a traditional Cree-style fishing strategy, many reproductive year-classes remain in the population even after fishing. At the same time, the reduction of the overall population density increases productivity by stimulating growth rates and earlier maturation in the remaining fish and helps the population renew itself.

TRADITIONAL KNOWLEDGE SYSTEMS AS ADAPTIVE MANAGEMENT

The Chisasibi Cree fishing system is as different as can be from the biological management system applicable to subarctic commercial fisheries. As regulated by government, commercial fisheries tend to be managed on the basis of gear and mesh size restrictions, season and area closures (as during spawning), and catch quotas. By contrast, Cree subsistence fishers use the most effective gear available, the mix of mesh sizes that gives the highest possible catch per unit of effort by area and by season, and they deliberately concentrate on aggregations of the most efficiently exploitable fish. In short, the subsistence fishery is a conventional resource manager's nightmare; it violates just about every conservation tool dear to the heart of government managers and biologists.

In turn, those practices that seem to contribute to the sustainability of Chisasibi fisheries do not seem to be much appreciated by the conventional Western management system: switching fishing areas according to the declining catch per effort; rotating fishing areas; using a mix of mesh sizes to thin out populations; keying harvest levels to needs; having a system of master fishers/stewards who regulate access and effort; and having a land use system in which resources are used under principles and ethics agreed upon by all. Does it work? The computer experiment helps understand how and why the Cree fishery is adaptive (Berkes and Gonenc 1982), but perhaps a stronger argument is the apparent sustainability of the age-class structure of the two major species over a fifty-year period (Berkes 1979). The Cree fishery is difficult to assess using the standards of conventional fisheries management, but there is one kind of Western resource management science that provides a good fit with a traditional system such as that of the Cree.

Adaptive Management has been discussed widely since Holling's 1978 book, and a number of researchers have pointed out the similarities of Adaptive Management with traditional systems. One of the first was Winterhalder (1983) who noted the relevance of one of the central ideas of Adaptive Management to subarctic hunters: how to manage when much is unknown, some things are uncertain, and the unexpected must be acknowledged. He pointed out that Cree-Ojibwa hunters of Northern Ontario were experts in using resources in an environment characterized by uncertainty and novelty, and that their foraging strategies used adaptive flexibility, as Holling's models would predict. A second researcher to make the connection was McDonald (1988, 70) who compared conventional and adaptive management systems, with special attention to the Arctic, and concluded that "the adaptive management process potentially provides a methodological framework in which resource scientists and indigenous peoples can work together."

Such a framework seems indeed feasible because, in many ways, there is a remarkable convergence between Adaptive Management and traditional ecological knowledge and management systems. We see in the Cree fishery system that there is learning by doing, a mix of trial-and-error and feedback learning, and social learning with elders and stewards in charge. Like Adaptive Management, there is no dichotomy between research and management in the Cree system. The Cree assume that they cannot control nature or predict yields; they are managing the unknown, as in Adaptive Management. Although the Cree would not use these terms, their thinking is nonlinear and multi-equilibrium. They are used to an unpredictable, ever-changing environment, and they are experts in using resources at different scales of space and time. As in Adaptive Management, the Cree hunter-fisher has respect for complexity and uses practices that conserve ecosystem resilience.

Obviously, there are differences between the two systems as well. Adaptive Management can and does incorporate elements of experimentation, use of advanced technology (e.g. computer simulations), and reductionistic thinking. Gunderson et al. (1995) have in mind large management agencies when they talk about social and institutional learning. Management policies can be systematically treated as experiments from which resource managers can learn. The differences are real. But the Cree fisher is also quite capable of conceiving and carrying out field experiments, as in the case of species selectivity of gill nets (see table 7.2, above). The Cree do not have formal management policies but they certainly have customary practices that, like the policies of management agencies, can change dramatically, as seen in the case of the caribou. The Cree do not have formal management agencies, but they do have informal institutions in which elders and stewards provide leadership, carry and transmit knowledge, and sometimes reinterpret new information to redesign management systems, again as in the case of the caribou. Traditional management can be reinterpreted as Adaptive Management. Alternatively, Adaptive Management can perhaps be considered a rediscovery of traditional management.

Part Three

Issues

Chapter Eight

How Local Knowledge Develops: Cases from the West Indies

Islands of the Eastern Caribbean provide laboratory-like settings in which the evolution of local knowledge and resource management systems can be studied. This chapter highlights four examples: a mangrove conservation and management project in St. Lucia, tropical forest management in Dominica with local entrepreneur-stewards, the cultivation of edible sea moss after the depletion of wild stocks, and a case of Adaptive Management inspired by traditional, community-based sea urchin resource use.

Throughout the world, rural people rely on local resources for their livelihoods and therefore have vested interests to defend. All traditional resource use systems are built on such self-interest, and some of them have persisted over long periods—long enough to become "traditional." However, the distribution of these traditional resource use systems is not geographically even. As the overview in chapter 4 shows, some parts of the world are rich in these systems but others are not.

Such factors as industrialization, urbanization, colonization, technology change, and stresses due to population pressure, loss of local control over resources, commercialization of subsistence resources, and changes in worldview as a result of loss of intimate contact with the land have resulted in the degradation and disappearance of traditional systems. In fact, much of the literature on traditional knowledge is concerned with its disappearance (e.g. Johannes 1978; Berkes 1985; Chapin 1991; Ruddle et al. 1992). These factors have acted in different geographical regions selectively, and in fits and starts that probably correspond to major periods of rapid social and environmental change. In previous chapters, we have seen the operation of some of these factors, such as the depletion of caribou, in part caused by the arrival of the repeating rifle in the early 1900s.

The loss of traditional knowledge is no doubt a serious issue. But on the positive side, local knowledge is being created all the time, and incipient "traditional systems" abound (Berkes and Folke 1998). Thus, a more useful, broader perspective would be to consider both the *creation* and the *destruction* of traditional systems. This chapter focuses on two aspects of this creation process: how new knowledge arises and is elaborated upon, and how new management systems are built on this knowledge and on self-interest. The creation process is of considerable practical interest. Knowing how to pursue self-interest in resource management presupposes that sufficient local knowledge exists to guide resource use. As the next step, sustainability can be supported by incorporating into management the self-interest aspect of traditional resource management. This involves the consideration of property rights, a topic elaborated upon in the concluding section of this chapter.

These points are illustrated with case studies from the Caribbean region. Strictly speaking, the West Indies is one part of the world in which traditional systems do *not* exist. The indigenous populations of the Eastern Caribbean islands, and whatever traditional knowledge and resource management systems they might have had, have almost completely disappeared. The present-day populations of Caribbean islands such as St. Lucia, Dominica, Jamaica, and Barbados are, to a large extent, the descendants of the people enslaved and brought over from Africa by colonists. Their transformation into independent agricultural communities and into groups of fishers and forest users is relatively new. Thus, the Caribbean islands provide good sites for field experiments in the creation of environmental knowledge, and in the evolution of community-based management systems that use this knowledge.

MANGROVE CONSERVATION AND
CHARCOAL MAKERS

In 1984, I was starting collaborative work with the Caribbean Natural Resources Institute (CANARI) in the island state of St. Lucia and its partner organizations. I had a chance to see the charcoal-making operation in Mankòtè, the largest mangrove stand on the island and a site identified earlier by CANARI as a priority area for conservation. At that time, Mankòtè seemed to be an unlikely area for either conservation or development. The mangrove area was strewn with garbage. There were hardly any mature trees. Much of the area was covered by thin shoots or branches growing out of stumps of the white mangrove (*Laguncularia racemosa*). In places, the forest floor was covered with recently cut branches from which the charcoal makers had selected the best pieces for their charcoal pits. The charcoal producers themselves were economically marginal rural people and looked about as impoverished as any group on the island.

The Mankòtè mangrove had been once covered with mature trees when it was part of a U.S. military base during World War Two. During this period, no one other than the military was allowed in and there was no extractive use; this effectively resulted in conservation. After the base closed down in 1960, the area became open-access public land and was used for a variety of purposes such as seasonal fishing, crabbing, bathing, animal grazing, and as a source of wood for charcoal production and for construction. The area was also used as an unauthorized waste disposal site. Two decades of uncontrolled use had left the mangrove in a highly degraded condition.

When I visited the area again in 1992, the changes were remarkable. The charcoal makers were the same people, but the ragged outfits had been replaced by clean, new work clothes. They looked healthy and self-confident. The charcoal-bagging operation was now an efficient assembly line that produced a uniformly bagged and weighed product ready for the market. The charcoal makers had become well-organized small businessmen. The mangrove forest itself looked different as well. There was very little slash on the forest floor, indicating that charcoal producers had become more selective in cutting branches for their charcoal pits. The coppices on the mangrove stumps looked healthy. There was still a dearth of mature trees, but the forest canopy was fuller and higher; Mankòtè mangrove was on the way to recovery.

What produced these changes was a combination of three factors: the evolution of a local knowledge base and management system over some twenty-five years; the recognition of charcoal producers' resource use rights; and the work of a nongovernmental organization (NGO) in helping organize the charcoal producers and carrying out an integrated conservation-development project for the benefit of both the people and the mangrove (Renard 1994).

The Mankòtè case is relatively unique among integrated conservation-development projects (projects that aim for conservation while simultaneously producing economic benefits for local people) because a time-series of information was available on three variables to test whether the project was achieving its goals of sustainability: the biological status of the mangrove, the amount of charcoal produced, and the evolution of local knowledge and management among the mangrove users.

Mangrove surveys had been conducted in 1986 before the main project intervention, and again in 1989 and 1992, after intervention. Using standard research techniques, the surveys showed that the density of mangrove stems above a certain size increased significantly from 1986 to 1992. The basal area (the sum of the base areas of all the stems) increased more than fourfold, also a statistically significant change. The mean diameter of the stems did not change much. Therefore, the observed increase in the basal area was the result of improved regeneration and stem density (Smith and Berkes 1993). While mangrove recovery was proceeding, charcoal production statistics showed that charcoal makers continued to make at least as much charcoal. Increased biological regeneration from 1989 to 1992 was particularly significant, as it followed a year of relatively high charcoal production in 1991 (Smith and Berkes 1993). What explains the reversal of the degradation trend and the apparent shift toward sustainability?

Management in Mankòtè is not a traditional system. The first evidence of local management only dates back to the 1980s when CANARI researchers noticed that some charcoal makers rotated their cutting areas. As it developed in the 1980s and the early 1990s, the Mankòtè practice was based on going to a location that had good-sized stems and cutting in zigzagging strips before relocating to a new area. There was no formalized rotation, no known rules of allocation, but simply constant communication and first-comer's rights within the group of users and mutual respect for one another's cutting areas.

Perhaps the most important factor for the improved regeneration in Mankòtè was the result of change in cutting practices. Until about the mid-1980s, harvesters practiced clear-cutting and indiscriminate slashing. A particularly important change occurred in the 1989–92 period. Clear-cutting and slashing were replaced by a practice of selective cutting of the larger stems and avoidance of damage to smaller stems. Cutting was done in such a way that did not kill the stump and allowed coppicing and approximated a two-year rotation. Since charcoal makers obtained their wood by selectively cutting the larger shoots from stumps, the stems actually harvested had usually been growing through longer than a two-year cutting cycle.

What were the conditions behind the change of management practices of the charcoal makers? The explanation, as confirmed by the users, was that the Mankòtè mangrove shifted in the 1980s from an open-access to a communal resource. Wood products that used to be freely open to all potential users were now harvested mainly by an organized community of a limited number of charcoal producers. Improved security of resource use rights precipitated a change in behavior and attitude. Instead of cutting indiscriminately, the security of rights to the resource made it possible to cut with more care and conserve for the long term. Charcoal producers could now count on being able to harvest what they had left behind.

Monitoring of charcoal production has continued, degradation by waste disposal has been stopped, and harvesters have been involved in self-help efforts such as the rehabilitation of drainage in the mangrove wetland (Renard 1994). A draft co-management plan has been prepared by which charcoal makers and government managers are to share management responsibility. But the plan has not been officially adopted, and rights to the mangrove forest have not been formalized. However, charcoal makers' self-regulation system has continued to evolve. The practice of zigzagging was apparently abandoned in the mid-1990s in favor of preferred areas, each controlled by one harvester. Within each area, the harvester moves from one stand to the next through the season. Charcoal makers have continued to practice selective cutting but have been experimenting with different arrangements for area rotation.

Hudson's (1997) work documents the kind of management-related knowledge that is elaborated by the charcoal makers and transmitted to the new generation: slash piled on top of the stumps prevents regeneration, thus stumps should be left clear; cuts should be made cleanly and at a sharp angle, without creating a jagged surface; and for maximum production, shoots should be harvested by cutting five centimeters above the topmost prop root of the mangrove. Although new biological data are not available to examine whether the recovery of the mangrove has continued since 1992, it is believed that the amount of charcoal production has been sustainable, and there has been no apparent decline in mangrove cover.

DOMINICAN SAWYERS: DEVELOPING PRIVATE STEWARDSHIP

After half an hour of work with the chain saw, the large *gommier* tree was finally on the forest floor. Now began the more difficult work. After trimming the branches and dividing the trunk into three segments with the help of his assistant and young son, the sawyer started cutting the segments, layer by layer, into planks that would be carried out of the valley by hand. Converting one large *gommier* into planks would take most of the day for the small work group, and they would leave behind only the branches and a large pile of sawdust.

This was participant observation research in Dominica. I was in the field assisting the project in part because I wanted to see firsthand how anyone could turn a *gommier* tree (*Dacryodes excelsa*), a species with exceptionally hard, silica-rich wood, into planks with only a handheld chain saw. The forest was alive with birds. Dominica contains a bird fauna that is the richest for its size of any island in the Caribbean (Evans 1986). This avifauna includes two endemic *Amazona* parrot species that dwell in the cavities of large old trees and are considered endangered. Given that the destruction of tropical forests and the associated loss of biodiversity are among the most serious environmental problems, was the Dominican sawyer part of the problem or part of the solution?

Dominica is portrayed as the "nature island" of the Caribbean, unspoiled by extensive agricultural plantations or by tourism development. It supports the most extensive tropical forest cover of the islands of the Eastern Caribbean. As late as 1985, between two-thirds and three-quarters of the island was still covered by forest, much of it on steep slopes (Evans 1986). The island is only 22 kilometers by 47 kilometers in size, but the rugged interior rises steeply to 1,420 meters. It is this ruggedness that has protected the forest cover: agriculture is hard to establish and commercial logging is difficult to carry out. But by the same token, the steep terrain is susceptible to erosion damage when agriculture and logging are attempted on the slopes.

Over the past decades, timber cutting in Dominica has exploited two distinct technologies: (a) mechanized harvesting, using skidders and other heavy equipment and relying on the construction of access roads through the forest; and (b) teams of sawyers, small-scale harvesters employing chain saws and cutting up logs into planks on site in the forest. The two technologies have very different impacts on the tropical forest ecosystem.

Rugged topography, high rainfall, and lack of roads in the interior make much of the productive forest area inaccessible to mechanized operations, and land capability studies indicate that large-scale timber extraction on a sustainable basis is not feasible (Putney 1989). Attempts at large and medium-scale timber harvesting in 1902, 1947, 1968, 1977, and 1991 all ended in failure, despite government subsidies, economic incentives, and development grants from external donors. In the meantime, the use of heavy machinery on Dominica's wet and difficult terrain led to soil erosion and compaction and damage to residual vegetation (Putney 1989).

In contrast to mechanized operations, the sawyers cut individually selected trees and convert logs into planks on site using chain saws. They carry the tree out of the forest on foot, plank by plank. Sawyers can operate in Dominica's rough terrain without the need for access roads, and with little residual effect on soil and vegetation. Sawyers "bring the mill to the tree rather than dragging the tree to the mill," says Putney (1989, 19). The mobility of the sawyers makes it possible to spread the harvesting effort in both space and time. Unlike the more capital-intensive operations, there is little financial pressure on sawyers to extract large volumes of timber per unit area to cover high capital costs. This permits light cuts and greater selectivity and care in harvesting.

Since woodcutting is a traditional occupation in Dominica, sawyers possess local knowledge that allows them to operate in an environment in which large-scale operations fail. They know the terrain, the distribution of tree species, how to access steep areas, and how to cut on steep slopes. Thus, the opportunity and background exist to link modern forest conservation with traditional practice. Historically, small sawyers used pit saws, large handsaws operated vertically by teams of two or three. After Hurricane David in 1979, chain saws became common, as they were necessary for the rapid clearance of the blowdown in the wake of the hurricane. This new technology in turn made it possible to exploit the valuable but hard to cut *gommier*.

The community of sawyers started to organize after Hurricane David and established a cooperative-like organization called Cottage Forest Industries (CFI) in 1987. CFI started with both business development and conservation objectives. For many of the members, livelihood issues were initially the primary concern. However, a survey and group interviews we carried out in 1991 showed an interesting transition taking place in the minds of sawyers, from financial concerns to sustainable use. Sawyers did indicate that they were in this line of work because it was a well-paying job in an economy that did not offer many opportunities. They enjoyed being sawyers also because they were their own bosses, took pride in their skills and self-reliance, liked the outdoors, and enjoyed working in a group. However, many sawyers also thought that being a CFI sawyer was more than being a woodcutter; it signified a greater knowledge of the forest and more responsibility for conservation.

How does a sense of stewardship evolve? One of the sawyer leaders observed that when he was younger, all he cared about was cutting and selling the wood. As he got older, his attitude toward the forest started changing. This change was the result of his experience in the forest, and his involvement in public education. CFI holds wood-sawing demonstrations at country fairs. Children would come up to him and ask if he cut large old trees. Would he cut one that had cavities and perhaps nesting parrots? These questions made the tough sawyer/businessman think, and they influenced his role as leader and proponent of selective cutting.

BOX 8.1
DOMINICA SAWYERS AS AN INTERNATIONAL MODEL
FOR TROPICAL FOREST SUSTAINABILITY

There is a growing opinion that conventional timber exploitation and tropical forest conservation are no longer compatible. The Dominica experiment holds the promise that it is possible to create incentive structures for small-scale operations to log sustainably, and it has been receiving international attention (Pearce 1993). The Dominica experiment was taken up by Frank Wadsworth of the U.S. Government's Institute of Tropical Forestry. Recognizing that the development of stewardship requires the incentive of secure resource tenure, the Wadsworth management plan included a government concession to CFI in Dominica's forest reserve in the interior of the island, which the sawyers started cutting in 1993.

The plan included strict controls regarding which trees can be felled. To maintain species diversity, only a certain number of mature *gommier* was to be selectively cut in any one block, with a harvesting cycle of forty-five years. A system of monitoring sites was set up, using birds as indicator species for measuring the health of the ecosystem, in such a way that warning signs can be detected within two or three years. The plan relied in part on "paraforesters," sawyers who were given additional training to allow them to play a central role in harvest management and monitoring not only the timber resource but the forest ecosystem. As quoted by Pearce (1993), "No tropical country has yet managed its forests for sustainable timber production," says the plan. "Dominica's success will literally be a model for the world to follow." But the design encountered a number of problems and was never fully implemented. As of 1998, "there is no organized community of sawyers co-managing the forest," says Yves Renard (pers. comm.); "we are very far from that."

Is the Dominica sawyer case merely an attractive story, or does it have significance beyond the Caribbean? Commercial logging, together with agricultural clearing, is a major cause of tropical deforestation worldwide, and there has been a search for alternatives. The local knowledge-based operations of Dominican sawyers show that it is in fact feasible to create incentive structures for small-scale local woodcutters, operating as associations of small independent businessmen, to use tropical forest resources sustainably. According to a management plan drawn up for Dominica by the Institute of Tropical Forestry, the aim is not merely the sustainability of the timber supply but the sustainability of the entire forest ecosystem and the users as well (see box 8.1).

CULTIVATING SEA MOSS IN ST. LUCIA

What happens when demands or stresses increase on a resource that produces a small supply or has limited capacity for replenishing itself? Can traditional knowledge help extend the supply? Or alternatively, if demand outstrips the supply and the resource crashes, is there a role for newly developed knowledge? These questions come up in many places and for many kinds of resources. The case of sea moss in St. Lucia provides a field study to pursue these questions in more detail.

Sea moss is the generic term for several species of edible red algae, mostly species of *Gracilaria*, traditionally used in the Caribbean. Sea moss contains polysaccharides that dissolve in boiling water and thicken to form a gel when the solution is cooled. It is a thickening agent traditionally used in many parts of the Caribbean in soups, porridge, and drinks, including a popular brew based on sea moss, milk, and rum.

Collection of sea moss in St. Lucia was traditionally done by hand from wild stocks. The traditional harvesters were people from several communities in three areas of St. Lucia. Harvesting was a seasonal activity, and sea moss collecting was part of a livelihood strategy that combined it with other seasonal activities. This presumably allowed the regeneration of sea moss beds between harvests. With increased demand and rising prices in the 1960s and the 1970s, there was an influx of nontraditional sea moss gatherers into the industry, mostly unemployed or underemployed youths who had no experience in sea moss collecting and who wanted to make quick profits. This created open-access (free-for-all) conditions that swamped any conservation-oriented practices that may have existed and resulted in the depletion of sea moss beds. With no pulsing of harvests to allow for regeneration of *Gracilaria* beds, and with the plants pulled from the substrate together with their holdfasts, natural growth and recruitment was no longer sufficient to maintain the resource. The shallower areas were depleted, leaving only small pockets of sea moss, as in the other depleted areas of the Caribbean, such as Barbados (Smith et al. 1986).

Sea moss aquaculture was started in St. Lucia in 1981 by the Department of Fisheries, as a response to declining wild stocks and to create alternative livelihoods for coastal communities based on the sustainable use of natural re-sources. The first commercial plot was started in 1984. In 1985, CANARI began a program of research and training in sea moss production. Various growing tech-niques were tested, all with the same basic method of seeding lines by inserting sea moss fronds between strands of rope: the Philippine stake-and-line method, bamboo rafts with floating lines, and most recently, floating longlines of ten to fifteen meters, anchored at each end.

The target group for training initially was fishers, partly because they were presumed to be knowledgeable about marine resources. It turned out that many fishers found the cultural switch to a "grower mentality" difficult. Similarly, wild sea moss gatherers were not attracted to aquaculture, presumably because they were unwilling to make the attitudinal adjustment from the immediate returns from wild harvesting to cultivation, which requires day-to-day work but intermittent returns. Thus, the assumption that resource users most familiar with the marine inshore environment were the people who could most easily adapt to strategies and attitudes associated with a different mode of resource production proved wrong (Renard 1994, 12). The sea moss project then targeted a mixed group (including women) of occupational pluralists, people who divided their time among a variety of cash- and subsistence-oriented activities, as typically found in West Indian rural society.

By the late 1980s, sea moss culture became established as a small-scale industry on the southeast and southwest coasts of St. Lucia. The barriers to further growth were not economic (prices were good) or biological (*Gracilaria* grew well on lines). The impediments included, in addition to the inability or unwillingness of many to adopt aquaculture, the short-term problem of loss to occasional hurricanes, and the long-term problem of insecurity of rights to aquaculture areas. If growers owned the *Gracilaria* lines but could not control the waters and the aquaculture sites, what was there to prevent the cultured sea moss from meeting the same fate as the wild *Gracilaria*?

A number of solutions have been devised in different parts of the world to solve the problem of rights. Many of these involve government recognition of individual or communal rights to productive waters. In many countries, coastal groups have traditional use rights to marine resources (see chapter 4), and in other countries, lagoons and coastal aquaculture sites are leased to individuals, companies, and cooperatives. The St. Lucia sea moss case is informative because it provides examples of some of the practical problems in making commons work. St. Lucia's Fisheries Act of 1984, section 21, provides for the leasing of "land, including areas of the foreshore or the sea-bed for the purposes of aquaculture."

The government of St. Lucia has demarcated aquaculture plots and encouraged sea moss growers to apply for formal leases. The problem, however, is that applications by growers have not been finalized over a period of more than ten years despite reapplication, and they have no greater legal right to aquaculture areas than before (Berkes and Smith 1995). In the absence of formal rights, growers have come to control their areas through joint supervision of the area with other growers and with government officers. They have to some extent developed a code of practice that resembles those in traditional resource use systems elsewhere and is similar to reciprocal help relations, based on the traditional rural Caribbean practice of *koudmen*.

REHABILITATING EDIBLE SEA URCHIN RESOURCES

One of the local delicacies that many of the visitors to the West Indies never get to try is the sea egg—it has been almost totally depleted from the shores of some of the more crowded islands such as Barbados and Martinique. The white-spined sea urchin, *Tripneustes ventricosus*, locally known as sea egg in the Eastern Caribbean, is traditionally harvested by family groups for their own needs and by small-scale producers for the local market. Sea eggs first reproduce at one year of age, live in shallow water sea grass beds, and are relatively easy to collect by free diving. The species is therefore vulnerable to overharvesting but appears capable of rapid recovery if protected.

The sea egg resource of St. Lucia seems to have been used sustainably until the 1980s. Sea urchins were traditionally collected by family groups and harvesting took place mainly during school vacation months. Parents and children shared the work of collecting and preparing the sea eggs. In the south part of the island, the major harvesting area, the bulk of the harvesting took place traditionally over a two-month period, allowing the resource to recover though ten months of the year. However, in recent decades, as demand increased, sea egg collecting increasingly became a commercial venture rather than a family-based activity, attracting young and underemployed people looking for part-time income. Year-round harvesting became the norm in areas where there was no community-based management.

Sea urchin populations in St. Lucia were severely affected by hurricanes in 1979 and 1980. Their recovery by 1983 was followed by uncontrolled harvesting in some areas, driven by strong demand from an external market (Martinique), resulting in severe depletion of stocks. To protect the remaining stocks, the government of St. Lucia closed sea urchin collecting in 1987. Year-round harvesting, as was the case in parts of St. Lucia before the ban, not only removes egg-bearing individuals but also results in the destruction of many individuals with unripe gonads. The explanation lies in the biology of the species. Although there are seasonal peaks in reproductive activity, the species produces eggs throughout the year, and hence at least some of the urchins would contain mature gonads at any given time. After the ban, some illegal harvesting continued in certain locations, although the regulation was enforced in other areas.

In 1987 CANARI started a project on sea urchins to determine the size and densities of sea egg populations in three different areas of the St. Lucia coast. The main objectives were to establish the conditions necessary for population recovery, and to formulate guidelines for sea urchin management. Given the government ban, the objectives were timely. The three locations were chosen on the basis of the similarity in ecological conditions. All three had been important traditional harvesting sites. The study also collected information on harvesting and marketing from sea urchin collectors and other people associated with the sea egg industry. The study continued until 1989, and the results were very revealing (Smith and Berkes 1991).

They showed that the traditional community-based management that existed in the coastal village of Laborie, one of the three locations of the study, was as effective as the government ban enforced in the Maria Islands Nature Reserve, one of the other locations of the study. Laborie, located on a small bay, had retained the traditional summer harvest of the sea egg, as practiced at least since the early 1900s. Sea egg collecting was not allowed in the bay at other times of the year, either for local residents or for outsiders. In the case of Maria Islands Nature Reserve, commercial sea egg collecting for the Martinique market had been stopped, in part through pressure from the local media to protect the waters of the reserve. In both locations, peak densities of 5.0 to 7.0 urchins per square mile occurred following the peak reproductive season.

By contrast, the sea urchin populations in Aupicon, the third study location, remained very low throughout the study: less than 0.1 urchins per square mile. There was no community management in the Aupicon area and no protected areas. Since there was no enforcement of the general government ban, sea egg collecting in Aupicon effectively remained open-access. But in any case, there were very few adults left and almost no young urchins, even after the peak reproductive season. The results of the study suggested that a necessary condition for sea urchin recovery was the presence of a certain minimum number of adult individuals in the environment. Once the adults had been as completely depleted as in Aupicon, few larvae settled at the site and recovery was not possible (Smith and Berkes 1991).

Sea urchin harvesters were kept informed of the progress of the study during the course of the research. CANARI's results were shared both with the Department of Fisheries and local sea urchin divers. Discussions began on the feasibility of establishing a co-management arrangement that would allow harvesting under controlled conditions. The government ban on harvesting was lifted in 1990 after nearly three years of closure, on three conditions, that the harvesters: observe an agreed starting date of harvest; observe a minimum size limit; and report to the Department of Fisheries when the stock above the minimum size was depleted (so that the harvesting season would be closed). As well, harvest zones would be established and harvesters licensed.

The sea egg research project provided not only the biological information needed to establish management guidelines, it also revealed the existence of a community-based management system in one of the study locations. It showed the traditional wisdom of a seasonal harvest, followed by a period in which the resource would recover. Given that the sea urchin has a one-year life cycle (but lives to at least three years), such a management practice would not deplete the stock, provided a certain critical number of adults were conserved. This traditional system design, emphasizing the importance of closed seasons and the maintenance of a minimum population density, provided useful guidelines in formulating new government regulations.

As well, part of the innovation in St. Lucia's new sea egg management was the arrangement in which harvesters would become partners with government managers in using feedback from the resource to adjust management regulations flexibly. Rather then relying on set seasons and set quotas, the co-management arrangement was designed to make use of the local knowledge of sea egg harvesters, their ability to monitor the harvestable population size, to determine when the sea egg season would open and when it would be closed. This system, which in effect uses principles of Adaptive Management, has been in place since 1989 and has continued to operate well (Renard 1994).

CONCLUSIONS: LESSONS IN COMMONS MANAGEMENT

These Caribbean cases provide informative examples regarding the creation or development of local knowledge and management systems, not only because the islands of the West Indies are compact, laboratory-like settings but also because they pose development issues similar to those in many areas elsewhere in the world. The subject of the previous chapters, the Cree of James Bay, a semi-isolated society until recent years, is not typical of rural societies of the world. In most regions, including the West Indies, communities do not possess detailed traditional ecological knowledge and time-tested management systems based on this knowledge. More typically, whatever exist of local traditional knowledge and management systems are often overwhelmed by population and resource pressures. And yet, as the St. Lucia and Dominica cases show, new local knowledge and management systems are arising all the time.

The mangrove case indicates that the beginnings of a rotational use system can emerge in two generations, or some twenty to thirty years, although local knowledge of charcoal making and woodcutting is no doubt multigenerational. Similarly, most Dominican sawyers are in possession of local knowledge and skills that are at least three or four generations old, perhaps old enough to be considered traditional. But in this case, there is no locally devised management system comparable to the St. Lucia mangrove case. The sea moss example is unusual in that it shows that a cultural orientation to *cultivation* (as opposed to harvesting from the wild) was more important than actual local knowledge and familiarity with the particular ecological setting (the marine inshore environment). However, sea moss growing is a new occupation, and it is not yet clear what knowledge and skills would be passed on to the next generation; there has not yet been a second generation. By contrast, sea urchin harvesting has a multigenerational background, long enough for the transmission of knowledge and elaboration of workable management strategies.

The examples from St. Lucia and Dominica are not unique in showing the creation and elaboration of local knowledge. Other examples can be given from the Caribbean, even though the area has never been considered to harbor much local-level management. For example, no marine tenure system had been documented from the Eastern Caribbean until the 1980s. In contrast to Oceania where reef and lagoon marine tenure systems abound (see chapter 4), the lack of such systems in the Eastern Caribbean was thought to be due to the relatively recent history of the postcolonial inhabitants of the area. More detailed studies have documented rudimentary territorial systems from the north shore of Jamaica. These systems lacked the sophistication of those from Oceania (Johannes 1978) but were real enough to be mapped and to function in limiting access to coral reef fish resources in a generally overfished area (Berkes 1987b).

Fishing communities included individuals with a great deal of local knowledge on the biology and habits of reef fish, some of it culturally transmitted, multigenerational knowledge. The technology used (dugout canoes and fish traps) was of mixed traditional heritage and came from indigenous people (now extinct in Jamaica) and from Africa. Other marine tenure systems have since been documented from the Caribbean. For example, Finlay (1995) studied the beach seine fisheries of Grenada and showed that the seining sites were used

---

BOX 8.2
GENERATING KNOWLEDGE: A DANISH INNOVATION
WITH POUND NETS

"In 1905 or 1906 two brothers Jensen, from Korsor Island on Seeland had noticed that the little plops they heard at their pound nets in the dark evenings of August came from eels crawling over the side of the nets. It seemed eels entered the pound nets, but left them again. So they tried attaching eel traps (fyke nets) to the head of the pound net, and it worked. . . . From then on, many traditional types of eel traps and weirs gradually gave way to pound nets which would catch other fish as well. The use of traditional eel weirs had mostly been a supplementary activity of farmers with coastal rights. With the advent of the eel pound nets, it was professional fishermen who took another step in the process that separated fishing from farming."

Source: Vestergaard 1991, 159

---

under ten rules, nine of which were universally accepted by all fishers, to ensure equity and to manage conflict.

Study methods similar to those used in Jamaica did not generate information on fishing territories in Barbados, and none was expected. Compared to Jamaica, Barbados has an insignificant shelf and coral reef area. Instead, traditional fishing in Barbados was oriented to the open sea. Before engines became available in the 1950s, Barbados fishers used sail to pursue flying fish within a day's travel of the island (and often risked being blown toward Africa). Increasingly greater mechanization allowed the Barbados fishing fleet to increase its range—all the way to Trinidad and Tobago by the early 1980s (Berkes 1987b).

In the process of adopting more sophisticated technology, the fishers no doubt lost some of their skills in reading the weather, wind, and waves. They picked up other skills in the meantime, such as the use of radio within groups of cooperating fishers to search for fish and to communicate information on fish concentrations. (Flying fish is a highly aggregated species.) At the same time, greater mobility on the high seas meant that fishers sharpened their knowledge and interpretation of environmental cues in search of aggregations of fish. Studies by Gomes et al. (1998) in the Eastern Caribbean show that there is a system of knowledge of sea color and distribution of debris as indicators of flying fish and large pelagic species such as dolphin fish. Some of this knowledge corresponds to Western science (oceanography and fisheries) and some of it does not. Some types of knowledge are inconsistent from island to island and are distributed unevenly among fishers of different islands.

It is not easy to document how knowledge is actually discovered and elaborated. The field of education is largely silent on traditional knowledge. There are few cases of detailed ethnographic studies on the transmission of traditional knowledge (e.g., Ohmagari and Berkes 1997) but almost nothing on its generation. The case described in box 8.2 is one of the exceptions. (See Nakashima

[1998] for another example.) It is a description of how Danish pound net fishers discovered at the turn of the century that these nets (which are large, fixed trap nets) could be adapted to catch eels, a valuable species in northern Europe. The innovation helped extend the fishing season and lowered equipment costs for commercial fishers, and at the same time made it difficult for farmer-fishers to compete against them (Vestergaard 1991).

Turning to the question of how new management systems are built on newly generated local knowledge and self-interest, the examples in this chapter show that there is always a general tendency for community self-organization toward sustainable practice. However, the examples also show that even though local knowledge is a necessary condition, it is often not a sufficient condition to achieve sustainability. What is to prevent other potential users from taking the mangrove wood conserved by the charcoal makers? To prevent other sea egg collectors from poaching on the brood population? To prevent cultured sea moss from meeting the same fate as the wild sea moss?

The issue is not specific to an individual resource such as mangrove wood, sea egg, or sea moss, nor is it specific to St. Lucia. It is a fundamental issue of property rights in the use of common property resources. Over historical time, property rights to resources in many parts of the world have been transformed from communal property (in which access and management rights are controlled by an identifiable group) to open access (a free-for-all in which the resource is accessible to all potential users). In the St. Lucia sea moss and sea egg cases, population and resource pressures have resulted in open access; in other cases, colonialism and the central government's economic policies have created open access (e.g., Johannes 1978; Berkes 1985).

As many studies of common property resources have made clear (McCay and Acheson 1987; Berkes 1989a; Ostrom 1990; Bromley 1992), it is this open-access regime (and not communal ownership) that leads to the *tragedy of the commons*, the phenomenon in which the individual offloads costs to society while pursuing private benefits, with disastrous consequences for the resource itself in the long run. Communal resource tenure such as that for sea eggs in Laborie, and individual tenure such as that in sea moss aquaculture, provide entry points for solving the tragedy of the commons in coastal waters. Resource tenure can pave the way to establish property rights in areas in which resource harvesting had previously operated under nonsustainable, open-access conditions.

Common-property (*common-pool*) *resources* are defined as a class of resources for which (a) exclusion is difficult and (b) joint use involves subtractability (Berkes et al. 1989; Feeny et al. 1990). There are thus two requirements for making commons work. The first is to solve the problem of exclusion by means of controlling access of all potential users by establishing property rights. These rights may be private or communal; the important point is to remove the open-access condition. The second is to solve the problem of subtractability (e.g., each user is capable of subtracting from the welfare of others). This involves the making and enforcing of resource use rules among the users themselves.

Once property rights and resource use rules have been established, both the costs and benefits of any management action will be borne by the same individual or group, thus providing *incentive to conserve*.

The emergence of coastal aquaculture for sea moss, and the recognition of community rights for sea egg harvesting (as in Laborie) may be seen as a change *back from* open-access *to* communal property or private property (Berkes and Smith 1995). Hence the cases in this chapter provide examples of the various ways in which local knowledge arises, in parallel with the development of resource use systems built on self-interest. The chapter merely considers a small region and a limited time scale. The emergence of local knowledge as an adaptive response has no doubt also operated over larger spatial and temporal scales in environmental history. This is a theme that is revisited in chapter 10 after examining some limitations and critiques of traditional ecological knowledge in chapter 9.

Chapter Nine

Challenges to Indigenous Knowledge

Did Chief Seattle say, "All things are connected"? More so than many other disciplines, indigenous knowledge has to contend with popular and academic myths about traditional peoples. Making sense of the contradictory evidence and providing a coherent picture of the real significance of traditional ecological knowledge for contemporary issues, such as biodiversity conservation, requires the development of a theory of indigenous knowledge that can account for changes in human-nature relations over time.

The study of traditional ecological knowledge is hampered by the existence of several, often contradictory, myths about traditional peoples. One of these myths (the "Exotic Other"), common among Western environmentalists, is that traditional peoples are close to the land and intrinsically attuned to nature, which makes it possible, in some vague way, to live "in balance" with their environment. They are "ecologically noble savages" (Buege 1996). They can do no wrong. Their photographs decorate the covers of popular magazines and provide lasting images in the education of the general public about traditional ecological knowledge (Linden 1991). As Ellen (1993, 126) puts it, the idea of lost ecological knowledge somehow associated with lost tribes is a view that unmistakably "reproduces the notion of a primitive, exotic Other. It is a view that the anthropologist Edmund Leach described with characteristic foresightedness as 'sentimental rubbish.' "

A second myth (the "Intruding Wastrel") holds humans as unnatural intruders, despoilers of pristine ecosystems, and aliens (Evernden 1993). Primitive peoples are no noble savages but tend to be ignorant, superstitious, careless, and backward. This view questions whether traditional peoples ever lived in "balance with nature," at least not due to any cultural adaptations. They lived as biological populations limited by their resources, at the mercy of natural forces and supernatural beliefs, and certainly not as organized communities with their own knowledge-practice-belief complex to adapt to and manage their environment. Their impact may have been small at a time when their population numbers were small and technology simple enough to be environmentally benign. But they had a tendency, even as primitive hunters many thousands of years ago, to cause environmental damage, as witnessed by ancient extinctions.

A third myth about traditional peoples portrays them in terms of a "Noble Savage/Fallen Angel" duality. They should continue to live as "primitives," lest they become a threat to the very ecosystems in which they live. Ramos (1994) describes cycles of adulation followed by denigration experienced by Brazilian Indians when they start to assert their land rights. As Alcorn (1994, 7) explains further, many northern conservationists (biological preservationists) "wish to keep biodiversity in untouched natural settings free of any human habitation. They see people who live and work there as threats.... On the other hand, Northern cultural preservationists wish to see exotic peoples preserved as idealized, superior cultures which live in 'harmony with nature,' untainted by the market economy." When such cultures are contaminated, the people became a threat to their environment and to themselves, as fallen angels who could not do anything right.

These three simplified images of traditional peoples sometimes overlap. It is probably fair to say that just about everyone who has a view about indigenous peoples holds preconceived and often ambiguous notions about them. Many people, including indigenous peoples themselves, may believe parts of one or more of these views, and their thinking may change depending on which groups of traditional people they are thinking about. Are they all incorrect? As with all myths, there are elements of truth at the basis of all three. On the whole, however, this volume argues that they are myths nonetheless.

The chapter starts by addressing the first myth, and the effort to create and nurture the image of the Exotic Other. It then proceeds to address the second (Intruding Wastrel) by focusing on the question of ancient extinctions, including that of the Paleolithic megafauna, and builds a cultural evolutionary perspective, distinguishing between *invaders* and *natives*. The third myth (Noble Savage/Fallen Angel) is addressed through the debate concerning the differences between Western and indigenous notions of conservation, and the notion of wilderness. Next, the chapter looks at the evidence on adapting traditional systems to the contemporary context, and its significance for sustainability. Finally, the chapter examines social learning as a way in which cultural evolution and the evolution of traditional systems proceeds.

LIMITATIONS OF INDIGENOUS KNOWLEDGE AND THE EXOTIC OTHER

Tradition is not always adaptive, and traditional people do not always act as wise stewards of the environment. For example, the caribou story in chapter 6 illustrates the gap between practice and ideology. When conservation practice in the caribou case was eventually restored, this was explainable in terms of social learning, environmental knowledge, oral history, and healthy indigenous institutions, and not in terms of noble savagery. Johannes and Lewis (1993, 106) observe that "the acceptance of all traditional ecological knowledge as infallible is an extreme position, almost as unfortunate as that of dismissing it. Traditional peoples are not infallible, and some of their misuses of natural resources have been, and are, substantial."

As well, indigenous interpretations may be at odds with Western science. Some traditional knowledge may indeed be incorrect, just as some Western scientific findings are later found to be incorrect. (As well, there are several well-known cases in which traditional knowledge has provided correction to Western science [Freeman 1992]). Some of the examples offered by Johannes and Lewis (1993) of errors or limitations of traditional ecological knowledge include the belief of Torres Strait islanders (between Australia and New Guinea) that marine resources were without limit; beliefs overriding objective observations, as in blaming sorcery for the decline in crop yields or hunting success; misinterpreting fish spawning for defecation, as in the case of some Pacific Island groups; and the indigenous belief in northern Alberta, Canada, that windfall areas in the forest attract lightning.

In many of the cases of excessive claims of indigenous wisdom, neither indigenous people themselves nor researchers can be held responsible. A case in point is the Chief Seattle story. Did Chief Seattle say, "All things are connected"? "The earth does not belong to man; man belongs to the earth"? Did he call the earth our mother, the rivers our brothers, or the perfumed flowers our sisters? He did not. Those words were not written until the early 1970s (Wilson 1992). Chief Seattle did make a speech in the 1850s in relation to treaties in the Pacific Northwest, but the content and the meaning of his talk have been altered considerably. The Washington Territory was created in 1853, and the governor was responsible, among other things, for settling relations with the Indians. To prepare the way for treaty making on Puget Sound, a gathering of the Duwamish was called in December 1854. The governor explained his plans to conclude treaties, and Chief Seattle of the Duwamish responded with a speech of his own.

The chief's speech made a profound impression on Henry A. Smith, who was one of the listeners. Smith published an account of Chief Seattle's speech in a local newspaper some years later. The speech was republished several times in the next few decades, and in the 1960s, William Arrowsmith, professor of classics at the University of Texas, modernized the language of the speech. Ted Perry, a writer, also at the University of Texas, who had heard the Arrowsmith version of the speech, decided to use parts of it for the script of a movie with an environmental theme, called *Home*. He paraphrased parts of the speech, and for good measure, added fictional text to bolster the ecological imagery. Visitors to the U.S. pavilion at Expo '74 in Spokane were confronted with yet another version of the speech, this one, an impressively concise and poetic ecological message, based on the script of the movie, *Home*, and of course attributed to Chief Seattle (Wilson 1992). Finally, Rudolf Kaiser, a German anthropologist, let the cat out of the bag in an international conference in 1984 and brought the story to the attention of scholars (Knudtson and Suzuki 1992). The myth itself continued to circulate for many more years.

There are several major differences between Smith's version of the speech and the modern accounts. The main difference, says Wilson (1992), is the de-

---

BOX 9.1
MANUFACTURING MYTHOLOGIES:
THE CASE OF CHIEF SEATTLE'S SPEECH

"If all the beasts were gone, men would die from a great loneliness of spirit. For whatever happens to the beasts, soon happens to man." These are great words, says science writer Stephen Strauss, but unfortunately Chief Seattle never uttered them; Ted Perry made them up. Strauss goes on to examine why we, as Western society, seem to be so susceptible to the perpetration of such sentimental fallacies. Strauss continues: "The fiction became part of the program called *Home* which aired in 1972. Initially, Mr. Perry said he attributed his fictional musings to Chief Seattle and later told the producer of his ruse.... From there the power of urban myth took over. Spurious speech or not, Mr. Perry's sentiments struck a chord. The speech was reprinted and translated widely. And the myth of the myth lives on...."

"What's going on here?" Strauss asks, "particularly when Mr. Perry tells everyone, including [the publishers of] *Brother Eagle, Sister Sky*, that the speech they are promoting as Chief Seattle's is fraudulent. There is a kind of bald-faced re-writing of history in the name of sentimentalized Indian environmentalism.... Historical record be damned, says [the publisher].... His company can put any words it wants into the mouth of Chief Seattle because 'we don't have access to [his] actual words.' ... All that matters is that people believe Chief Seattle uttered the sentiments. 'These words have been attributed to the Chief or to the Chief's intent and have been used by the ecological movement for some time,' he says. But others point out that the issue is really one of the packaging of wisdom. It only has true resonance if it were said by a wise native person. 'It doesn't sound the same if it was produced by a guy named Ted,' says Rick Caldwell, librarian at the Seattle Museum of History and Industry, who regularly demythologizes the speech for the curious."

Source: Strauss 1992

---

velopment of Chief Seattle as a native ecologist. A sense of love of the land is present in the Smith version: "Every part of this county is sacred to my people. Every hillside, every valley, every plain and grove has been hallowed by some fond memory or some sad experience of my tribe" as quoted by Wilson (1992, 15). But in the modern versions, ecological imagery is pervasive and the text is full of human-nature relationships. The Chief Seattle story is reminiscent of the Eskimo snow hoax in many ways (see chapter 3). It documents the susceptibility of Western society to embrace exaggerated claims of native ecological knowledge and wisdom (see box 9.1). This is obviously no fault of indigenous peoples and researchers, but it does underscore the need for traditional knowledge scholars to be ever-vigilant.

INVADERS AND NATIVES:
A HISTORICAL PERSPECTIVE

In a backlash against excessive claims for the ecological wisdom of indigenous peoples, some researchers have pointed out examples of tribal people who did overexploit local resources (e.g., Diamond 1993). For example, researchers are finding in the neotropics large areas of forest with few animals (Redford 1992).

Others point out the issue of waves of species extinctions accompanying migrations of early humans to the Americas and to major and minor islands around the world.

Martin (1973) proposed the hypothesis that Ice Age humans, at that time already proficient hunters, were responsible for the extinction of much of the megafauna (mostly large mammals) in the Americas. Their extinction had previously been explained in terms of Pleistocene glaciation and the shift of climate belts. Martin's provocatively entitled story, the "Discovery of America," begins with the end of the last Ice Age when big game hunters from Siberia crossed over to North America. Finding an unpopulated continent full of big game, the invaders expanded southward. Their exploding populations provided a moving front of death and destruction for the inexperienced prey that they encountered—mammoths, horses, camels, and ground sloths. According to Martin, the coexistence of hunters and megafauna probably lasted no more than ten years in any one area before extinction occurred. This did not give animals time to learn defensive behavior, nor for other adaptations to develop.

Martin's overkill hypothesis provides, certainly no proof, but a plausible model for the extinction of the megafauna. It addresses some of the paradoxes that had puzzled paleontologists for a long time: the almost total absence of kill sites, and sudden (as opposed to gradual) extinctions. For example, the timing of ground sloth extinctions at specific areas coincides almost exactly with the arrival of Stone Age hunters. Even though confounding factors such as climate change indicate that the original model may be simplistic, there is general agreement about the contribution of early Americans to the extermination of many large species (Martin and Klein 1984).

More certain is the role of invaders in bringing about the extinction of many species that once occupied islands such as Madagascar, New Zealand, and Hawaii. Perhaps the clearest cases come from New Zealand and the extermination of flightless Moas and many other species of large birds by the ancestors of the Maori. Coinciding with prehistoric human settlement, at least forty-four endemic species of land birds became extinct in the past 1,000 years (Steadman 1995). The larger picture in the Pacific indicates a major crisis of extinctions. About 3,500 years before the present, humans arrived in Western Polynesia and Micronesia, reaching virtually all of Oceania by 1,000 years before the present. Detailed island-by-island archeological studies by Steadman (1995) and others have shown that most species of land birds and populations of seabirds on those islands were exterminated by human activities, not only by hunting but also as a result of habitat change and predation by nonnative mammals. The loss of bird biodiversity in the tropical Pacific, largely attributable to pre-European invaders, may exceed 2,000 species and represent a 20 percent reduction worldwide in the number of bird species.

To recap, the overkill hypothesis may be elaborated to argue that the development of hunting in Africa led to technologically skilled hunters capable of killing at a distance, unlike other predators. The long coexistence of humans and African wildlife allowed the animals to coevolve with the human predator, thus limiting extinctions. However, the expansion of these hunters out of Africa brought them into contact with naive animals, those unaccustomed to the human hunter. The hunters had their largest impact on large-sized animals, not only because they targeted them, but also because large animals tend to have relatively few young and low rates of population renewal. If extinctions had been explainable on the basis of Pleistocene climate change alone, both large and small species would have been affected—which is not the case (Owen-Smith 1987).

In terms of the geography of extinctions, the most noticeable impacts of invaders occurred on islands. Species diversity is often lower on islands than the mainland, and the impacts of newly arrived predators are further magnified because there is no place to escape and the native species have evolved in the absence of native predators. Many island animals are relatively easy to kill, and such tameness can also be found today on remote islands and in areas in which there has been no hunting. As well, extinctions on islands are easier to document, especially if they were relatively recent (Steadman 1995). In the case of very large "islands" such as Australia, the evidence is much less clear. There is some evidence that early hunters are associated with the extinction of some large marsupials and birds. But there is also evidence that people may have been present in Australia for thousands of years before the major wave of extinctions, which argues against the simple version of the overkill hypothesis (Bahn 1996).

Just what do these findings signify for traditional ecological knowledge and human ecology in general? They destroy the myth of the Exotic Other, imbued with environmental wisdom, but they do not necessarily support the Intruding Wastrel myth either.

A number of human ecologists, notably Dasmann (1988) have pointed out that a distinction must be made between invaders and natives. When humans invade a new and unfamiliar ecosystem, their impact on the environment may be substantial initially. This initial relationship may change as the people develop a knowledge base, learn from their mistakes, and come to terms with the limits of their new environment. Long-settled natives tend to coevolve with their environment, and they often achieve a level of symbiosis with their environment (Dasmann 1988; Callicott 1994). This is not likely to happen over short periods. A knowledge base takes a long time to develop, and practices based on such knowledge even longer. Practices will be grounded in institutions, as in land and marine tenure systems.

The transition from invader to native is not easy to study and document. Most of the evidence is indirect. For example, the ancestors of the Maori may have exterminated the Moa and other large land birds, but the contemporary Maori (and many other Pacific island peoples) have well-developed systems of ecological knowledge, practice, and indigenous environmental ethics (Roberts et al. 1995), indicating that the Maori evidently learned from the experience. Similarly, the ancestors of American Indians may have contributed to the extinction of the American megafauna, but their descendants have some of the most sophisticated systems of ecological ethics (Callicott 1982, 1994); we do not need to resort to Chief Seattle's speech to make that point.

The relationship of the eastern James Bay Cree to their animals such as beaver (Feit 1986), goose (Berkes 1982; Scott 1986), moose (Feit 1987), black bears (see chapter 5; Tanner 1979), and caribou (see chapter 6) all indicate a relationship involving careful resource stewardship and respect. In contrast to the rapid pace and large magnitude of megafaunal overkill in Martin's (1973) hypothesis, there is no record of even a single species of large mammal extinction in the eastern James Bay since the glaciers covering the area retreated several thousand years ago. To make sense of this contradiction in evidence, we need a theory to explain the transition from invader to native.

INDIGENOUS PEOPLES AS CONSERVATIONISTS?

Much of the debate on traditional peoples can be reduced to one question: are they natural conservationists or not? The myth of the Exotic Other would hold that they are; the myth of the Intruding Wastrel, that they are not. The myth of the Noble Savage/Fallen Angel acknowledges that either case is possible but does not allow for a third choice or nuanced solutions. The question itself is part of the problem: One should instead ask, what kind of conservation?

In the Western tradition, there are two fundamentally different kinds of conservation: "wise use" conservation, and preservation (Worster 1977; Norton 1991; Evernden 1993). Modern conservation combines elements of both. It differs from wise use conservation in its rejection of utilitarianism and instrumental values, or nature-as-commodity. It differs from preservationism in its rejection (as unrealistic) of a pure hands-off approach to nature, in the form of extensive wilderness areas unoccupied by humans. Modern conservation seeks to sustain species and ecosystems and has come to focus on biodiversity as an overarching goal. How biodiversity conservation interacts with traditional conservation is one of the major issues of the traditional ecological knowledge field, as the exchange between Redford & Stearman and Alcorn, discussed below, shows.

Although biodiversity as a concept has its roots in the field of conservation biology, many people other than biologists have claimed standing, especially the indigenous people inhabiting the rain forests of the Amazon basin (Redford and Stearman 1993; Redford and Mansour 1996). The message from these indigenous peoples and their supporters has been that "tribal land rights and sovereignty must be supported in order to save both indigenous peoples *and the world's remaining natural areas*" (as quoted by Redford and Stearman 1993, 250). But are the agendas of the indigenous peoples consistent with the interests of biodiversity conservation?

The authors argue that well-meaning but perhaps overzealous attempts to portray all indigenous peoples as natural conservationists places an unrealistic expectation on native groups to preserve land ceded to them in the same state as they received it. This is happening at a time when many indigenous groups are linked to the market economy and may be compelled to engage in activities that differ in type and intensity from traditional patterns of resource use.

In the indigenous view, according to the authors, preserving biodiversity apparently means preventing large-scale destruction (hydroelectric development, mines, large ranches, and so on) and conserving certain "acceptable" levels of biodiversity. Such a view of biodiversity does not preclude practices of shifting cultivation for the market, small-scale cattle ranching, selective logging for commerce, and subsistence and even commercial hunting. Some of these activities may conserve elements of biodiversity, but not the full range of biodiversity.

For example, the activities of rubber tappers in the extractive reserves of Brazil have been shown to alter forest biodiversity. "If the full range of genetic, species, and ecosystem diversity is to be maintained *in its natural abundance* on a given piece of land, then virtually any significant activity by humans must not be allowed. ... Even low levels of indigenous activity alter biodiversity" (Redford and Stearman 1993, 252). Hence, if an area is expected to meet biodiversity conservation as well as indigenous needs, there are necessarily trade-offs that must be addressed explicitly (Redford and Stearman 1993).

In the view of Alcorn (1993), the indigenous notion of biodiversity conservation as provided by Redford and Stearman ("preventing large-scale destruction") is inadequate and misleading. There are several other elements of indigenous conservation. Many groups demonstrate a concern for maintaining ecological processes and the species that mediate those processes. In many indigenous communities, there are well-respected local experts interested in rare plants. In Asia and Africa, there are traditions of maintaining sacred forest areas (Gadgil and Vartak 1976; Castro 1990; Dei 1993). Many indigenous groups have community-enforced rules for resource use. Indigenous peoples' goals may not match the narrower conservation goals as indicated by Redford and Stearman, but "they more closely match the broader goals espoused by many conservationists who recognize that most of the world's biodiversity is found, and will continue to be found, in landscapes occupied by people" (Alcorn 1993, 425).

Partnership of conservationists and indigenous peoples, Alcorn continues, offers the best option for achieving conservation. One barrier to such partnerships is the attitude that conservationists are in a position of authority to "cede" rights. "When Redford and Stearman write about indigenous people 'claiming standing' to enter conservation discussions, their statement implicitly acknowledges the problem [that] 'conservationists' are acting as gatekeepers to a discussion table that does not have a place set for those whose homeland's future hangs in the balance" (Alcorn 1993, 426).

The debate between Redford & Stearman and Alcorn is covered here in some detail because it highlights not only the political dimension of the issue (more on this in chapter 10) but also the larger question of the difference between Western versus indigenous notions of conservation. Bridging the gap between the two positions in the debate depends on the feasibility of having indigenous peoples as *participants* and co-managers in conservation, instead of either Noble Savages or Fallen Angels. This, in turn, depends on the search for a universal, cross-cultural concept of conservation, if such a thing is possible.

Forcing indigenous conservation into the mold of Western conservation is not likely to work. Dwyer (1994, 91) states the problem succinctly: "The resource management systems of indigenous people often have outcomes that are analogous to those desired by Western conservationists. They differ, however, in context, motive and conceptual underpinnings. To represent indigenous management systems as being well suited to the needs of modern conservation, or as founded in the same ethic, is both facile and wrong." That they are not founded on the same ethic is clear, for example, from chapter 5 on the Cree Indians. The Cree believe that the use of a resource is necessary for its continued productivity. Use is, in fact, an obligation. Many other examples can be given. The Maori environmental ethic, for instance, is oriented to conservation for human use. Traditional prohibitions are intended to ensure resource productivity, not to safeguard some notion of so-called intrinsic value—simply because there is no human:nature or self:other duality in the Maori worldview (Roberts et al. 1995).

A practical consequence of this is that the Maori conservation ethic of sustainable utilization conflicts with New Zealand's 1987 Conservation Act, which stipulates "preservation" and "setting aside of land" to meet conservation objectives (Roberts et al. 1995). The issue, according to the authors, is not merely the political control of land, but (from the Maori point of view) the unacceptable notion of conservation driven by the Western concept of a human:nature dichotomy that "only serves to further alienate all humans, but particularly Maori, from their land, and thus from their *kaitiaki* [guardianship, stewardship] responsibilities" (Roberts et al. 1995, 15).

"WILDERNESS" AND A UNIVERSAL CONCEPT
OF CONSERVATION

To appreciate the arguments of Alcorn, Dwyer, and Roberts and her colleagues, it is useful to examine the notion of *wilderness*, which is central to the preservationist school of the two streams of Western thought that make up modern conservation. The preservationist belief holds that there is an inverse relationship between human presence and the well-being of the natural environment. Wilderness areas, enhanced and maintained in the absence of people, are seen as pristine environments similar to those that existed before human interference. According to the 1964 U.S. Wilderness Act, wilderness is a place "where man himself is a visitor who does not remain" (Gómez-Pompa and Kaus 1992a). To examine the idea of wilderness as the basis of a universal concept of conservation, there are two considerations: (a) Does wilderness as a notion stand up to a cross-cultural critique? (b) Is wilderness ecologically real?

For many indigenous peoples and for much of the rest of the non-Western world, including the great Asian religions, the distinction between nature and culture is meaningless. Strict dichotomies, such as nature:culture or mind:nature, are alien to many non-Western traditions. For example, in the symbol for the yin-yang principle in Chinese philosophy, it is considered that there is some yin within the yang and vice versa (Hjort af Ornas 1992). As noted above (in chapter 2), the concept of an external environment or nature separate from human society is the basis of the Cartesian dichotomy of mind versus matter, and hence humans versus environment (Bateson 1972, 337).

"Wilderness" is the thought product of a people who see themselves as separate from environment, a value appropriate for a technological-industrial society no longer in direct contact with nature, a value not shared by native cultures (Klein 1994). For indigenous peoples from the Arctic to the tropics, there is no wilderness but home. Hence, a kind of conservation that is based on preserving wilderness and maintaining the Cartesian dualism between mind and matter, which itself is at the roots of our environmental problem (e.g., Bateson 1972, 1979), cannot provide a universal concept of conservation.

Wilderness as an ecological notion is also questionable. No doubt there are areas that satisfy the usual definitions of wilderness as places free of human presence (Antarctica comes to mind). Many other areas, however, previously considered wilderness turn out to be anthropogenic landscapes on closer examination. Many apparently pristine areas did in fact support large numbers of people in the past, whose activities influenced what remains today. For example, much of the "wilderness" found by early Europeans in North America, "what Longfellow erroneously referred to as the 'forest primeval,' was in most parts of the continent and in varying degrees a human artifact" (Lewis 1993b, 395).

> Scientific findings indicate that virtually every part of the globe, from the boreal forests to the humid tropics, has been inhabited, modified, or managed throughout our human past. . . . The concept of wilderness as the untouched or untamed land is mostly an urban perception, the view of people who are far removed from the natural environment they depend on for raw resource. The inhabitants of rural areas have different views of the areas that urbanites designate as wilderness, and they base their land-use and resource management practices on these alternative visions. Indigenous groups in the tropics, for example, do not consider the tropical forest environment to be wild; it is their home (Gómez-Pompa and Kaus 1992a, 273).

These considerations indicate that wilderness and wilderness preservation cannot be the basis of a universal, cross-cultural concept of conservation. More promising is the notion of *sustainability*, as in the broad-based definition of conservation in *Caring for the Earth*: "the management of human use of organisms or ecosystems to ensure such use is sustainable. Besides sustainable use, conservation includes protection, maintenance, rehabilitation, restoration, and enhancement of populations and ecosystems" (IUCN/UNEP/WWF 1991). This definition has been criticized by preservationists as being too use-oriented, but it represents a trend in conservation thinking that is trying to put humans back into the landscape (McNeely 1994, 1996). Much effort and thought have been expended to reconcile conservation and local needs. According to some, conservation is achievable by making it an attractive economic choice for people:

> The debate between "sustainable use" of wildlife and "pure preservation" hinges on a very simple economic problem. If peasant farmers in Latin America, Asia and Africa cannot make wildlife pay, then they will destroy the wildlife, plant their crops and bring in their domestic animals. The challenge for planners who care about the earth's wilds is to make wildlife conservation a sensible economic choice for the poor farmers concerned. Sometimes—not always—that will mean allowing those farmers to kill some of the animals concerned and trade in wildlife products (Harland 1993).

A major paradigm change among many Western conservationists is that some kinds of human use are acceptable as part of conservation planning. This has been a debate of over one hundred years in the United States, featuring preservationists versus wise-use conservationists. In the context of indigenous peoples, the debate has a cross-cultural dimension as well. Indigenous practices of conservation differ from Western conservation in context and motive, and it may never be possible (or desirable) to integrate the two but rather to find common ground in sustainability. Perhaps the most useful way to think about indigenous conservation is that it is complementary to Western conservation, not a replacement for it. Indigenous conservation is legitimate in its own right, just as indigenous knowledge is legitimate in its own right. It does not have to be recast in Western idiom or legitimized through Western science.

Redford and Stearman (1993) are correct in their analysis that there are trade-offs that must be addressed explicitly, if an area is expected to meet both biodiversity conservation and indigenous needs. Many indigenous practices are conservative of biodiversity (Berkes et al. 1995; also see chapter 4). In many cases, indigenous peoples' capacity to maintain and to adapt their systems can be enhanced through the defense of their property rights and resource tenure systems, which provide incentives to conserve (see chapter 8). However, hunters and fishers behave in the short term as "optimal foragers" maximizing their catch per unit of effort (see chapter 7; Alvard 1993). No one has ever documented a so-called traditional preservation ethic, except perhaps with sacred sites. Indigenous peoples do not have a concern necessarily with the preservation of *all* the species in their environment (and neither do most nonindigenous peoples).

The acceptance of the validity of indigenous conservation would in itself be a major paradigm change in the conservation field. In the dominant positivist paradigm of Western science, conservation professionals assume that they know best. This style of conservation has neglected the needs and aspirations of local people, their knowledge and management systems, their institutions, and their worldviews. The old ideology of conservation has attempted to exclude people from nature. The new trend in conservation is to treat people as part of the landscape to be conserved, enable local participation in decision making, and encourage pluralistic ways of thinking about the world (Pimbert and Pretty 1995).

ADAPTING TRADITIONAL SYSTEMS TO
THE MODERN CONTEXT

Can traditional systems be adapted to the contemporary context? How do traditional practices evolve to respond to modern pressures? An examination of change and adaptation in a variety of cases provides an understanding of the limits and capabilities of traditional management systems. Since the area of common interest between Western and indigenous conservation is sustainability, one way of assessing the complementarity of the two systems is to look for examples in which the combination enhances or at least maintains the potential for sustainability, as in caribou management in chapter 6.

Examples are many and span the larger field of indigenous knowledge from agriculture (Warren et al. 1995), to soil and water conservation (Reij et al. 1996), environmental assessment (Emery 1997), and development (Richards 1985). They include examples of technological innovation, such as the use of Nishga'a (also spelled Nishga) fish wheels to improve salmon management in the Pacific Northwest. In an effort to improve salmon returns on the Nass River, the local aboriginal management authority, the Nishga'a Fisheries Board, combines traditional and modern biological approaches. Observing that electronic fish sensors can be inaccurate, the Nishga'a have devised a fish-counting system that combines the ancient fish wheel technology with modern statistical methods and data analysis. Salmon are sampled at an upriver fish wheel station at which the proportion of tagged fish is used to calculate returns. Reportedly, this procedure provides more accurate and reliable data than those collected by electronic tracking systems (Corsiglia and Snively 1997).

Many of the examples of complementarity come from applied areas of conservation. Box 9.2 contains an example of the use of local knowledge of the indigenous Dusun people to build a botanical inventory in a Malaysian national park. Note that the researcher himself is Dusun, and this joint project of UNESCO, the World Wildlife Fund, and Kew Botanical Gardens starts with the useful plants, including locally important cane species. The result is a two-way interaction; local people share their knowledge and the results help community economic development.

A different kind of two-way interaction is apparent in the Zulu herbalist case (see box 9.3). The solution was precipitated by a resource crisis, as the demand for medicinal plants exceeded the supply. At the time the nursery was established, some species such as the *mathithibala* (*Haworthia* spp.), for warding off evil spirits and purifying the blood, had already disappeared, and conservationists wanted to secure medicinal plants for the future. If the managers had tried to stop overexploitation, they would simply have driven the trade underground. Instead, they involved a local university, obtained funding from a donor

---

BOX 9.2
ANCESTRAL ECOLOGY FOR CONSERVATION

As Martin tells the story, Dius Tadong knows a great deal about the tropical forest in his country, Malaysia. After working for several years all over his native island, Borneo, for the Sabah State Forest Authority, he decided to return to his home village, part of the Dusun community. The Dusun are an indigenous group who still depend to a large extent on what nature provides. They live on the edge of the Kinabalu National Park, a large protected area of 753 square kilometers. Tadong works with the villagers to collect and list plants. The project aims at providing better knowledge and use of plant species in protected regions by providing training and assistance.

"In Kinabalu Park," Martin writes, "the first stage consists of drawing up an inventory on the rich flora, believed to include about 4,000 species, starting with plants that are useful to humanity. Studies of medicinal, edible and decorative plants are planned. Dius Tadong continues to cultivate the land, just as other five plant collectors still work in their villages. They concentrate on palm trees, including those used to make cane, which are of crucial importance to the local population. The trees are used as food and in traditional medicine, as roofing material, to make rope, and in arts and crafts....

"Similar projects are underway elsewhere—in Bolivia, Cameroon, Mexico, Uganda and the Caribbean for instance—in the hope of building ecological awareness based on ancestral knowledge. These projects may turn out to be more rewarding than previous efforts because they are being conducted in cooperation with the local people who know the forest intimately."

Source: Martin 1993, 5

BOX 9.3
ZULU HERBALISTS OF SOUTH AFRICA AS ESSENTIAL INGREDIENTS
IN PLANT CONSERVATION

"Squeezed between gritty Umlazi (a black township) and the neighboring Indian township of Chatsworth, a solitary 220-hectare green lung breathes a future into local conservation and the medicinal plant trade. The Durban Parks Department's Silverglen Nature Reserve is home to Umlaas Nursery, South Africa's first and largest medicinal plant nursery, which grows thousands of specimens of 350 plant species commonly used for traditional medicine....

"Plant growing is a matter of science: seeds, bulbs, and cuttings provide sprouts, and high-tech tissue culture generation is done in a Durban Parks Department laboratory. But the nursery's success depends on the arcane knowledge of Zulu herbalists such as Mkhuluwe Cele—heirs to a mystic oral tradition—who identified the important plants disappearing from the wild and explained their uses.

" 'I was caught a number of times by the Natal Parks Board for picking protected plants,' Cele admits with a smile. 'When I saw the plants in Silverglen I felt jealous. After all, I thought, I also had soil and could plant.' Today Cele grows thousands of plants in his own nursery which he started with the help of a grateful Silverglen team. One of Cele's 11 children is learning nursery management and ethnobotany at Silverglen."

Source: Mbanefo 1992, 11, 12

agency, and started growing medicinal plants, including the pepperbark tree of northern Zululand, now extremely rare in the wild. Part of the success of the nursery project is in its involvement of traditional herbalists. They contribute their knowledge to the project and, in turn, receive the means of growing their own plants. Their knowledge is returned to the community as well; for example, the nursery instructs gatherers to put mud on a tree's wound when they peel bark, a traditional Zulu practice.

The Chagga of Tanzania are a mixture of ethnic groups who settled in the area of the great Kilimanjaro. Different groups contributed their crop species, and over time, a rich mixture of domestic plants inspired a form of land use known as *vihamba*, multistory tree gardens characterized by great biodiversity, giving the visitors the impression of being in the Garden of Eden (Kuchli 1996). The Chagga are experts in combining many types of plants requiring different amounts of light and having roots of varying depths. *Vihamba* incorporates patches of the original forest where useful species remain standing; other parts of the natural forest are replaced by cultivated species. By the turn of the century, the Chagga were successfully growing coffee as a cash crop, incorporating the shade-tolerant coffee bush into their *vihambas*. Contemporary Chagga farmers cultivate up to sixty different species of trees on an area the size of a football field.

The Chagga case is not an isolated example. Beaucage et al. (1997) provide a remarkably similar case of a biologically diverse and productive coffee agro-forestry system from the Nahua of the Lower Sierra Norte, Mexico. Chapter 4 in the present volume makes the argument that many traditional systems, such as shifting cultivation, *kebun-talun*, and *pekarangan*, maintain tropical ecosystem resilience and sustain productive landscapes through a variety of uses. Some of the uses are subtle. For example, many groups of indigenous people recognize species used as famine and survival foods. Turner and Davis (1993) identified over one hundred species of plants used by the tribes of the Pacific Northwest that are not normally eaten but saved as special foods, alternative foods, emergency foods, hunger suppressants, and thirst quenchers.

Such redundancy of food species parallels the emerging view of biodiversity as consisting of functionally redundant species that help maintain ecosystem resilience in fluctuating environments (Holling et al. 1995). There is little doubt that all of these traditional systems help maintain high degrees of biodiversity. But since "even low levels of activity alter biodiversity" (Redford and Stearman 1993, 252), they obviously do not live up to the ideals of preservationists!

Are other kinds of sustainable transformations of natural systems possible? In some instances it is possible to convert a tropical forest ecosystem into a completely different system. A case in point is the transition from traditional shifting cultivation to irrigated rice production, as studied in Palawan, the Philippines, by Conelly (1992). During the 1950s and the 1960s, settlers in the area produced their rice, the local staple, in long-fallow swidden fields cleared from the forest. By 1970, land was becoming scarce due to population pressure, and by 1980 typical fallow periods had declined from more than ten years to only two to four years, together with declining yields. A widely held theory of agricultural change holds that the adoption of intensive cultivation techniques allows the farmer to support a larger population by increasing the yield per unit area. This growth in carrying capacity, however, will be achieved at the cost of lower labor efficiency (Boserup 1965). Intensive cultivation, as in wet rice agriculture, requires more work than does shifting cultivation; thus, Conelly had to address the question of why the local people did not resist the change.

What Conelly found was that the long-term consequence of the change probably did entail lower labor efficiency (i.e., more work for the farmer) as well as increased carrying capacity. But in the short term, standards of living improved. The reason for this was that farmers did not make the transition directly from long-fallow shifting cultivation to wet rice culture. Rather, they were forced to make the transition from a short-fallow swidden *that had already become unproductive*, to a more intensive form of cultivation that at least fed the population (Conelly 1992). The example of the Palawan irrigated rice system is fundamentally different from the shifting cultivation, *kebun-talun*, *pekarangan*, and *vihamba* examples. It shows that it is possible to convert a tropical forest into a productive rice monoculture. In this case, the forest ecosystem no longer exists; it has been replaced by a different ecosystem. (As well, it should be added that such conversions are obviously not going to work everywhere.)

TOWARD AN EVOLUTIONARY THEORY OF TRADITIONAL KNOWLEDGE

It is important to recognize indigenous resource management systems not as mere traditions but as adaptive responses that have evolved over time. These adaptations may involve the evolution of similar systems in geographically diverse areas (what evolutionary biologists call *convergent evolution*), as in the case of shifting agriculture found in virtually all tropical areas of the world (Brookfield and Padoch 1994). They may involve the elaboration of one basic model of management into a diversity of variations (what evolutionary biologists call *adaptive radiation*), as one finds, for example, in the reef and lagoon tenure systems of Oceania (Johannes 1978). They may involve the major transformation of the landscape from one productive system to another, as in the Palawan irrigated rice example (Conelly 1992). They may involve the synthesis of several traditions, and current commercial pressures, into a new, sustainable, and beautiful system, as in the *vihambas* of Kilimanjaro (Kuchli 1996). The examples show that adaptive responses can be recreated to solve emerging resource management problems. The Caribbean cases in chapter 8 illustrate how societies are constantly self-organizing in various ways to respond to resource management needs.

Two features of these adaptations stand out. The first, alluded to above, is the extraordinary similarity of basic designs shared by different cultures in comparable ecosystems worldwide, coupled with a remarkable diversity in practice even in adjacent areas. For example, Kuchli (1996) comments that the *vihambas* are complex agroforestry systems "without parallel." In fact, that is not true. Indonesian home gardens (*pekarangan*) as described in chapter 4 share many of the characteristics of the *vihamba*. Neither is the *vihamba* as unique as a coffee agroforesty system. Locally developed, diverse, tropical agroforestry systems that include coffee as a cash crop are found, among other places, in Nigeria (Warren and Pinkston 1998), Kenya, New Guinea (Brookfield and Padoch 1994), and Mexico (Beaucage et al. 1997).

The second feature of these adaptations is that they tend not to proceed in smooth and even steps but rather in fits and starts. The Palawan case is unusual in that it catches the process of transformation of agricultural systems. It shows that change proceeds in discontinuous steps, from long-fallow swidden to short-fallow and then to wet rice culture. The same kind of rapid transformation is also apparent in the way Chisasibi Cree hunters readjusted their caribou hunts in the 1980s (see chapter 6). The relevant theory in evolutionary biology is *punctuated equilibrium*, which states that evolution does not occur gradually (as Darwin thought) but rather through long periods of relative stability punctuated by periods of rapid change. The renewal of ecosystems and resource management institutions also seems to proceed that way (Gunderson et al. 1995).

The mechanism of the transition from invader to native is likely to proceed in a similar fashion as well. The fortuitous observation of the modification of caribou hunting practice based on experience and oral history, as summarized in chapter 6, provides insights in this regard. Social learning and cultural evolution based on ecological knowledge, following an ecological crisis, seem to be the major ingredients of developing a symbiotic relationship between a group of people and their resources.

Another line of evidence is provided by archaeology. McGovern et al. (1988) studied Viking-age colonization of North Atlantic offshore islands by Scandinavian settlers. They found that medieval farming technology exported by the settlers resulted in soil erosion through pasture mismanagement and forest depletion. The colonists eventually took some measures to correct their mistakes. Many environmental feedback messages, however, were difficult to interpret due to the masking effect of climate change, and the impacts of poor management practices were often difficult to reverse. For example, it was not easy to judge pasture overgrazing until after it had occurred. In this case, learning did not occur rapidly enough (in the period, eighth to eleventh century) for adaptation and redesign to proceed, presumably because the message of resource crisis was not clearly received by the population.

These findings, as well as the caribou case and many others (Gunderson et al. 1995), suggest that the experience of a resource crisis is not only a major, but a *necessary* ingredient of social learning. As part of this, signals from the environment have to be received and properly interpreted by the people in question if they are to be successful in adapting to the new circumstances. The development of an appropriate conservation ethic, as part of the belief system or the worldview guiding practice, may also proceed via periods of rapid change punctuating long periods of relative stability. There is insufficient evidence to develop principles regarding the relationship between the ethics and practice of resource management. We may hypothesize, however, that belief or ethics is the *slower variable* in a knowledge-practice-belief complex. One evidence for this is that the Cree Indian trappers of James Bay apparently suspended their conservation *ethics* and changed their *practice* between 1920 and 1930, contributing to the depletion of beaver. After their resource tenure was recognized by law, proper practice was restored after about 1950, based on the same ethic as had existed previously (Feit 1986; Berkes et al. 1989).

A conservation ethic may never develop, if the group in question fails to experience a crisis or is unable to interpret it. The Torres Strait islanders constitute a case in point (Johannes and Lewis 1993). This group lives in a particularly productive area in the path of migratory species and is probably unable to receive feedbacks of resource depletion as do most Pacific island peoples, such as those in Palau (Robert Johannes, pers. comm.). In some cases, it is unclear why a conservation ethic fails to develop. A disturbing case is Easter Island, one of the more remote and larger islands of the Pacific, colonized by the ancestors of the Polynesians about 1,500 years before the present. Environmental degradation was gradual but severe, and included the loss of more of the terrestrial biota than in any other island of its size in Oceania. Deforestation of the island was virtually complete by about 550 before present (Steadman 1995). Unlike the Easter Islanders, many societies seem to be able to learn from experience and develop appropriate ethics and practices to solve their environmental problems, a significant lesson for our industrial society as well.

Chapter Ten

Toward a Unity of Mind and Nature

There are only a few places in the world, often in isolated areas, where traditional systems of resource management are still in force. The globalization of Western culture has meant, among other things, the globalization of Western resource management. The remaining pockets of traditional systems probably cannot escape history, but they can inspire new approaches to environmental stewardship and suggest more participatory and locally grounded alternatives to top-down, centralized resource management.

During the past century, a diversity of resource management systems all over the world has been replaced by a monolithic Western resource management science, while many traditional approaches have disappeared. Until only a few years ago, the spread of modern, rational, scientific resource management was considered a part of "natural progress." The problem is that Western scientific resource management, despite all of its power, seems unable to halt the depletion of resources and the degradation of the environment. Part of the reason for this paradox may be that Western resource management, and reductionist science in general, developed in the service of a utilitarian, exploitive, dominion-over-nature worldview of colonists and industrial developers (Worster 1977; Gadgil and Berkes 1991). Utilitarian sciences were best geared for the efficient use of resources as if they were limitless, consistent with the laissez-faire doctrine still alive in today's neoclassical economic theory (e.g., Daly and Cobb 1989). But utilitarianism is ill-suited for sustainability, which requires a new philosophy that recognizes ecological limits and strives to satisfy social as well as economic needs.

Perhaps the most fundamental lesson of traditional ecological knowledge is that worldviews and beliefs do matter. Almost all traditional ecological knowledge systems may be characterized as a complex of knowledge, practice, *and belief*. Almost universally, one encounters an ethic of nondominant, respectful human-nature relationship, a sacred ecology, as part of the belief component of traditional ecological knowledge. This is true not only for the Cree Indians (see chapter 5) or for Australian aborigines (see box 2.2), but for many other groups as well. For example, the Fijian expressions of spiritual affinity with land, *ne qau vanua* ("the land which supports me and to which I belong") and *na vanua na tamatu* ("the people are the land") (Ravuvu 1987), could have just as easily come from traditional peoples of the Americas, Africa, Australia, or New Guinea (Ballard 1997). The notion of unity of people and land is not absent in

Western societies, either. For example, witness the Gaelic greeting, "where do you belong to?" signifying specific connections to land (Mackenzie 1998).

In general, the idea of identification with nature goes back to the dominant pantheistic (many gods) traditions before the rise of monotheistic (single god) religions. These beliefs existed in pre-Christian Europe and survived for a time in the Christian mysticism of St. Francis (White 1967). They may be found in the Sufi mysticism of Islam, and in Hindu, Buddhist, and Taoist traditions (Callicott 1994). Pantheistic religions have all but disappeared, but the worldview associated with them has survived longer, as in the case of the James Bay Cree. The decline of the worldview that identifies with nature seems to be related to the decline of pantheism, as well as to the rise of the modern industrial state with its ethos of control of nature and a utilitarian, depersonalized science.

The science of ecology occupies a unique position. Although much of ecology continues as a conventional reductionistic science, the more holistic approaches in ecology provide a new vision of the earth as an ecosystem of interconnected relationships in which humans are part of the web of life. However, Roszak's (1972, 404) question still remains open: "which will ecology be, the last of the old sciences or the first of the new?" This is not an easy question for ecologists. Many would not be comfortable, for example, with the contention that ecology is "discovering a new version of the 'enchanted world' that was part of the natural mind for most of human history" (Berry 1988). Although Leopold (1949) explained his land ethic in ecological terms, an ethic of ecology has not caught on among ecologists, probably for the simple reason that Western science, by definition, does not include an ethical or belief component. Traditional ecological knowledge does, however, and it is not surprising that many of the thinkers of alternative visions (such as Leopold) incorporate a component of value, wisdom, ethics, or belief in environmental stewardship.

This chapter opens with a consideration of the political ecology of traditional knowledge, and its role in the empowerment of indigenous peoples and other marginalized groups dependent on local resources. The main argument is that the use of indigenous knowledge is *political* because it threatens to change power relations between indigenous groups and the dominant society. The chapter then turns to a consideration of traditional knowledge as a challenge to the positivist-reductionist paradigm in Western science, on the basis of the critique of conventional resource management and the development of alternative resource management approaches in Western science, such as Adaptive Management. The chapter then addresses the question of integrating traditional ecological knowledge with Western science and concludes that the two kinds of knowledge may be best pursued in parallel. Contact points may be provided by certain kinds of holistic western science consistent with the stewardship of nature, rather than its domination and control. The chapter ends with a recap of some of the main lessons of traditional ecological knowledge, its compelling argument for conceptual pluralism, its inspiration of more participatory, community-based alternatives to top-down resource management, and its potential to inject a measure of ethics into the science of ecology and resource management, thereby restoring the "unity of mind and nature" (Bateson 1979).

POLITICAL ECOLOGY OF INDIGENOUS KNOWLEDGE

Mac Chapin (pers. comm.) observes that, "In all the discussions of 'indigenous knowledge' there is seldom talk of the wider social, political context. It is not just systems of knowledge that come into play, but social systems that have different ways of going about things: different beliefs and values, different priorities, different decision-making systems." Political ecology is a historical outgrowth of the central questions asked by the social sciences about the relations between human society, in its political and cultural complexity, and human-dominated nature (Greenberg and Park 1994). As a field, it differs from political economy, which has tended to reduce everything to social constructions, disregarding ecological relations. To a significant degree, both nature and society are socially constructed. "Political ecology expands ecological concerns to respond to the inclusion of cultural and political activity within an analysis of ecosystems that are significantly but not always entirely socially constructed" (Greenberg and Park 1994).

The application of political ecology to indigenous knowledge starts by focusing on the familiar political-economic divisions among the actors (interest groups or stakeholders), "divisions between international, national and local interests; between North and South; between science and politics; official and folk; and power relations at the local level deriving from differences of class, ethnicity and gender" (Blaikie and Jeanrenaud 1996, 1).

Following Blaikie (1985), Colchester (1994), Long and Long (1992), and Blaikie and Jeanrenaud (1996), the complexity of traditional knowledge issues may be interpreted and made more comprehensible by considering that:

1 There exist different actors who relate in different ways to the resource in question;

2 The actors define knowledge, ecological relations, and resources in different ways and at different levels or geographic scales;

3 They bring to bear on these definitions their culture and their experience; and

4 They will use different definitions in pursuit of their own "projects" or political agendas.

The controversial issue of intellectual property rights provides a useful example. Some industries and governments have pressed for the extension of intellectual property rights to biological products so they can be patented. Under debate is the issue of privatization (through patenting) of agricultural varieties, individual genes, and biochemical products from natural or bioengineered species (Posey and Dutfield 1996). But what about agricultural varieties developed by traditional management systems, or species that have long-established traditional uses?

Such a species is the neem tree (*Azadirachta indica*) which has been used for centuries by traditional doctors and farmers in India. Chemical properties of neem make it suitable for the extraction of a number of medicinal substances and natural pesticides. These properties have been known to Indians for many generations, and scientific research on neem has been carried out by Indian institutions, but these chemical properties have never been patented. In fact, under Indian law, medicinal or agricultural products cannot be patented. However, since 1985, a number of U.S. patents have been registered by U.S. and Japanese firms on neem-based biological products. This has created a bitter controversy, with the Indians charging that multinationals have no right "to expropriate the fruit of centuries of indigenous experimentation" (Shiva and Holla-Bhar 1993). One response in India has been the formation of an alliance of farmers and scientists to develop an alternative form of intellectual property. The *goan samoj*, a village-level collective, would hold "collective intellectual property rights" to assert that knowledge is a social product, subject to local common rights. These would give the community the right to benefit commercially from traditional knowledge (Shiva and Holla-Bhar 1993).

The neem case illustrates the divisions between international, national, and local interests, and between North and South. As well, the case shows that different actors relate in different ways to the resource, define knowledge in different ways and at different geographic scales, and use different definitions in pursuit of their own projects. Given that intellectual property rights laws are generally inappropriate for defending local rights (Posey and Dutfield 1996, 92), and that Western legal tools of copyrights and patents cannot readily be used for indigenous knowledge (Brush and Stabinsky 1996), it is not clear what the *goan samoj* can do to protect community interests against multinationals. However, even if the communal right to benefit commercially from traditional knowledge can be enforced, one might expect other kinds of equity dilemmas at the local level, for communities are not homogenous entities. There often is a multiplicity of interests and actors within a community who relate to resources in different ways (Agrawal 1997).

A second example is the controversy over the use of traditional knowledge in environmental assessment in the Northwest Territories (NWT), Canada. The NWT was the first jurisdiction in Canada to develop policies for the use of traditional knowledge. A report prepared after several years of study by a working group (Legat 1991) was adopted by the NWT government recognizing that "aboriginal traditional knowledge is a valid and essential source of information about the natural environment and its resources, the use of natural resources, and the relationship of people to the land and to each other." The policy was put into effect during an environmental assessment process in 1995 leading to the approval of a major mining project. The government's environmental assessment panel issued a directive to the proponent (BHP Diamonds Inc.) to give traditional knowledge equal consideration with science in assessing the impacts of the proposed mine (Stevenson 1996).

The objections subsequently raised by Howard and Widdowson (1996) to the directive and to its implications touched off a heated public policy debate in Canada about the nature and role of traditional knowledge ("TK"), a debate that attracted several rejoinders and even news media coverage. Howard and Widdowson (1996) argued that "TK, because of its spiritual component, is a threat to environmental assessment" because "rational understanding of the world is impeded by spiritualism." They talked about how "aboriginal groups obfuscated the Panel's attempts to understand" TK, and how "the aboriginal leadership then went on to argue that TK holders must be involved directly to protect the 'intellectual property rights' of First Nations." They concluded that traditional knowledge is "a cash cow for TK consultants and aboriginal leaders" and "has limited value and little to do with knowledge," and that "interest in TK is politically motivated." The point subsequently picked up by the media was "spiritualism," thus making traditional knowledge sound like a version of New Age thinking.

The BHP case illustrates the divisions between North (in this case, the aboriginal-dominated NWT government) and South (the dominant Euro-Canadian culture, which has only superficial sympathy for aboriginal concerns and values). As well, the case shows that different actors relate in different ways to the resource and define knowledge in different ways. In fact, by choosing carefully the definition used, one can manipulate ethnic prejudices. Howard and Widdowson (1996) used an NWT government definition of traditional knowledge ("knowledge and values ... from the land or *from spiritual teachings*," emphasis added by the authors), to make their point that spiritualism was the key issue. This helped portray traditional knowledge as vague and unworthy of serious consideration by the dominant culture, which of course values the "rational" (Berkes and Henley 1997).

The Howard and Widdowson argument is interesting in part because it questions the validity and applicability of traditional knowledge on the basis of its belief component. This assumes that there are other kinds of science that do not have a belief component or a cultural context, a point rejected by philosophers such as Feyerabend (1987). Howard and Widdowson's points bring to mind Holmes's (1996) observation in chapter 2 that Westerners are often unable to understand indigenous values or cosmologies, except as either "myth" or "data." The objection to *spiritualism* (a term emotionally more loaded than *belief* or *value*) is merely an excuse to denigrate traditional knowledge; the real issue is resource management power. This can be deduced from Howard and Widdowson's (1996) objection, not only to the use of traditional knowledge, but also to the devolution of environmental management responsibilities to native groups, as a "conflict of interest."

This debate is not an isolated example. A similar debate has raged in New Zealand for a number of years. Dickison (1994, 6) notes: "The idea of a separate indigenous science, practiced by Maori before European settlement and passed on to their descendants, is an appealing one." But, he asks, how does Maori knowledge measure up to the conventional definition of science? "The answer, it seems, is not very well," because "Maori knowledge acquisition was neither objective (relying as it did on religious faith), nor rational (it mixed supernatural with mundane explanations)."

However, if one uses instead the perspective of such thinkers as Levi-Strauss (1962) and Feyerabend (1987), the answer, it seems, is that Maori science is science—but *not* Western science. More to the point, Maori science, or any indigenous knowledge system, is not necessarily inconsistent with all of Western science. It is, however, definitely inconsistent with the positivist-reductionist tradition in Western science, and the assumption that the professional expert knows best. There is more to come on this point, after we further explore the use of indigenous knowledge for empowerment and note that the use of traditional knowledge is, after all, often very political.

INDIGENOUS KNOWLEDGE FOR EMPOWERMENT

It is often assumed that indigenous peoples have only two options: to return to an ancient and "primitive" way of life, or to abandon traditional beliefs and practices and become assimilated into the dominant society. Increasingly, indigenous groups have been expressing preference for a third option: to retain culturally significant elements of a traditional way of life, combining the old and the new in ways that maintain and enhance their identity while allowing their society and economy to evolve. Traditional knowledge has become a symbol for indigenous groups in many parts of the world to regain control over their own cultural information, and reclaiming this knowledge has become a major strategy for revitalization movements.

Indigenous peoples across North America, Latin America, Northern Europe, South Asia, and Southeast Asia are making similar claims: the right to control their lands and resources; the right to self-determination and self-government; and the right to represent themselves through their own political organizations (Colchester 1994). All of these claims have their basis in indigenous peoples' knowledge of and attachment to the land, their traditional knowledge and management systems, and their local institutions. The first four examples described here deal with the use of traditional knowledge for mapping aboriginal land claims. The next two deal with its use for environmental and social impact assessment, and the final example deals with its use for co-management of resources, that is, the sharing of power and responsibility between the government and local users, in this case, the Maori of New Zealand.

Inuit Land Use Maps for Self-Government

Aboriginal land use studies in the Canadian North have been undertaken since the 1970s mainly to document land claims (Duerden and Kuhn 1998). The pioneering study that provided inspiration and methodology for many of the subsequent ones was *The Inuit Land Use and Occupancy Project* (Freeman 1976). Southern researchers and northern knowledge holders collaborated to document Inuit (Eskimo) land use in the Canadian Arctic. They detailed how communities understand their environment and dealt with the cultural organization of land use and its social meaning. Composite maps, combining those for different resources and for different time periods, showed that the Inuit used almost all of the Arctic—a land that southerners had always considered "empty." The maps were regarded with disbelief in some circles until the overwhelming evidence of many other mapping studies showed that not only the Inuit but many indigenous groups still use their lands and resources extensively as part of a mixed-economic strategy for livelihoods. Riewe's (1992) *Nunavut Atlas* extended the work of Freeman and his colleagues and provided a comprehensive series of land use maps that were used in land selection by the Inuit as part of a comprehensive claims settlement, the Nunavut Agreement of 1993, leading to the creation of the self-governing Inuit territory of Nunavut in 1999 in the Canadian Eastern Arctic.

Defending the Land with Maps in Honduras

Indigenous peoples of Latin America have often lost their land because they could not "prove" they owned it. In 1992, native leaders and cultural activists in the northeast corner of Honduras decided to remedy the situation by making indigenous land ownership more visible. They put together a project by which the Garifuna, Miskito, Pesch, and Tawahka Sumu tribes of the Mosquitia region could create detailed, graphic records of their homelands (Denniston 1994; Chapin 1998). These maps gave the indigenous groups a chance for the first time to be heard by the government and other influential groups, such as international conservation organizations. By organizing a series of forums, indigenous groups sought to communicate with government agencies, national and international NGOs, and other native groups. The maps showed that the remaining areas of forest, savanna, and wetland closely coincided with Indian territories, debunking the myth that indigenous homelands were degraded. The political momentum created by the process raised regional awareness, empowering other indigenous groups to pursue legal protection for their homelands, with the result that "indigenous land rights are now taken seriously for the first time in Honduras by national politicians" (Denniston 1994).

Panama: Ethnocartography in the Darién

Until the 1960s, eastern Panama was a region of largely intact tropical rain forest inhabited by three indigenous groups, the Emberá, the Wounaan, and the Kuna. The construction of Bayano Dam and the extension of the Pan-American Highway opened up the region in the 1970s. In more recent years, the area has come under the siege of loggers, cattle ranchers, land speculators, and landless colonists from overcrowded areas (González et al. 1995). The Darién mapping project borrowed the techniques and approaches of the Honduras project and was largely carried out in 1994. It was designed as a tool to protect indigenous lands, to show conservationists that the areas of native use were also areas of good forest cover, and to document the damage caused by loggers, cattle ranchers, and landless peasants (González et al. 1995). The projects in Panama and Honduras not only provided an education for the local communities but also stimulated struggles for land rights in indigenous lands along the length of the Caribbean coast of Central America. In southern Belize, the Toledo Maya Cultural Council has been working to establish a Mayan homeland; in Nicaragua, the Miskito are establishing protected areas on the coast to conserve their resources; in Costa Rica, the Bribri and Cabecar peoples are establishing councils of elders to help manage La Amistad Biosphere Reserve near Talamanca (Denniston 1994).

Reconstructing Aboriginal Land Ownership in Australia

Early European settlers widely believed that Australian Aborigines did not have territories or boundaries and were "aimless wanderers." But as anthropological, geographic, and linguistic studies demonstrated, especially since the 1970s, Aboriginal groups held communal rights and responsibilities, usually through lineage groups, for distinct areas of land and resources, through the use of ecological and spiritual knowledge (Young 1992; Kalit and Young 1997). Recent land claims legislation, based primarily on the establishment of proof of traditional ownership, has made the issue of Aboriginal territories crucially important both politically and economically. Once land passes into Aboriginal control, mining companies no longer have unimpeded access to it. One of the consequences of increased attention to ownership and boundary issues was that Aboriginal land tenure in Australia was found to be more complex than previously thought. Sutton (1995) brought together a huge amount of information on Aboriginal land use, initially as a critique of some existing maps and analyses of traditional territories. Maps in Sutton (1995) showed that the complexities and multiple layerings often make it impossible to delineate boundaries as simple lines. As well, similar complexities have emerged in the definition of "traditional owners" because of fluidity of group membership (Sutton 1995; Kalit and Young 1997).

Omushkego Cree of Ontario: Fighting Development

A cooperative project was originally undertaken to assist the Omushkego (or West Main) Cree of subarctic Ontario, to formulate culturally appropriate economic development strategies (George and Preston 1992). Partway through the project, plans were announced for hydroelectric development in the area. The

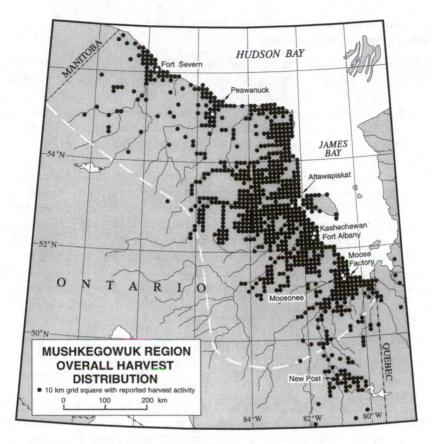

Map 10.1 Distribution of fish and wildlife harvesting activity over one annual cycle (1990) of eight communities of Omushkego Cree Indian people of Ontario. *Source:* Berkes et al. (1995); cartography by A. Hughes.

Cree responded by mobilizing all available information to show that the land-based economy was still an essential part of their livelihoods and would be at unacceptable risk from hydroelectric development. They used the results of the cooperative project to show that the value of subsistence was one-third as large as the total cash economy (Berkes et al. 1994). They also used the wildlife harvest area maps that documented aboriginal resource use by species and by season (Berkes et al. 1995). The composite map (map 10.1) indicated that the Cree indeed used a large part of their traditional territory, some 250,000 square kilometers, even though they officially controlled only 900 square kilometers as reserve land. They put forward an alternative view of development, "culturally sustainable" development that is consistent with the traditional Cree worldview, as opposed to environmentally damaging development based on large-scale projects (Preston et al. 1995).

Traditional Knowledge for Cumulative Impact Assessment in Hudson Bay

In the late 1980s and the early 1990s, aboriginal residents of the communities around Hudson Bay nervously anticipated the construction of the Great Whale hydro project. An environmental assessment was carried out, but it addressed only the specific impacts of Great Whale. Governments were not willing to authorize studies of the combined effects (or cumulative impacts) of existing and proposed development. The tiny Inuit (Eskimo) community of Sanikiluaq on Belcher Islands took the lead to organize a project involving twenty-eight Inuit and Cree communities on Hudson Bay. Carried out in 1992–95, the project aimed to build an integrated regional-scale picture of environmental change from the point of view of aboriginal people, drawing upon the day-to-day and year-to-year observations of hunters and fishers. The picture that emerged from the exercise is that the pace of environmental change in Hudson Bay has been accelerating, with large-scale changes in goose migration patterns and in the sea ice and currents of the bay. The changes are narrated in quotations and through maps. The Hudson Bay study provides details of changes based on cues or indicators monitored by indigenous experts but rarely measured by Western scientists; thus, it shows how traditional knowledge can complement scientific data (Fenge 1997; McDonald et al. 1997).

Conflicting Worldviews in New Zealand

The Treaty of Waitangi, signed by the English Crown and chiefs of the Maori tribes in 1840, sets out indigenous land rights in New Zealand. The Conservation Act of 1987 directs the Department of Conservation to establish co-management arrangements with the Maori, in accordance with the principles of the Treaty of Waitangi. The problem is that the conservation ethic adopted by the act involves "the preservation and protection of ... resources for the purpose of maintaining their intrinsic values," whereas the conservation ethic of the Maori is motivated by a different philosophy (Roberts et al. 1995, 15). Maori conceptualize humans "as part of a personified, spiritually imbued 'environmental family.' ... Earth's bounty is considered to be a gift necessitating reciprocity on the part of human users in order to maintain sustainability" and requiring a sense of guardianship (*kaitiaki*) (Roberts et al. 1995, 14). The imposition of the Western concept of a dichotomy between humans and nature, and the setting aside of land for preservation, merely serve to alienate Maori from their land and *kaitiaki* responsibilities. Some New Zealand scientists and Maori have jointly developed creative solutions to this impasse, involving the co-management of contentious resources as a means of bridge-building and dialogue between the two cultures (Taiepa et al. 1997). One of the mechanisms developed to signify mutual respect and to safeguard the intellectual property rights of Maori traditional knowledge-holders is the Cultural Safety contract (see box 10.1).

BOX 10.1
INSTITUTING MUTUAL RESPECT OF KNOWLEDGE SYSTEMS
IN NEW ZEALAND

The Rakiura Island at the southern tip of New Zealand supports a traditional Maori harvest of the sea bird, *titi* or sooty shearwater. It is the last full-scale bird harvest controlled by the Maori, and it is under pressure from some conservation NGOs who allege that *titi* are declining. University researchers have entered into a co-management agreement with the Rakiura Maori to research and monitor *titi* ecology and harvest. A major component of the project is the traditional knowledge of the birders, which is proving to be considerable. University of Otago's Henrik Moller comments: "We are stunned by the long series of data that the birders have recorded and are beginning to reveal to us. One of the *kaitiaki* (guardians) went to her mother and provided us with a 40-year data score on the fatness and the relative number of *titi* chicks."

A formal "Cultural Safety" contract was drawn up to clarify rules for disclosure and ownership of information coming out of the study. According to the contract, the Rakiura Maori retain complete ownership of intellectual property rights over traditional knowledge. The scientific data gathered on *titi* ecology and harvests are jointly owned by the University and the Rakiura Maori. The contract guarantees that *titi* population data would be published, whether or not it predicts the sustainability of the resource, thus safeguarding the scientific integrity of the university researchers.

The contract requires university researchers to communicate study results to the Rakiura Maori first. At the end of the ten-year project, there will be a maximum of one-year delay before the final scientific findings may be submitted for publication. This will give the Rakiura Maori time to meet and formulate their collective response to the final results, before the findings are disclosed to the general public. Interim results of the project will be communicated to Maori on an ongoing basis by the use of an informal newsletter prepared in nontechnical language. The contract guarantees the *kaitiaki* of the Rakiura Maori full access to research data, the right to submit the data for a second opinion, and the right to see and comment on anything proposed for publication.

Source: Taiepa et al. 1997; Moller (pers. comm.)

Each of the cases above deals with the use of traditional knowledge for empowerment in different parts of the world. In each case, the use of indigenous knowledge is political because it threatens to change the balance of power between indigenous groups on the one hand versus governments, developers, and conventional resource management scientists on the other. Consistent with the cultural importance of indigenous peoples' attachment to land, many of the examples of empowerment deal with land use mapping and land claims. "Maps are the most effective, legitimate, and convincing means available [to indigenous groups] for demonstrating to outsiders that they manage their natural resources, and hence for providing claims to their customary lands" (Fox 1998, 2).

Mapping has become a political process but is also one of the most innovative and dynamic areas in traditional knowledge research because mapping has stimulated the development of techniques using modern technology such as GIS and remote sensing, and the development of participatory, cross-cultural approaches to the research process itself (Weinstein 1993; Duerden and Kuhn 1998; see table 10.1).

Table 10.1   Methodologies for using traditional knowledge for documenting aboriginal land use.

Methodology	Description
Map biographies	Land use and occupancy studies in the Northwest Territories, Canada, have relied primarily on the map biography method in which researchers record on large-scale maps the lifetime extent of land use (resource harvesting, habitation, travel routes, and sometimes place names, stories and legends associated with places, and sacred sites) of individual traditional people. These individual map biographies are then combined, often by time period, into composite maps representing many individuals and families, to provide the land use map of a community (Freeman 1976; Riewe 1992).
Oral history, sketch maps and GIS	A number of studies in various parts of the world, for example, in East Kalimantan, Indonesia, have used a methodology that includes the collection of oral history, local information as recorded on sketch maps, and the use of geographic information system (GIS) technology to overlay this information with government land use maps. Such mapping may be designed to help with resource planning and to identify management alternatives, for example in documenting customary forest territories or in river basin planning (Sirait et al. 1994; Ontario Ministry of Natural Resources 1994).
Resource use area mapping	The spatial extent and the quantitative importance of resource use (wildlife, fisheries and other resources) can be determined with a questionnaire-based study over a specific time period. Using a GIS system, the maps so produced provide a snapshot of land use by season and by activity. They can be scaled to show the quantitative values of various kinds of resources harvested, for example, the intensity of waterfowl or large game hunting, over that specific period of time (Berkes et al. 1995).
Ethnocartography	As developed for indigenous land use studies in Honduras and Panama, information from land use questionnaires can be summarized into cartographic records by geographic zone and by community, showing all the resources and land features that are of importance to local groups. By combining these records with other information, such as government base maps and aerial photographs, composite maps are constructed. These are then combined into 1:50,000 zonal maps and a 1:250,000 master map (González et al. 1995).

The two cases on environmental assessment are notable in that the use of traditional knowledge not only brings local knowledge of land and ecological processes into the assessment, but it also forces the governments and developers to deal with indigenous values and worldviews. This is perhaps the real reason why "the current attempts to use TK to understand the effects of proposed development projects ... have disturbing implications" to the critics (Howard and Widdowson 1996). Indigenous peoples, once empowered to become actors in environmental assessment, do not necessarily play the game according to the rules established by others. For example, Stoffle and colleagues (1990) used Turner's (1988) "index of cultural significance" to determine protection priorities for local plant species used by the Paiute and Shoshone Indians and potentially affected by the nuclear waste disposal site to be set up in the Yucca Mountain project in Nevada. Undertakings of this sort, however rigorous their scientific methodology, may still be unacceptable to indigenous worldviews. Turner (1988) herself was not able to convince the Salish people to use the index for prioritizing the importance of plant species. One woman informant simply refused to go along with the exercise, saying "they are all important" (Turner 1988).

The New Zealand case is particularly telling because the controversy is directly on the issue of worldviews. The Maori are asserting the legitimacy of their views of conservation and are willing to reach out to the dominant society by going into partnerships with university researchers. However, the Cultural Safety contract (see box 10.1, above) is not merely a research protocol; it is used as a tool to share political power, in this case, the power of knowledge. Similar cases of conflicting conservation views, accompanied by power struggles, are found in many parts of the world. Cox and Elmqvist (1997, 84), writing about rain forest reserves in Samoa, found that "the principles of indigenous control were unexpectedly difficult to accept by Western conservation organizations who, ultimately, were unwilling to cede decision-making authority to indigenous peoples."

Elsewhere, struggles have been internal as well as external. For example, the Marovo Lagoon Project in the Solomon Islands was undertaken to assert traditional land and marine tenure in the face of development pressures. But the major struggle did not involve outsiders or foreign views. Research results on customary tenure and traditional management institutions were used to resolve internal differences—the differences between those who believed that customary tenure was an impediment to "progress" and development, versus those who saw opportunities to work with, rather than against, customary rights and traditional social institutions (Baines 1991; Baines and Hviding 1993).

These examples concentrate on politics, but issues of politics and philosophy in the use of traditional knowledge are often intertwined. The use of indigenous knowledge may threaten to break the monopoly of conventional resource management science on "truth." The next section shifts the focus of inquiry from political ecology to philosophy of science, for a more detailed examination of the extent to which indigenous knowledge systems are consistent with Western science.

INDIGENOUS KNOWLEDGE AS CHALLENGE TO
THE POSITIVIST-REDUCTIONIST PARADIGM

Since the early seventeenth century, science has been dominated by the Cartesian paradigm, often termed positivism or rationalism, which is based on the search for universal truths. It is an approach that assumes the existence of a reality driven by immutable laws. The role of science is to discover these truths, with the ultimate aim of predicting and controlling nature. The assumption is that scientists themselves are detached from the world and operate in a value-free environment. They use reductionism, which involves breaking a system into discrete components, analyzing the components, and making predictions on the basis of the analysis of the parts. Knowledge about the world is then synthesized into generalizations and principles independent of context, space, and time (Capra 1996). The above summary of the positivist-reductionist paradigm of science is simplistic to be sure; not too many scientists would subscribe to all the assumptions of the paradigm. But it is also true that the positivist-reductionist (also referred to as the positivist-rationalist) approach has dominated conventional resource management (Berkes and Folke 1998) and conservation thinking (Pimbert and Pretty 1995), as seen in the New Zealand case and elsewhere.

The limitations of reductionistic thinking are becoming obvious in a number of disciplines. In recent years, ecology has made great strides in understanding and analyzing complexity and natural variability. Ecosystems are increasingly perceived as being in a state of continuous change, thus necessitating the development of multi-equilibrium thinking and attention to system resilience (Holling 1973, 1986; Gunderson et al. 1995). Few contemporary ecologists would defend the equilibrium concept, and yet the equilibrium-centered idea of maximum sustained yield (MSY) is still used in fisheries, wildlife, and forestry, even though it ignores ecosystem interactions and environmental variability. Emphasis on quantitative targets such as MSY is a consequence of the positivist-reductionist tradition. In the short term, such targets are well-suited to the efficient utilization of fisheries and other resources, as if stocks were discrete commodities in space and time. To the extent that these assumptions are faulty, however, the MSY is part of the problem and an impediment to sustainability in the larger context of the long-term maintenance of healthy ecosystems.

The point is that both ecology and resource management science that developed under the conventional and mechanistic worldview, shaped by the utilitarian premises of the industrial age, had more to say about the human mission to extract rather than to conserve (Worster 1977, 53). The managers who were in charge of such resource management were not only the technocrats who knew how to calculate quantitative targets, but they were also the high priests of the positivist-reductionist paradigm. These managers rejected traditional knowledge and management systems because their fundamental characteristics did not fit the new paradigm: embeddedness of knowledge in the local culture; boundedness of local knowledge in space and time; the importance of community; lack of separation between nature and culture, and between subject and object; attachment to the local environment; and a noninstrumental approach to nature (Banuri and Apffel Marglin 1993).

The development of a technocratic-bureaucratic class, the separation of the user from the manager and the governed from the governor were justified in terms of the rise of the modern state, whose affairs had become too complicated for the ordinary citizen. In place of traditional management systems, the high priests enforced a system characterized by disembeddedness; universalism; supremacy of individualism; nature/culture and subject/object dichotomy; mobility; and an instrumental, utilitarian attitude toward nature (Banuri and Apffel Marglin 1993).

These changes in resource management science should not be seen in isolation. Rather, they should be regarded in the larger context of a great transformation of society and values that characterized the period after the seventeenth century, the period of the Enlightenment. The development of positivist-reductionist science was closely linked to the emergence of industrialization and to economic theories of both capitalism and communism. Through the technological domination of the earth, scientists and economists promised to "deliver a more fair, rational, efficient, and productive life for everyone, themselves above all" (Worster 1988, 11). Their method was simply to free individual enterprise from the bonds of traditional hierarchy and community, whether the bondage derived from other humans or the earth (Kellert 1997). That meant teaching everyone to treat the earth, as well as each other, with a "frank, energetic self-assertiveness, unembarrassed by too many moral or aesthetic sentiments" (Worster 1988, 11).

In pursuing individual wealth, people were taught to regard land, resources, and their own labor as potential commodities for the market. As explored by Polanyi (1964), this "great transformation" of the scientific-economic system was also linked to a radical transformation of social attitudes. "Everyday dealings of people with nature were altered too, that ecological relations, deriving as they did from human social relations, also became more destructive as they grew more distant. Just as capitalists organized the new underclass of workers into instruments of profit, so they organized the earth as the raw material for that labor to exploit" (Worster 1988, 12).

In exploring the relationship of traditional knowledge to Western science, these considerations led to the conclusion that indigenous knowledge systems are fundamentally inconsistent with a certain kind of Western science, the positivist-reductionist tradition. It is this paradigm that displaced traditional knowledge in the first place, insisted that "professionals know best," and asserted that users of resources cannot be the managers at the same time. Given its bias for individualism over community, its utilitarian attitude toward nature, and its nature:culture and subject:object dichotomies, it is clear that the positivist-reductionist paradigm is ill-suited as a framework for integrating Western science and traditional knowledge.

Many Westerners believe that knowledge has been converging into a coherent whole. Norgaard has used the metaphor of sciences as islands of knowledge, gradually growing and pushing back the sea of ignorance. The belief in the ultimate and final victory of Western science has been accompanied by the belief that all cultures would merge into one "correct" way of thinking about human development and well-being. For example, development economists have typically projected social and economic change in a way that leads all cultures to adopt one correct Western way of thinking. This then justified, for example, policies like exporting "development" to Africa and assimilating indigenous peoples. To the extent that such development and "progress" after the Western pattern have not worked, a re-visioning of the future becomes necessary (Norgaard 1994).

If our sciences were truly merging, one would expect to find that our growing islands of knowledge would seamlessly come together. What one finds instead is a fundamental questioning of old paradigms in those sciences centrally involved in the management of resources and the environment. For example, the assumptions of neoclassical economics have run into biophysical limits dictated by ecological considerations, and equilibrium-centered supply/demand analyses are providing poor predictions, thus making a paradigm change likely (Daly and Cobb 1989). Both ecology and economics are in a state of flux as new paradigms threaten to take over the old.

In resource management, many critics have highlighted the inadequacy of conventional science—reductionistic, mechanistic, detached from people and politics. The rival stream is represented by systems thinking and an evolutionary approach. The applied form of this stream is represented by alternative resource management approaches, in particular Adaptive Management, in which uncertainty and surprises become an integral part of an anticipated set of adaptive responses (Holling 1978; Gunderson et al. 1995). As it has been developing, Adaptive Management is fundamentally interdisciplinary and combines historical, comparative, and experimental approaches. Resource and environmental problems are dealt with as systems problems in which the behavior of the system is complex and unpredictable, and causes are usually multiple. Ecological relationships are nonlinear in nature, cross-scale in space and time, and have an evolutionary character (Holling et al. 1998). Adaptive Management involves multi-equilibrium thinking and attention to system integrity and focuses on ecosystem processes rather than ecosystem products.

Adaptive Management is part of the holistic tradition in Western science, which includes systems theory, gestalt psychology, quantum physics, and ecology (Capra 1996). Many of these holistic sciences are potentially suitable to provide frameworks for integrating Western and indigenous knowledge in general. As discussed through chapters 4 to 8, Adaptive Management is a good match for traditional ecological knowledge, and a bridge between Western and indigenous ways of knowing in the area of ecology and resource management.

Much needs to be done to explore the ways in which Western and traditional knowledge can be used together—and whether such integration is desirable in the first place. Attempts at integration inevitably come up against the questions of power sharing and decision making. The cases summarized in this chapter, as well as in chapter 2 and elsewhere, indicate that the use of indigenous knowledge can provide both empowerment for local peoples and improvement of the knowledge base for decision making. However, in many cases, indigenous knowledge has been ignored or dismissed; conversely, there have been other cases in which indigenous peoples have been reluctant to work with Western scientists or to share their knowledge.

As discussed in chapter 9 in the context of sustainability and conservation, the most useful way to think about indigenous knowledge is that it is complementary to Western scientific knowledge, and not a replacement for it. Rooted in different worldviews and unequal in power, Western and traditional knowledge are not easy to combine. It may never be possible or desirable to meld the two, even if Western knowledge is represented by one of the holistic traditions. Each is legitimate in its own right, within its own context; each has its own strengths. The two kinds of knowledge may be pursued separately but in parallel, with opportunities to enrich one another, as in the case of the Alaska-Yukon caribou "knowledge co-op" (Kofinas 1998). They can be brought together to be used on common grounds such as sustainability.

LEARNING FROM TRADITIONAL KNOWLEDGE AND RESOURCE MANAGEMENT

The explosion of interest in traditional ecological knowledge in recent years reflects the need for ecological insights from indigenous practices of resource use, and the need to develop a new ecological ethic based in part on indigenous wisdom. By treating traditional ecological knowledge as a knowledge-practice-belief complex, it is possible to examine ecological practices and worldviews, and their dynamics, together. The main lessons of traditional ecological knowledge, as summarized here, fall into three clusters: the first addresses the unity and diversity of indigenous systems; the second, the importance of participatory and community-based resource management; and the third, the ethics of a sacred ecology.

1. Unity and Diversity of Traditional Indigenous Systems

Traditional management systems pose a paradox. On the one hand, they are characterized by an extraordinary similarity of basic designs shared by different cultures in different geographic areas in comparable ecosystems. Examples include shifting cultivation developed by peoples of tropical forests worldwide, and reef and lagoon tenure systems of island peoples dependent on marine resources. On the other hand, they are characterized by a remarkable diversity in practice, even in adjacent areas. For example, in shifting cultivation, the actual crop mix used and the details of practice vary; in reef and lagoon tenure, the set of rules used and the mix of exploitation-control mechanisms differ; and in semiarid-area herding systems, the details of rotation and migration are all fine-tuned to the local environment and vary from one area and group to the next. Also notable is the evidence that rules may be used flexibly and may vary from one year to the next, using cues from the ecosystem as feedback to adjust for environmental fluctuations, based on an accumulation of traditional knowledge (Berkes et al. 1997).

Traditional ecological knowledge is considered by some to be merely locally relevant because it is locally developed. This is a very limited view. Many practices are common enough to be called principles; these include rotation of exploited areas and use of territorial systems, as found in different kinds of ecosystems. The practice of monitoring the fat content of caribou as a qualitative management measure is found not only in adjacent areas and related cultural groups, but right across North America from Alaska to Labrador. The use of fat content as a monitoring tool that integrates a range of ecosystem information is also found in seabird management by the Maori of New Zealand, indicating the potential for generating universal management principles from some locally developed practices.

These findings are consistent with the historical and evolutionary view of indigenous resource management systems as adaptive responses that have evolved over time, not as mere traditions. Scholars have paid relatively little attention to the evolution of traditional knowledge systems, but there is evidence of what evolutionary biologists call convergent evolution, adaptive radiation, and punctuated equilibrium. Similarly, relatively little attention has been paid to knowledge diffusion and transmission (Ohmagari and Berkes 1997). Chapter 6 provides some evidence that adaptive responses resulting in a change in management practice and worldview may be explained by social learning and cultural evolution, based on local knowledge, oral history, and myth. A resource crisis seems to be a necessary condition for social learning leading to a re-design of management systems (Gunderson et al. 1995). However, signals from the environment have to be received and correctly interpreted by the group in question.

The lesson for Western science is that we should perhaps be building resource management systems that are open to alternative ways of thinking, rather than being conceptually closed, a science compatible with pluralistic ways of thinking about the world. This requires an explicit recognition that our multiple models in Western science "do not fit into a single, coherent understanding. . . . Conceptual pluralism is what we have" (Norgaard 1994, 96). This pluralism can include non-Western knowledge about specific ecosystems as well as non-Western perspectives in interpreting that knowledge. Western science, as a product of Western culture, represents but one cultural perspective. There are different ways of knowing and no one standard for determining the validity of knowledge, a controversial view that runs counter to conventional wisdom in positivist science.

2. Participatory, Community-based Resource Management

A second lesson from traditional systems concerns the central importance of community-based resource management in traditional systems, and hence the necessity of incorporating participatory processes into contemporary resource management. There is evidence for a general tendency for community self-organization toward sustainable practice. However, examples such as those in chapter 8 also show that even though the development of local knowledge is a necessary condition, it is often not a sufficient condition to achieve sustainability. The fundamental issue is one of defining property rights to common property resources such as forests, grazing lands, wildlife, and fisheries. Over historical time, property rights in resources in many parts of the world have been transformed from communal property (in which access and management rights are controlled by an identifiable group) to open access (free-for-all). Restoring traditional resource tenure can pave the way to establishing property rights in areas in which resource harvesting had previously operated under nonsustainable, open-access conditions. Once property rights and resource use rules have been established, both the costs and benefits of any management action will be borne by the same individual or group, thus providing incentive to conserve.

Whether traditional peoples practice conservation or not depends more on this fundamental point than on any supposed natural inclination of a group to act as conservers or nonconservers. Traditional peoples, like all peoples, respond to incentives. Self-interest, coupled with social sanctions, is key to biodiversity conservation and sustainable resource use in general. Resource rights, balanced against responsibilities, strengthen the traditional conservation ethic wherever it may exist, together with communal-property resource management systems that sustain them (Berkes 1989a; Trosper 1998).

Traditional systems inspire a new resource management science open to the participation of resource users in management, one that uses locally grounded alternatives to top-down centralized resource management. The point is important not only for humanizing resource management, but also for making sure that local needs are addressed and that relevant local knowledge, practice, and values are part of management decision making. In regard to common property resource management and co-management, the general principle, also called the subsidiarity principle, may be stated as, "using as much local-level management as possible; only so much government regulation as necessary" (Berkes et al. 1991, 14).

The use of traditional knowledge is important especially in the context of indigenous peoples' empowerment. Many aboriginal people, from the Australian outback to the Brazilian Amazon, are raising concerns about resource depletion and are demanding a share in management decisions. The use of traditional knowledge provides a mechanism, a point of entry, to implement co-management and self-government and to integrate local values into decision making (Berkes and Henley 1997). Respect for indigenous knowledge and management systems levels the playing field and helps find a new balance against an expert-dominated positivistic science.

3. Ethics of Sacred Ecology

A third lesson from traditional systems concerns the potential to forge new ethical principles for ecology and resource management. Traditional knowledge has the power to address some of the shortcomings of the contemporary Western knowledge-practice-belief complex, as identified by various scholars: restoring the unity of mind and nature (Bateson); providing intuitive wisdom for developing awareness of the nonlinear nature of our environment (Capra); addressing the problem of a self-identity distinct from the world around us (Evernden); and restoring a cosmology based on morality toward nature (Skolimowski).

A fundamental lesson of traditional ecological knowledge is that worldviews do matter. Positivist science, despite claims to the contrary, is not value-free. If the notion of man's dominion over nature symbolizes the positivist paradigm of Western science, the community-of-beings worldview symbolizes traditional ecological knowledge. The science of ecology comes close to accepting the latter idea; but much of contemporary ecological research uses reductionistic thinking. Thus, not all ecological science is sympathetic to traditional ecology.

The challenge is to cultivate a kind of ecology that rejects the materialist tradition and questions the Newtonian, machinelike view of ecosystems, the one with ecological cycles pictured as giant gears powered by the sun. The indigenous knowledge systems of diverse groups, from the Dene of the North American subarctic to the Fijians of the South Pacific, provide an alternative view of ecosystems. This is a view of an ecosystem pulsating with life and spirit, incorporating people who *belong* to that land and who have a relationship of peaceful coexistence with other beings.

However, in many indigenous views, such a coexistence does not preclude the human use of resources. In Leopold's (1949) land ethics, it is the humans who are to extend *their* ethics to include nature; animals have no obligations toward humans, at least no explicit obligations. By contrast, in James Bay Cree ethics (as outlined in chapter 5), and in North American Indian ethics in general, the relationship is not one-way, and there is explicit human-nature reciprocity in which animals have obligations to nourish humans in return for respect and other proper behavior (Trosper 1995).

Some authors reject indigenous peoples' ethics as human-centric and use-oriented and confuse it with utilitarianism. Many systems of indigenous ethics not only include human-nature reciprocity but are deeply moral. This point sharply distinguishes most indigenous ethics from utilitarianism, which is characterized by an amoral approach and the commodification of nature. In building new ecological ethics, traditional ecological knowledge bridges the gap between utilitarianism (as a kind of human-centric ethics) and biocentric ethics. A series of ideas in environmental ethics, including Leopold's land ethics, deep ecology, Gaia, topophilia/love of land, sense of place, bioregionalism, and biophilia/love of living beings, has explored the personal meaning and sacred dimensions of ecology that have been missing in scientific ecology. The knowledge-practice-belief complex of many indigenous traditions incorporates wisdom that has implicitly or explicitly inspired many of these ideas about the centrality and beauty of the larger whole and the place of humans in it.

References

Acheson, J. M. 1975. "The lobster fiefs": Economic and ecological effects on territoriality in the Maine lobster industry. *Human Ecology* 3: 183–207.

Agrawal, A. 1995a. Indigenous and scientific knowledge: Some critical comments. *Indigenous Knowledge and Development Monitor* 3(3): 3–6.

Agrawal, A. 1995b. Dismantling the divide between indigenous and scientific knowledge. *Development and Change* 26: 413–39.

Agrawal, A. 1997. Community in conservation: Beyond enchantment and disenchantment. Gainesville, Fla.: Conservation and Development Forum Discussion Paper.

Ahmed, M., A. D. Capistrano, and M. Hossain. 1997. Experience of partnership models for the co-management of Bangladesh fisheries. *Fisheries Management and Ecology* 4: 233–48.

Alcorn, J. B. 1984. *Huastec Mayan Ethnobotany*. Austin: University of Texas Press.

Alcorn, J. B. 1989. Process as resource. *Advances in Economic Botany* 7: 63–77.

Alcorn, J. B. 1990. Indigenous agroforestry strategies meeting farmers' needs. In *Alternatives to Deforestation* (A. B. Anderson, ed.). New York: Columbia University Press.

Alcorn, J. B. 1993. Indigenous peoples and conservation. *Conservation Biology* 7: 424–26.

Alcorn, J. B. 1994. Noble savage or noble state? Northern myths and southern realities in biodiversity conservation. *Ethnoecológica* 2(3): 7–19.

Alegret, J. L. 1995. Co-management of resources and conflict management: The case of the fishermen's *confreries* in Catalonia. MARE Working Paper No. 2. Aarhus, Denmark: Aarhus University.

Alvard, M. S. 1993. Testing the "ecologically noble savage" hypothesis: Interspecific prey choice by Piro hunters of Amazonian Peru. *Human Ecology* 21: 355–87.

Amarasinghe, U. S., W. U. Chandrasekara, and H. M. P. Kithsiri. 1997. Traditional practices for resource sharing in an artisanal fishery of a Sri Lankan estuary. *Asian Fisheries Science* 9: 311–23.

Anderson, E. N. 1996. *Ecologies of the Heart: Emotion, Belief, and the Environment*. New York: Oxford University Press.

André, N. 1989. Shamanism among the Montagnais. *Rencontre* 10(3): 5–6.

Aswani, S. 1997. Troubled waters in south-western New Georgia, Solomon Islands. *Traditional Marine Resource Management and Knowledge Information Bulletin* 8: 2–16.

Bahn, P. G. 1996. Further back down under. *Nature* 383: 577–78.

Baines, G. B. K. 1989. Traditional resource management in the Melanesian South Pacific: A development dilemma. In *Common Property Resources* (F. Berkes, ed.). London: Belhaven, 273–95.

Baines, G. B. K. 1991. Asserting traditional rights: Community conservation in Solomon Islands. *Cultural Survival Quarterly* 15(2): 49–52.

Baines, G., and E. Hviding. 1993. Traditional environmental knowledge for resource management in Marovo, Solomon Islands. In *Traditional Ecological Knowledge: Wisdom for Sustainable*

Development (N. M. Williams and G. Baines, eds.). Canberra: Centre for Resource and Environmental Studies, Australian National University, 56–65.

Ballard, C. 1997. It's the land, stupid! The moral economy of resource ownership in Papua New Guinea. In *The Governance of Common Property in the Pacific Region* (P. Larmour, ed.). Canberra: Australian National University, 47–65.

Banfield, A. W. F., and J. S. Tener. 1958. A preliminary study of the Ungava caribou. *Journal of Mammalogy* 39: 560–73.

Banuri, T., and F. Apffel Marglin, editors. 1993. *Who Will Save the Forests?* London: United Nations University/Zed Books.

Barnston, G. 1861. Recollections of the swans and geese of Hudson's Bay. *Canadian Naturalist and Geologist* 6: 337–44.

Barreiro, J. 1992. The search for lessons. *Akwe:kon Journal* 9(2): 18–39.

Barrows, D. P. 1900. The ethno-botany of the Coahuila Indians of Southern California. Chicago. (Cited in Levi-Strauss, 1962.)

Barsh, R. L. 1997. Fire on the land. *Alternatives Journal* 23(4): 36–40.

Basso, K. H. 1972. Ice and travel among the Fort Norman Slave: Folk taxonomies and cultural rules. *Language in Society* 1: 31–49.

Bateson, G. 1972. *Steps to an Ecology of Mind.* New York: Ballantine.

Bateson, G. 1979. *Mind and Nature: A Necessary Unity.* New York: Dutton.

Bearskin, J., G. Lameboy, R. Matthew, J. Pepabano, A. Pisinaquan, W. Ratt, and D. Rupert. 1989. *Cree Trappers Speak* (compiled and edited by F. Berkes). Chisasibi, Quebec: Cree Trappers Association's Committee of Chisasibi and the James Bay Cree Cultural Education Centre.

Beaucage, P., and Taller de Tradición Oral del Cepec. 1997. Integrating innovation: The traditional Nahua coffee-orchard (Sierra Norte de Puebla, Mexico). *Journal of Ethnobiology* 17: 45–67.

Behnke, R. H., I. Scoones, and C. Kerven, editors. 1993. *Range Management at Disequilibrium: New Models of Natural Variability and Pastoral Adaptation in African Savannas.* London: Overseas Development Institute.

Bielawski, E. 1992. Inuit indigenous knowledge and science in the Arctic. *Northern Perspectives* 20(1): 5–8.

Berkes, F. 1977. Fishery resource use in a subarctic Indian community. *Human Ecology* 5: 289–307.

Berkes F. 1979. An investigation of Cree Indian domestic fisheries in northern Quebec. *Arctic* 32: 46–70.

Berkes, F. 1981a. Some environmental and social impacts of the James Bay hydroelectric project, Canada. *Journal of Environmental Management* 12: 157–72.

Berkes, F. 1981b. Fisheries of the James Bay area and northern Quebec: A case study in resource management. In *Renewable Resources and the Economy of the North* (M. M. R. Freeman, ed.). Ottawa: Association of Canadian Universities for Northern Studies/Man and the Biosphere Program, 143–60.

Berkes, F. 1982. Waterfowl management and northern native peoples with reference to Cree hunters of James Bay. *Musk-Ox* 30: 23–35.

Berkes, F. 1985. Fishermen and the "tragedy of the commons." *Environmental Conservation* 12: 199–206.

Berkes, F. 1986a. Common property resources and hunting territories. *Anthropologica* 28: 145–62.

Berkes, F. 1986b. Chisasibi Cree hunters and missionaries: Humour as evidence of tension. In *Actes du Dix-Septième Congrès des Algonquinistes* (W. Cowan, ed.). Ottawa: Carleton University Press, 15–26.

Berkes, F. 1987a. Common property resource management and Cree Indian fisheries in subarctic Canada. In *The Question of the Commons* (B. J. McCay and J. M. Acheson, eds.). Tucson: University of Arizona Press, 66–91.

Berkes, F. 1987b. The common property resource problem and the fisheries of Barbados and Jamaica. *Environmental Management* 11: 225–35.

Berkes, F. 1988a. The intrinsic difficulty of predicting impacts: Lessons from the James Bay hydro project. *Environmental Impact Assessment Review* 8: 201–20.

Berkes, F. 1988b. Environmental philosophy of the Cree people of James Bay. In *Traditional Knowledge and Renewable Resource Management in Northern Regions* (M. M. R. Freeman and L. Carbyn, eds.). Edmonton: Boreal Institute, University of Alberta, 7–21.

Berkes, F., editor. 1989a. *Common Property Resources: Ecology and Community-Based Sustainable Development*. London: Belhaven.

Berkes, F. 1989b. Cooperation from the perspective of human ecology. In *Common Property Resources: Ecology and Community-Based Sustainable Development* (F. Berkes, ed.). London: Belhaven, 70–88.

Berkes, F. 1992. Success and failure in marine coastal fisheries of Turkey. In *Making the Commons Work* (D. W. Bromley, ed.). San Francisco: Institute for Contemporary Studies Press, 161–82.

Berkes, F. 1993. Traditional ecological knowledge in perspective. In *Traditional Ecological Knowledge: Concepts and Cases* (J. T. Inglis, ed.). Ottawa: Canadian Museum of Nature and the International Development Research Centre, 1–9.

Berkes, F., J. Colding, and C. Folke. 1997. Rediscovery of traditional ecological knowledge as adaptive management. Beijer Discussion Paper Series No. 109.

Berkes, F., and H. Fast. 1996. Aboriginal peoples: The basis for policy-making towards sustainable development. In *Achieving Sustainable Development* (A. Dale and J. B. Robinson, eds.). Vancouver: University of British Columbia Press, 204–64.

Berkes, F., D. Feeny, B. J. McCay, and J. M. Acheson. 1989. The benefits of the commons. *Nature* 340: 91–93.

Berkes, F. and C. Folke, editors. 1998. *Linking Social and Ecological Systems: Management Practices and Social Mechanisms for Building Resilience*. Cambridge: Cambridge University Press.

Berkes, F., C. Folke, and M. Gadgil. 1995. Traditional ecological knowledge, biodiversity, resilience and sustainability. In *Biodiversity Conservation* (C. Perrings, K.-G. Maler, C. Folke, C. S. Holling, and B.-O. Jansson, eds.). Dordrecht: Kluwer, 281–99.

Berkes F., P. J. George, and R. J. Preston. 1991. Co-management. *Alternatives* 18(2): 12–18.

Berkes, F., P. J. George, R. J. Preston, A. Hughes, J. Turner, and B. D. Cummins. 1994. Wildlife harvesting and sustainable regional native economy in the Hudson and James Bay Lowland, Ontario. *Arctic* 47: 350–60.

Berkes F., and T. Gonenc. 1982. A mathematical model on the exploitation of northern lake whitefish with gillnets. *North American Journal of Fisheries Management* 2: 176–83.

Berkes, F., and T. Henley. 1997. Co-management and traditional knowledge: Threat or opportunity? *Policy Options* (March 1997): 29–31.

Berkes, F., A. Hughes, P. J. George, R. J. Preston, B. D. Cummins, and J. Turner. 1995. The persistence of aboriginal land use: Fish and wildlife harvest areas in the Hudson and James Bay Lowland, Ontario. *Arctic* 48: 81–93.

Berkes, F., K. Kislalioglu, C. Folke, and M. Gadgil. 1998. Exploring the basic ecological unit: Ecosystem-like concepts in traditional societies. *Ecosystems* 1: 409–415.

Berkes, F. and M. MacKenzie. 1978. Cree fish names from eastern James Bay, Quebec. *Arctic* 31: 489–95.

Berkes, F., and A. H. Smith. 1995. Coastal marine property rights: The second transformation. In *Philippine Coastal Resources Under Stress* (M. A. Juinio-Menez and G. F. Newkirk, eds.). Quezon City: University of the Philippines, 103–13.

Berlin, B. 1973. Folk systematics in relation to biological classification and nomenclature. *Annual Review of Ecology and Systematics* 4: 259–71.

Berlin, B. 1992. *Ethnobotanical Classification: Principles of Categorization of Plants and Animals in Traditional Societies*. Princeton: Princeton University Press.

Berlin, B., D. E. Breedlove, and P. H. Raven. 1966. Folk taxonomies and biological classification. *Science* 154: 273–75.

Berlin, B., D. E. Breedlove, and P. H. Raven. 1974. *Principles of Tzeltal Plant Classification: An Introduction to the Botanical Ethnography of a Mayan-Speaking People of Highland Chiapas*. New York: Academic Press.

Berry, T. 1988. *The Dream of the Earth*. San Francisco: Sierra Club Books.

Bishop, C. A., and T. Morantz, editors. 1986. Who owns the beaver? Algonquian land tenure reconsidered. Special issue of *Anthropologica* 28(1 & 2).

Blackburn, T. C., and K. Anderson, editors. 1993. *Before the Wilderness: Environmental Management by Native Californians*. Menlo Park: Ballena Press.

Blaikie, P. 1985. *The Political Economy of Soil Erosion in Developing Countries*. Harlow, U.K.: Longman.

Blaikie, P., and S. Jeanrenaud. 1996. Biodiversity and human welfare. Geneva: United Nations Research Institute for Social Development (UNRISD) Discussion Paper No. 72.

Boas, F. 1934. *Geographical Names of the Kwakiutl Indians*. New York: Columbia University Press.

Bocco, G. 1991. Traditional knowledge for soil conservation in Central Mexico. *Journal of Soil and Water Conservation* 46: 346–48.

Borrini-Feyerabend, G. 1996. Collaborative management of protected areas: Tailoring the approach to the context. Gland, Switzerland: IUCN (International Conservation Union).

Boserup, E. 1965. *The Conditions for Agricultural Growth: The Economics of Agrarian Change Under Population Pressure*. Chicago: Aldine.

Brascoupe, S. 1992. Indigenous perspectives on international development. A*kwe:kon Journal* 9(2): 6–17.

Brightman, R. A. 1993. *Grateful Prey: Rock Cree Human-Animal Relationships*. Berkeley: University of California Press.

Brokensha, D., D. M. Warren, and O. Werner, editors. 1980. *Indigenous Knowledge Systems and Development*. Washington, D.C.: University Press of America.

Bromley, D. W., editor. 1992. *Making the Commons Work*. San Francisco: Institute for Contemporary Studies Press.

Bronowski, J. 1978. *The Origins of Knowledge and Imagination*. New Haven and London: Yale University Press.

Brookfield, H., and C. Padoch. 1994. Appreciating agrodiversity: A look at the dynamism and diversity of indigenous farming practices. *Environment* 36(5): 6–11, 37–45.

Brown, J. E., recorder and editor. 1953. *The Sacred Pipe: Black Elk's Account of the Seven Rites of the Oglala Sioux*. Norman: University of Oklahoma Press.

Brush, S., and D. Stabinsky. 1996. *Valuing Local Knowledge: Indigenous People and Intellectual Property Rights*. Washington, D.C.: Island Press.

Bruun, O., and A. Kalland, editors. 1995. *Asian Perceptions of Nature: A Critical Approach*. London: Curzon Press.

Buege, D. J. 1996. The ecologically noble savage revisited. *Environmental Ethics* 18: 71–88.

Butz, D. 1996. Sustaining indigenous communities: Symbolic and instrumental dimensions of pastoral resource use in Shimshal, Northern Pakistan. *Canadian Geographer* 40: 36–53.

Callicott, J. B. 1982. Traditional American Indian and Western European attitudes toward nature: An overview. *Environmental Ethics* 4: 293–318.

Callicott, J. B., editor. 1989. *In Defense of the Land Ethic: Essays in Environmental Philosophy*. Albany: State University of New York Press.

Callicott, J. B. 1994. *Earth's Insights: A Survey of Ecological Ethics from the Mediterranean Basin to the Australian Outback*. Berkeley: University of California Press.

Capra, F. 1982. *The Turning Point*. New York: Simon and Schuster.

Capra, F. 1996. *The Web of Life*. New York: Anchor Books, Doubleday.

Castro, P. 1990. Sacred groves and social change in Kirinyaga, Kenya. In *Social Change and Applied Anthropology* (M. Chaiken and A. Fleuret, eds.). Boulder, Colo.: Westview Press, 277–89.

Ceci, L. 1978. Watchers of the Pleiades: Ethnoastronomy among native cultivators in northeastern North America. *Ethnohistory* 25: 301–17.

Chambers, R. 1983. *Rural Development: Putting the Last First*. London: Longmans.

Chapin, M. 1988. The seduction of models: *Chinampa* agriculture in Mexico. *Grassroots Development* 12(1): 8–17.

Chapin, M. 1991. Losing the way of the Great Father. *New Scientist* 10: 40–44.

Chapin, M. 1998. Mapping and the ownership of information. *Common Property Resource Digest* 45: 6–7.

Chapman, M. D. 1985. Environmental influences on the development of traditional conservation in the South Pacific region. *Environmental Conservation* 12: 217–30.

Chapman, M. D. 1987. Traditional political structure and conservation in Oceania. *Ambio* 16: 201–05.

Christianty, L., O. S. Abdoellah, G. G. Marten, and J. Iskandar. 1986. Traditional agroforestry in West Java: The pekarangan (homegarden) and kebun-talun (annual-perennial rotation) cropping systems. In *Traditional Agriculture in Southeast Asia* (G. G. Marten, ed.). Boulder, Colo.: Westview, 132–58.

Christy, F. T. 1982. Territorial use rights in marine fisheries: Definitions and conditions. Rome: FAO Fisheries Technical Paper No. 227.

Clement, D. 1995. *La Zoologie des Montagnais*. Paris: Editions Peeters.

Colby, B. N. 1966. Ethnographic semantics: A preliminary survey. *Current Anthropology* 7: 3–17.

Colchester, M. 1994. Salvaging nature: Indigenous peoples, protected areas and biodiversity conservation. Geneva: UNRISD Discussion Paper No. 55.

Colding, J. 1998. Analysis of hunting options by the use of general food taboos. *Ecological Modelling* 110: 5–17.

Colding, J., and C. Folke. 1997. The relation between threatened species, their protection, and taboos. *Conservation Ecology* 1: article 6, 19 (URL:http://www.consecol.org/vol1/iss1/art6)

Collier, R., and D. Vegh. 1998. Gitxsan mapping workshop. Crossing Boundaries: 7th Conference of the International Association for the Study of Common Property, June 1998, Vancouver, British Columbia. (For details see URL: http://www.native.maps.org)

Colorado, P. 1988. Bridging native and western science. *Convergence* 21: 49–70.

Conelly, W. T. 1992. Agricultural intensification in a Philippine frontier community: Impact on labor efficiency and farm diversity. *Human Ecology* 20: 203–23.

Conklin, H. C. 1957. Hanunoo agriculture. Report of an integral system of shifting cultivation in the Philippines. Rome: FAO Forestry Development Paper No. 5.

Cordell, J. 1995. Review of *Traditional Ecological Knowledge* (ed. N. M. Williams and G. Baines). *Journal of Political Ecology* 2: 43–47.

Cordova, V. F. 1997. Ecoindian: A response to J. Baird Callicott. *Ayaangwaamizin: The International Journal of Indigenous Philosophy* 1: 31–43.

Corsiglia, J., and G. Snively. 1997. Knowing home. *Alternatives Journal* 23(3): 22–27.

Costa-Pierce, B. A. 1987. Aquaculture in ancient Hawaii. *BioScience* 37: 320–30.

Costa-Pierce, B. A. 1988. Traditional fisheries and dualism in Indonesia. *Naga* 11(2): 34.

Couturier, S., J. Brunelle, D. Vandal, and G. St.-Martin. 1990. Changes in the population dynamics of the George River caribou herd, 1976–87. *Arctic* 43: 9–20.

Cox, P. A., and T. Elmqvist. 1997. Ecocolonialism and indigenous-controlled rainforest peserves in Samoa. *Ambio* 26: 84–89.

Cronon, W. 1983. *Changes in the Land: Indians, Colonists, and the Ecology of New England*. New York: Hill and Wang.

Cruikshank, J. 1995. Introduction: Changing traditions in northern ethnography. *The Northern Review* 14: 11–20.

Daly, H. E., and J. B. Cobb. 1989. *For the Common Good*. Boston: Beacon Press.

Dasmann, R. F. 1988. Towards a biosphere consciousness. In *The Ends of the Earth* (D. Worster, ed.). Cambridge: Cambridge University Press, 277–88.

Dei, G. J. S. 1992. A Ghanaian town revisited: Changes and continuities in local adaptive strategies. *African Affairs* 91: 95–120.

Dei, G. J. S. 1993. Indigenous African knowledge systems: Local traditions of sustainable forestry. *Singapore Journal of Tropical Geography* 14: 28–41.

Dene Cultural Institute. 1993. *Traditional Dene Environmental Knowledge: A Pilot Project Conducted in Ft. Good Hope and Colville Lake, NWT, 1989–1993*. Hay River, Northwest Territories: Dene Cultural Institute.

Denevan, W. M., J. M. Treacy, J. B. Alcorn, C. Padoch, J. Denslow, and S. F. Paitan. 1984. Indigenous agroforestry in the Peruvian Amazon: Bora Indian management of swidden fallows. *Interciencia* 9: 346–57.

Denniston, D. 1994. Defending the land with maps. *World Watch* 7(1): 27–31.

Denslow, J. S. 1987. Tropical rainforest gaps and tree species diversity. *Annual Review of Ecology and Systematics* 18: 431–51.

De Schlippe, P. 1956. *Shifting Cultivation in Africa: The Zande System of Agriculture*. London: Routledge Kegan Paul.

Diamond, J. 1966. Zoological classification system of a primitive people. *Science* 151: 1102–04.

Diamond, J. 1993. New Guineans and their natural world. In *The Biophilia Hypothesis* (S. R. Kellert and E. O. Wilson, eds.). Washington, D.C.: Island Press, 251–71.

Dickison, M. 1994. Maori science? *New Zealand Science Monthly* (May 1994): 6–7.

Dove, M. R. 1993. A revisionist view of tropical deforestation and development. *Environmental Conservation* 20: 17–24.

Drolet, C. A., A. Reed, M. Breton, and F. Berkes. 1987. Sharing wildlife management responsibilities with native groups: Case histories in Northern Quebec. *Transactions of the 52nd North American Wildlife and Natural Resources Conference*, 389–98.

Dubos, R. 1972. *A God Within*. New York: Scribner's.

Duerden, F., and R. G. Kuhn. 1998. Scale, context and the application of traditional knowledge of the Canadian North. *Polar Record* 34: 31–38.

Duffield, C., J. S. Gardner, F. Berkes, and R. B. Singh. 1998. Local knowledge in the assessment of resource sustainability: Case studies in Himachal Pradesh, India, and British Columbia, Canada. *Mountain Research and Development* 18: 35–49.

Dunbar, M. J. 1973. Stability and fragility in Arctic ecosystems. *Arctic* 26: 179–85.

Dwyer, P. D. 1994. Modern conservation and indigenous peoples: In search of wisdom. *Pacific Conservation Biology* 1: 91–97.

Dymond, J. R. 1933. Biological and oceanographic conditions in Hudson Bay. 8. The Coregonine fishes of Hudson and James bays. *Contributions to Canadian Biology and Fisheries* 8 (NS) No. 28: 1–12.

Dyson-Hudson, R., and E. A. Smith. 1978. Human territoriality: An ecological assessment. *American Anthropologist* 80: 21–41.

Ellen, R. 1993. Rhetoric, practice and incentive in the face of the changing times. In *Environmentalism: The View from Anthropology* (K. Milton, ed.). London and New York: Routledge, 126–43.

Elton, C. 1942. *Voles, Mice and Lemmings: Problems in Population Dynamics*. London: Oxford University Press.

Emery, A. R. 1997. *Guidelines for Environmental Assessment and Traditional Knowledge*. A Report from the Centre of Traditional Knowledge to the World Council of Indigenous People. Ottawa: Centre for Traditional Knowledge.

Engel, J. R., and J. G. Engel, editors. 1990. *Ethics of Environment and Development*. London: Belhaven.

Evans, P. H. G. 1986. Dominica multiple land use project. *Ambio* 15: 82–89.

Evernden, N. 1993. *The Natural Alien: Humankind and Environment*. 2d ed. Toronto: University of Toronto Press.

Fairhead, J., and M. Leach. 1996. Rethinking the forest-savanna mosaic. In *The Lie of the Land: Challenging Received Wisdom on the African Environment* (M. Leach and R. Mearns, eds.). London: The International African Institute, 105–21.

Fathy, H. 1986. *Natural Energy and Vernacular Architecture*. Chicago: University of Chicago Press.

Feeny, D., F. Berkes, B. J. McCay, and J. M. Acheson. 1990. The tragedy of the commons: Twenty-two years later. *Human Ecology* 18: 1–19.

Feit, H. A. 1973. Ethno-ecology of the Waswanipi Cree; or how hunters can manage their resources. In *Cultural Ecology* (B. Cox, ed.). Toronto: McClelland and Stewart, 115–25.

Feit, H. A. 1986. James Bay Cree Indian management and moral considerations of fur-bearers. In *Native People and Resource Management*. Edmonton: Alberta Society of Professional Zoologists, 49–65.

Feit, H. A. 1987. North American native hunting and management of moose populations. *Swedish Wildlife Research Vitlrevy Suppl.* 1: 25–42.

Feit, H. A. 1991. Gifts of the land: Hunting territories, guaranteed incomes and the construction of social relations in James Bay Cree society. *Senri Ethnological Studies* 30: 223–68.

Felt, L. F. 1994. Two tales of a fish: The social construction of indigenous knowledge among Atlantic Canadian salmon fishers. In *Folk Management in the World's Fisheries* (C. L. Dyer and J. R. McGoodwin, eds.). Niwot: University Press of Colorado, 251–86.

Fenge, T. 1997. Ecological change in the Hudson Bay bioregion: A traditional ecological knowledge perspective. *Northern Perspectives* 25(1): 2–3.

Feyerabend, P. 1987. *Farewell to Reason*. London: Verso.

Fienup-Riordan, A. 1990. *Eskimo Essays*. New Brunswick, N.J., and London: Rutgers University Press.

Finlay, J. A. 1995. Community-level sea use management in the Grenada beach seine fishery. Master's thesis, University of the West Indies, Cave Hill, Barbados.

Fox, J. 1998. Mapping the commons: The social context of spatial information technologies. *Common Property Resource Digest* 45: 1–4.

Francis, D., and T. Morantz. 1983. *Partners in Furs: A History of the Fur Trade in Eastern James Bay 1600–1870*. Montreal: McGill–Queens University Press.

Freeman, M. M. F. 1970. The birds of Belcher Islands, NWT, Canada. *The Canadian Field-Naturalist* 84: 277–90.

Freeman, M. M. R., editor. 1976. *Report of the Inuit Land Use and Occupancy Project*. 3 volumes. Ottawa: Department of Indian and Northern Affairs.

Freeman, M. M. R. 1984. Contemporary Inuit exploitation of the sea-ice environment. In *Sikumiut: "The People Who Use the Sea Ice."* Ottawa: Canadian Arctic Resources Committee, 73–96.

Freeman, M. M. R. 1989. Gaffs and graphs: A cautionary tale in the common property resource debate. In *Common Property Resources: Ecology and Community-Based Sustainable Development*. London: Belhaven, 92–109.

Freeman, M. M. R. 1992. The nature and utility of traditional ecological knowledge. *Northern Perspectives* 20(1): 9–12.

Freeman, M. M. R. 1993a. The International Whaling Commission, small type whaling, and coming to terms with subsistence. *Human Organization* 52: 243–51.

Freeman, M. M. R. 1993b. Traditional land users as a legitimate source of environmental expertise. In *Traditional Ecological Knowledge: Wisdom for Sustainable Development* (N. M. Williams and G. Baines, eds.). Canberra: Centre for Resource and Environmental Studies, Australian National University, 153–61.

Freeman, M. M. R., and L. N. Carbyn, editors. 1988. *Traditional Knowledge and Renewable Resource Management in Northern Regions*. Edmonton: Boreal Institute for Northern Studies, University of Alberta.

Freeman, M. M. R., Y. Matsuda, and K. Ruddle, editors. 1991. Adaptive Marine Resource Management Systems in the Pacific. Special Issue of *Resource Management and Optimization* 8(3/4): 127–245.

Friedman, J. 1992. Myth, history and political identity. *Cultural Anthropology* 7: 194–210.

Gadgil, M. 1987. Diversity: Cultural and biological. *Trends in Ecology and Evolution* 2: 369–73.

Gadgil M., and F. Berkes. 1991. Traditional resource management systems. *Resource Management and Optimization* 8: 127–41.

Gadgil, M., F. Berkes, and C. Folke. 1993. Indigenous knowledge for biodiversity conservation. *Ambio* 22: 151–56.

Gadgil, M., and R. Guha. 1992. *This Fissured Land: An Ecological History of India*. Delhi: Oxford University Press.

Gadgil, M., and R. Thapar. 1990. Human ecology in India: Some historical perspectives. *Interdisciplinary Science Reviews* 15: 209–23.

Gadgil, M., and V. D. Vartak. 1976. The sacred groves of the Western Ghats of India. *Economic Botany* 30: 152–60.

Galaty, J. G., and D. L. Johnson, editors. 1990. *The World of Pastoralism: Herding Systems in Comparative Perspective*. New York: Gildford Press.

George, P., and R. J. Preston. 1992. The TASO research program: Retrospect and prospect. *Anthropologica* 34: 51–70.

Giarelli, G. 1996. Broadening the debate: The Tharaka participatory action research project. *Indigenous Knowledge and Development Monitor* 4(2): 19–22.

Glacken, C. 1967. *Traces on the Rhodian Shore: Nature and Culture in Western Thought from Ancient Times to the End of the Eighteenth Century*. Berkeley: University of California Press.

Gomes, C., R. Mahon, W. Hunte, and S. Singh-Renton. 1998. The role of drifting objects in pelagic fisheries in the southeastern Caribbean. *Fisheries Research* 34: 47–58.

Gómez-Pompa, A., and A. Kaus. 1992a. Taming the wilderness myth. *BioScience* 42: 271–79.

Gómez-Pompa, A., and A. Kaus. 1992b. Letters. *BioScience* 42: 580–81.

González, N., F. Herrera, and M. Chapin. 1995. Ethnocartography in the Darién. *Cultural Survival Quarterly* (winter 1995): 31–33.

Gottesfeld, L. M. J. 1994. Conservation, territory and traditional beliefs: An analysis of Gitksan and Wet'suwet'en subsistence, northwest British Columbia. *Human Ecology* 22: 443–65.

Gould, S. J. 1980. *The Panda's Thumb*. New York and London: Norton.

Grenier, L. 1998. *Working with Indigenous Knowledge: A Guide for Researchers*. Ottawa: International Development Research Centre.

Greenberg, J. B., and T. K. Park. 1994. Political ecology. *Journal of Political Ecology* 1: 1–12.

Groenfelt, D. 1991. Building on tradition: Indigenous irrigation knowledge and sustainable development in Asia. *Agriculture and Human Values* 8: 114–20.

Gulland, J. A. 1974. *The Management of Marine Fisheries*. Bristol: Scientechnica.

Gunderson L. H., C. S. Holling, and S. S. Light, editors. 1995. *Barriers and Bridges to the Renewal of Ecosystems and Institutions*. New York: Columbia University Press.

Hardesty, D. L. 1977. *Ecological Anthropology*. New York: Wiley.

Harland, D. 1993. Letters. *Time* June 14.

Healey, C. 1993. The significance and application of TEK. In *Traditional Ecological Knowledge: Wisdom for Sustainable Development* (N. M. Williams and G. Baines, eds.). Canberra: Centre for Resource and Environmental Studies, Australian National University, 21–26.

Healey, M. C. 1975. Dynamics of exploited whitefish populations and their management with special reference to the Northwest Territories. *Journal of the Fisheries Research Board of Canada* 32: 427–48.

Heffley, S. 1981. The relationship between North Athapaskan settlement patterns and resource distribution. In *Hunter-Gatherer Foraging Strategies, Ethnographic and Archeological Analyses* (B. Winterhalder and E. A. Smith, eds.). Chicago: University of Chicago Press, 126–47.

Heywood, V. H., exec. editor. 1995. *Global Biodiversity Assessment*. Cambridge, U.K.: United Nations Environmental Program and Cambridge University Press.

Hjort af Ornas, A. 1992. Cultural variation in concepts of nature. *GeoJournal* 26: 167–72.

Holling, C. S. 1973. Resilience and stability of ecological systems. *Annual Review of Ecology and Systematics* 4: 1–23.

Holling, C. S., editor. 1978. *Adaptive Environmental Assessment and Management*. London: Wiley.

Holling, C. S. 1986. The resilience of terrestrial ecosystems: local surprise and global change. In *Sustainable Development of the Biosphere* (W. C. Clark and R. E. Munn, eds.). Cambridge: Cambridge University Press, 292–317.

Holling, C. S., F. Berkes, and C. Folke. 1998. Science, sustainability and resource management. In *Linking Social and Ecological Systems: Management Practices and Social Mechanisms for Building Resilience* (F. Berkes and C. Folke, eds.). Cambridge: Cambridge University Press, 342–62.

Holling, C. S., D. W. Schindler, B. W. Walker, and J. Roughgarden. 1995. Biodiversity in the functioning of ecosystems: An ecological synthesis. In *Biodiversity Loss* (C. Perrings, K.-G. Maler, C. Folke, C. S. Holling, and B.-O. Jansson, eds.). Cambridge: Cambridge University Press, 44–83.

Holmes, L. 1996. Elders' knowledge and the ancestry of experience in Hawai'i. Ph.D. dissertation, University of Toronto.

Howard, A., and F. Widdowson. 1996. Traditional knowledge threatens environmental assessment. *Policy Options* (November 1996): 34–36.

Hudson, B. 1997. A socio-economic study of community-based management of mangrove resources of St. Lucia. Master's thesis, University of Manitoba, Winnipeg.

Hughes, J. D. 1983. *American Indian Ecology*. El Paso: University of Texas Press.

Hunn, E. 1993a. What is traditional ecological knowledge? In *Traditional Ecological Knowledge: Wisdom for Sustainable Development* (N. M. Williams and G. Baines, eds.). Canberra: Centre for Resource and Environmental Studies, Australian National University, 13–15.

Hunn, E. 1993b. The ethnobiological foundation for TEK. In *Traditional Ecological Knowledge: Wisdom for Sustainable Development* (N. M. Williams and G. Baines, eds.). Canberra: Centre for Resource and Environmental Studies, Australian National University, 16–20.

Hunt, C. 1997. Cooperative approaches to marine resource management in the South Pacific. In *The Governance of Common Property in the Pacific Region* (P. Larmour, ed.). Canberra: Australian National University, 145–64.

Hutchings, J. 1998. Discarding, catch rates and fishing effort in Newfoundland's inshore and offshore cod fisheries: Analytical strengths and weaknesses of interview-based data. Workshop on Bringing Fishers' Knowledge into Fisheries Science and Management, May 1998, St. John's, Newfoundland.

Hviding, E. 1990. Keeping the sea: Aspects of marine tenure in Marovo Lagoon, Solomon Islands. In *Traditional Marine Resource Management in the Pacific Basin: An Anthology* (K. Ruddle and R. E. Johannes, eds.). Jakarta: UNESCO/ROSTSEA.

Inuit Circumpolar Conference. 1992. Development of a program for the collection and application of indigenous knowledge. Presented at the United Nations Conference on Environment and Development (UNCED), Rio de Janeiro.

Irvine, D. 1989. Succession management and resource distribution in an Amazonian rain forest. In *Resource Management in Amazonia: Indigenous and Folk Strategies* (D. A. Posey and W. L. Balee, eds.). New York: New York Botanical Garden, 223–37.

IUCN (International Conservation Union). 1986. *Tradition, Conservation and Development*. Occasional Newsletter of the Commission on Ecology's Working Group on Traditional Ecological Knowledge. No. 4.

IUCN/UNEP/WWF. 1991. *Caring for the Earth: A Strategy for Sustainable Living*. Gland, Switzerland: International Conservation Union.

Jackson, L. 1986. World's greatest caribou herd mired in Quebec-Labrador boundary dispute. *Canadian Geographic* 105(3): 25–33.

Jantsch, E. 1972. *Technological Planning and Social Futures*. London: Casell.

Janzen, D. 1986. The future of tropical ecology. *Annual Review of Ecology and Systematics* 17: 305–06.

Johannes, R. E. 1978. Traditional marine conservation methods in Oceania and their demise. *Annual Review of Ecology and Systematics* 9: 349–64.

Johannes, R. E. 1981. *Words of the Lagoon: Fishing and Marine Lore in the Palau District of Micronesia*. Berkeley: University of California Press.

Johannes, R. E., editor. 1989. *Traditional Ecological Knowledge: A Collection of Essays*. Gland, Switzerland: International Conservation Union (IUCN).

Johannes, R. E. 1994. Pacific island peoples' science and marine resource management. In *Science of the Pacific Island Peoples* (J. Morrison, P. Geraghty, and L. Crowl, eds.). Suva, Fiji: Institute of Pacific Studies, University of the South Pacific, 81–89.

Johannes, R. E. 1998. The case for data-less marine resource management: Examples from tropical nearshore fisheries. *Trends in Ecology and Evolution* 13: 243–46.

Johannes, R. E., P. Lasserre, S. W. Nixon, J. Pliya, and K. Ruddle. 1983. Traditional knowledge and management of marine coastal systems. *Biology International*, Special Issue 4.

Johannes, R. E., and H. T. Lewis. 1993. The importance of researchers' expertise in environmental subjects. In *Traditional Ecological Knowledge: Wisdom for Sustainable Development* (N. M. Williams and G. Baines, eds.). Canberra: Centre for Resource and Environmental Studies, Australian National University, 104–08.

Johannes, R. E., and W. MacFarlane. 1991. *Traditional Fishing in the Torres Strait Islands*. Hobart: Commonwealth Scientific and Industrial Research Organization.

Johnson, L. 1976. Ecology of Arctic populations of lake trout, *Salvelinus namaycush*, lake whitefish, *Coregonus clupeaformis*, Arctic char, *S. alpinus*, and associated species in unexploited lakes of the Canadian Northwest Territories. *Journal of the Fisheries Research Board of Canada* 33: 2459–88.

Johnson, M., editor. 1992. *Lore: Capturing Traditional Environmental Knowledge*. Ottawa: Dene Cultural Institute/International Development Research Centre.

Juniper, I. 1979. Problems in managing an irrupting caribou herd. *Proceedings of the Second International Caribou Symposium*, Roros, Norway, 722–24.

Kalit, K., and E. Young. 1997. Common property conflict and resolution: Aboriginal Australia and Papua New Guinea. In *The Governance of Common Property in the Pacific Region* (P. Larmour, ed.). Canberra: Australian National University, 183–208.

Kalland, A. 1994. Indigenous knowledge—local knowledge: Prospects and limitations. In *Arctic Environment: A Report on the Seminar on Integration of Indigenous Peoples' Knowledge*. Copenhagen: Ministry of the Environment/The Home Rule of Greenland, 150–67.

Keesing, R. M. 1989. Creating the past: Custom and identity in the contemporary Pacific. *Contemporary Pacific* 1: 19–42.

Keith, R. F., and M. Simon. 1987. Sustainable development in the northern circumpolar world. In *Conservation with Equity* (P. Jacobs and D. A. Munro, eds.). Cambridge: International Union for the Conservation of Nature and Natural Resources, 209–25.

Kellert, S. R. 1997. *Kinship to Mastery: Biophilia in Human Evolution and Development*. Washington, D.C.: Island Press.

Kellert, S. R. and E. O. Wilson, editors. 1993. *The Biophilia Hypothesis*. Washington, D.C.: Island Press.

Klee, G., editor. 1980. *World Systems of Traditional Resource Management*. London: Edward Arnold.

Klein, D. R. 1994. Wilderness: A Western concept alien to Arctic cultures. *Arctic Institute of North America, Information North* 20(3): 1–6.

Knudtson, P., and D. Suzuki. 1992. *Wisdom of the Elders*. Toronto: Stoddart.

Kofinas, G. P. 1998. The costs of power sharing: Community involvement in Canadian porcupine caribou co-management. Ph.D. thesis, University of British Columbia, Vancouver. (For caribou information partnership, "knowledge co-op," see URL:http://www.taiga.net)

Kothari, A. 1996. India's protected areas: The journey to joint management. *World Conservation* 2(96): 8–9.

Kuchli, C. 1996. Tanzania: A second Garden of Eden. *People and the Planet* 5(4): 20–21.

Kuhn, T. S. 1970. *The Structure of Scientific Revolutions*. 2d ed. Chicago: University of Chicago Press.

Lansing, J. S. 1987. Balinese water temples and the management of irrigation. *American Anthropologist* 89: 326–41.

Lansing, J. S. 1991. *Priests and Programmers*. Princeton: Princeton University Press.

Leach, M. 1994. *Rainforest Relations: Gender and Resource Use Among the Mende of Gola, Sierra Leone*. Edinburgh: Edinburgh University Press.

Leach, M., and R. Mearns, editors. 1996. *The Lie of the Land: Challenging Received Wisdom on the African Environment*. London: The International African Institute.

Leacock, E. B. 1954. The Montagnais "hunting territory" and the fur trade. Menasha, WI: American Anthropological Association, Memoir No. 78.

Lee, K. N. 1993. *Compass and Gyroscope: Integrating Science and Politics for the Environment.* Washington, D.C.: Island Press.

Lee, R. B., and I. Devore, editors. 1968. *Man the Hunter.* Chicago: Aldine.

Legat, A., editor. 1991. Report of the Traditional Knowledge Working Group. Yellowknife: Department of Culture and Communications, Government of the Northwest Territories.

Legat, A., S. A. Zoe, and M. Chocolate. 1995. The importance of knowing. In *NWT Diamonds Project Environmental Impact Statement.* Volume 1, Appendices. Vancouver: BHP Diamonds Inc.

Leopold, A. 1949. *A Sand County Almanac.* Reprinted 1966. Oxford: Oxford University Press.

Lévi-Strauss, C. 1962. *La pensee sauvage.* Paris: Librarie Plon. (English translation, *The Savage Mind,* Chicago: University of Chicago Press, 1966.)

Lewis, H. T. 1973. *Patterns of Indian Burning in California: Ecology and Ethnohistory.* Ramona, CA: Ballena Press.

Lewis, H. T. 1989. Ecological and technological knowledge of fire: Aborigines versus park managers in northern Australia. *American Anthropologist* 91: 940–61.

Lewis, H. T. 1993a. Traditional ecological knowledge: Some definitions. In *Traditional Ecological Knowledge: Wisdom for Sustainable Development* (N. M. Williams and G. Baines, eds.). Canberra: Centre for Resource and Environmental Studies, Australian National University, 8–12.

Lewis, H. T. 1993b. In retrospect. In *Before the Wilderness: Environmental Management by Native Californians* (T. C. Blackburn and K. Anderson, eds.). Menlo Park: Ballena Press, 389–400.

Lewis, H. T., and T. A. Ferguson. 1988. Yards, corridors and mosaics: How to burn a boreal forest. *Human Ecology* 16: 57–77.

Lind, A. W. 1938. *An Island Community: Ecological Succession in Hawaii.* Chicago: University of Chicago Press.

Linden, E. 1991. Lost tribes, lost knowledge. *Time* 138(12): 44–56 (Sept. 23).

Linnekin, J. 1983. Defining tradition: Variations on the Hawaiian identity. *American Ethnologist* 10: 241–52.

Long, N., and A. Long. 1992. *Battlefields of Knowledge.* London: Routledge.

Lovelock, J. E. 1979. *Gaia: A New Look at Life on Earth.* London and New York: Oxford University Press.

Ludwig, N. A. 1994. An Ainu homeland: An alternative solution for the Northern Territories/Southern Kuriles imbroglio. *Ocean and Coastal Management* 25: 1–29.

Lugo, A. 1995. Management of tropical biodiversity. *Ecological Applications* 5: 956–61.

Maass, A., and R. L. Anderson. 1986. *. . . and the Desert Shall Rejoice; Conflict, Growth, and Justice in Arid Environments.* Malabar, FL: Krieger.

Mabry, J. B., editor. 1996. *Canals and Communities: Small-Scale Irrigation Systems.* Tucson: University of Arizona Press.

Mackenzie, F. 1998. "Where do you belong to?" Land and the construction of community in the Isle of Harris, Outer Hebrides, Scotland. Crossing Boundaries: 7th Conference of the International Association for the Study of Common Property, June 1998, Vancouver, British Columbia.

Majnep, I., and R. Bulmer. 1977. *Birds of My Kalam Country.* London: Oxford University Press.

Malmberg, T. 1980. *Human Territoriality.* The Hague: Mouton.

Manseau, M., editor. 1998. *Traditional and Western Scientific Environmental Knowledge.* Workshop Proceedings. Goosebay, Labrador: Institute for Environmental Monitoring and Research.

Martin, G. 1993. Dius Tadong: Ancestral ecology. *UNESCO Sources* 50: 5.

Martin, L. 1986. "Eskimo words for snow": A case study in the genesis and decay of an anthropological example. *American Anthropologist* 88: 418–33.

Martin, P. S. 1973. The discovery of America. *Science* 179: 969–74.

Martin, P. S., and R. G. Klein, editors. 1984. *Quaternary Extinctions.* Tucson: University of Arizona Press.

Mathew, S. 1991. Study of territorial use rights in small-scale fisheries: Traditional systems of fisheries management in Pulicat Lake, Tamil Nadu, India. Rome: FAO Fisheries Circular No. 890.

Mathias-Mundy, E., and C. M. McCorkle. 1995. Ethnoveterinary medicine and development—A review of the literature. In *The Cultural Dimension of Development* (D. M. Warren, L. J. Slikkerveer, and D. Brokensha, eds.). London: Intermediate Technology Publications.

Mayr, E. 1963. *Animal Species and Evolution*. Cambridge: Belknap Press of Harvard University Press.

Mbanefo, S. 1992. Medicine men. *World Wide Fund for Nature, WWF News* 76: 11–12.

McCay, B. J., and J. M. Acheson, editors. 1987. *The Question of the Commons: The Culture and Ecology of Communal Resources*. Tucson: University of Arizona Press.

McClanahan, T. R., H. Glaesel, J. Rubens, and R. Kiambo. 1997. The effects of traditional fisheries management on fisheries yields and the coral-reef ecosystems of southern Kenya. *Environmental Conservation* 24: 105–20.

McDonald, M. 1988. An overview of adaptive management of renewable resources. In *Traditional Knowledge and Renewable Resource Management in Northern Regions* (M. M. R. Freeman and L. N. Carbyn, eds.). Edmonton: Boreal Institute, University of Alberta, 65–71.

McDonald, M., L. Arragutainaq, and Z. Novalinga, compilers. 1997. *Voices from the Bay: Traditional Ecological Knowledge of Inuit and Cree in the Hudson Bay Bioregion*. Ottawa: Canadian Arctic Resources Committee and municipality of Sanikiluaq.

McGovern, H., G. F. Bigelow, T. Amorosi, and D. Russell. 1988. Northern islands, human error and environmental degradation. *Human Ecology* 16: 225–70.

McHarg, I. L. 1969. *Design with Nature*. Garden City, N.Y.: Doubleday/Natural History Press.

McNeely, J. A. 1994. Lessons from the past: Forests and biodiversity. *Biodiversity and Conservation* 3: 3–20.

McNeely, J. A. 1996. Conservation—the social science? *World Conservation* 2(96): 2.

McNeely, J. A., and D. Pitt, editors. 1985. *Culture and Conservation*. London: Croom Helm.

Messier, F., J. Huot, D. Le Henaff, and S. Luttich. 1988. Demography of the George River caribou herd: Evidence of population regulation by forage exploitation and range expansion. *Arctic* 41: 279–87.

Moorehead, R. 1989. Changes taking place in common-property resource management in the Inland Niger Delta of Mali. In *Common Property Resources* (F. Berkes, ed.). London: Belhaven, 256–72.

Morauta, L., J. Pernetta, and W. Heaney, editors. 1982. *Traditional Conservation in Papua New Guinea: Implications for Today*. Port Moresby, Papua New Guinea: Institute for Applied Social and Economic Research.

Morseth, C. M. 1997. Twentieth-century changes in beluga whale hunting and butchering by the Kanigmiut of Buckland, Alaska. *Arctic* 50: 241–55.

Munsterhjelm, E. 1953. *The Wind and the Caribou*. New York: Macmillan.

Murphy, G. I. 1968. Pattern of life history and the environment. *American Naturalist* 102: 391–403.

Murray, S. O. 1982. The dissolution of classical ethnoscience. *Journal of the History of Behavioral Sciences* 18: 163–75.

Nabhan, G. P. 1985. *Gathering the Desert*. Tucson: University of Arizona Press.

Naess, A. 1989. *Ecology, Community and Lifestyle: Outline of an Ecosophy*. Translated and edited by D. Rothenberg. Cambridge: Cambridge University Press.

Nakashima, D. J. 1991. The ecological knowledge of Belcher Island Inuit: A traditional basis for contemporary wildlife co-management. Ph.D. thesis, McGill University, Montreal.

Nakashima, D. J. 1993. Astute observers on the sea ice: Inuit knowledge as a basis for Arctic co-management. In *Traditional Ecological Knowledge: Concepts and Cases* (J. T. Inglis, ed.). Ottawa: Canadian Museum of Nature/International Development Research Centre, 99–110.

Nakashima, D. J. 1998. Conceptualizing nature: The cultural context of resource management. *Nature and Resources* 34(2): 8–22.

Neihardt, J. G. 1932. *Black Elk Speaks*. Lincoln and London: University of Nebraska Press.

Neis, B. 1992. Fishers' ecological knowledge and stock assessment in Newfoundland. *Newfoundland Studies* 8: 155–78.

Neis, B., L. Felt, D. C. Schneider, R. Haedrich, J. Hutchings, and J. Fischer. 1996. Northern cod stock assessment: What can be learned from interviewing resource users? Department of Fisheries and Oceans, Atlantic Fisheries Research Document No. 96/45.

Nelson, R. K. 1969. *Hunters of the Northern Ice*. Chicago: University of Chicago Press.

Nelson, R. K. 1982. A conservation ethic and environment: The Koyukon of Alaska. In *Resource Managers: North American and Australian Hunter-Gatherers* (N. M. Williams and E. S. Hunn, eds.). Washington, D.C.: American Association for the Advancement of Science, 211–28.

Nelson, R. 1993. Searching for the lost arrow: Physical and spiritual ecology in the hunter's world. In *The Biophilia Hypothesis* (S. R. Kellert and E. O. Wilson, eds.). Washington, D.C.: Island Press, 201–28.

Netting, R. M. 1981. *Balancing on an Alp: Ecological Change and Continuity in a Swiss Mountain Community*. Cambridge: Cambridge University Press.

Netting, R. M. 1986. *Cultural Ecology*. 2d ed. Prospect Heights, IL: Waveland Press.

Newsome, A. 1980. The eco-mythology of the Red Kangaroo in Central Australia. *Mankind* 12: 327–34.

Niamir, M. 1990. Herders' decision-making in natural resources management in arid and semi-arid Africa. Rome: FAO Community Forestry Note No. 4.

Niamir-Fuller, M. 1998. The resilience of pastoral herding in Sahelian Africa. In *Linking Social and Ecological Systems: Management Practices and Social Mechanisms for Building Resilience* (F. Berkes and C. Folke, eds.). Cambridge: Cambridge University Press, 250–84.

Norgaard, R. B. 1994. *Development Betrayed: The End of Progress and a Coevolutionary Revisioning of the Future*. London and New York: Routledge.

Norton, B. 1991. *Toward Unity Among Environmentalists*. New Haven: Yale University Press.

Odum, E. P. 1971. *Fundamentals of Ecology*. 3d ed. Philadelphia: Saunders.

Ohmagari, K., and F. Berkes. 1997. Transmission of indigenous knowledge and bush skills among the Western James Bay Cree women of subarctic Canada. *Human Ecology* 25: 197–222.

Oldfield, M. L., and J. B. Alcorn, editors. 1991. *Biodiversity: Culture, Conservation and Ecodevelopment*. Boulder, CO: Westview Press.

Ontario Ministry of Natural Resources. 1994. *A Proposal for an Environmental Information Partnership in the Moose River Basin*. Kapuskasing, Ontario: Moose River Basin Project.

Orlove, B. S., and S. B. Brush. 1996. Anthropology and the conservation of biodiversity. *Annual Reviews of Anthropology* 25: 329–52.

Ostrom, E. 1990. *Governing the Commons: The Evolution of Institutions for Collective Action*. Cambridge: Cambridge University Press.

Owen-Smith, N. 1987. Pleistocene extinctions: The pivotal role of megaherbivores. *Paleobiology* 13: 351–62.

Palsson, G. 1982. Territoriality among Icelandic fishermen. *Acta Sociologica* 25(supplement): 5–12.

Pawluk, R. R., J. A. Sandor, and J. A. Tabor. 1992. The role of indigenous soil knowledge in agricultural development. *Journal of Soil and Water Conservation* 47: 298–302.

Pearce, F. 1993. Living in harmony with forests. *New Scientist* 23 (September 11–12).

Pepper, D. M. 1984. *The Roots of Modern Environmentalism*. London: Croom Helm.

Pimbert, M. P., and B. Gujja. 1997. Village voices challenging wetland management policies. *Nature and Resources* 33: 34–42.

Pimbert, M. P., and J. N. Pretty. 1995. Parks, people and professionals. Geneva: United Nations Research Institute for Social Development (UNRISD) Discussion Paper No. 57.

Poffenberger, M., B. McGean, and A. Khare. 1996. Communities sustaining India's forests in the twenty-first century. In *Village Voices, Forest Choices* (M. Poffenberger and B. McGean, eds.). Delhi: Oxford University Press, 17–55.

Polanyi, K. 1964. *The Great Transformation*. (Original edition, 1944.) Boston: Beacon Press.

Polunin, N. V. C. 1984. Do traditional marine "reserves" conserve? A view of Indonesian and New Guinean evidence. *Senri Ethnological Studies* 17: 267–83.

Posey, D. A. 1985. Indigenous management of tropical forest ecosystems: The case of the Kayapo Indians of the Brazilian Amazon. *Agroforestry Systems* 3: 139–58.

Posey, D. A., and W. L. Balee, editors. 1989. *Resource Management in Amazonia: Indigenous and Folk Strategies*. New York: New York Botanical Garden.

Posey, D. A., and G. Dutfield. 1996. *Beyond Intellectual Property: Toward Traditional Resource Rights for Indigenous Peoples and Local Communities*. Ottawa: International Development Research Centre.

Posey, D. A., and G. Dutfield, principal writers. 1997. *Indigenous Peoples and Sustainability: Cases and Actions*. Utrecht: International Books/IUCN (International Conservation Union).

Power, G. 1978. Fish population structure in Arctic lakes. *Journal of the Fisheries Research Board of Canada* 35: 53–59.

Preston, R. J. 1975. *Cree Narrative: Expressing the Personal Meanings of Events*. Ottawa: National Museum of Man Mercury Series, Canadian Ethnology Service Paper No. 30. National Museum of Canada.

Preston, R. J. 1979. The development and self control in the eastern Cree life cycle. In *Childhood and Adolescence in Canada* (K. Ishwaran, ed.). Toronto: McGraw-Hill, 83–96.

Preston, R. J., F. Berkes, and P. J. George. 1995. Perspectives on sustainable development in the Moose River Basin. *Papers of the 26th Algonquian Conference*: 378–93.

Pruitt, W. O. 1960. Animals in the snow. *Scientific American* 202(1): 60–68.

Pruitt, W. O. 1978. *Boreal Ecology*. London: Edward Arnold.

Pruitt, W. O. 1984. Snow and living things. In *Northern Ecology and Resource Management* (R. Olson, F. Geddes, and R. Hastings, eds.). Edmonton: University of Alberta Press, 51–77.

Pullum, G. 1991. *The Eskimo Vocabulary Hoax and Other Irreverant Essays on the Study of Language*. Chicago: University of Chicago Press.

Putney, A. D. 1989. Getting the balance right. *World Wildlife Fund Reports* (June/July): 19–21.

Ramakrishnan, P. S. 1992. *Shifting Agriculture and Sustainable Development: An Interdisciplinary Study from North-Eastern India*. Paris: UNESCO/Parthenon.

Ramos, A. 1994. From Eden to limbo: The construction of indigenism in Brazil. In *Social Construction of the Past: Representation as Power* (G. C. Bond and A. Gillam, eds.). London: Routledge, 74–88.

Rappaport, R. A. 1979. *Ecology, Meaning and Religion*. Richmond, CA: North Atlantic Books.

Rappaport, R. A. 1984. *Pigs for the Ancestors: Ritual in the Ecology of a New Guinea People*. 2d ed. New Haven and London: Yale University Press.

Ravuvu, A. D. 1987. *The Fijian Ethos*. Suva, Fiji: Institute of Pacific Studies, University of the South Pacific.

Ray, A. J. 1975. Some conservation schemes of the Hudson's Bay Company, 1821–50. *Journal of Historical Geography* 1: 49–68.

Redford, K. H. 1992. The empty forest. *BioScience* 42: 412–22.

Redford, K. H., and J. A. Mansour, editors. 1996. *Traditional Peoples and Biodiversity Conservation in Large Tropical Landscapes*. Arlington: America Verde/The Nature Conservancy.

Redford, K. H., and C. Padoch, editors. 1992. *Conservation of Neotropical Forests: Working from Traditional Resource Use*. New York: Columbia University Press.

Redford, K. H., and A. M. Stearman. 1993. Forest-dwelling native Amazonians and the conservation of biodiversity. *Conservation Biology* 7: 248–55.

Regier, H. A. 1978. *A Balanced Science of Renewable Resources with Particular Reference to Fisheries*. Seattle and London: Washington Sea Grant/University of Washington Press.

Regier, H. A., and G. L. Baskerville. 1986. Sustainable redevelopment of regional ecosystems degraded by exploitive development. In *Sustainable Development of the Biosphere* (W. C. Clark and R. E. Munn, eds.). Cambridge: Cambridge University Press, 75–103.

Reichel-Dolmatoff, G. 1976. Cosmology as ecological analysis: A view from the rain forest. *Man* 11(NS): 307–18.

Reid, R. S., and J. E. Ellis. 1995. Impacts of pastoralists in South Turkana, Kenya: Livestock-mediated tree recruitment. *Ecological Applications* 5: 978–92.

Reij, C., I. Scoones, and C. Toulmin, editors. 1996. *Sustaining the Soil: Indigenous Soil and Water Conservation in Africa*. London: Earthscan.

Renard, Y. 1994. *Community Participation in St. Lucia*. Washington, D.C.: Panos Institute, and Vieux Fort, St. Lucia: Caribbean Natural Resources Institute.

Richards, P. 1985. *Indigenous Agricultural Revolution: Ecology and Food Production in West Africa*. London: Hutchinson.

Richardson, A. 1982. The control of productive resources on the Northwest coast of North America. In *Resource Managers: North American and Australian Hunter-Gatherers* (N. M. Williams and E. S. Hunn, eds.). Washington, D.C.: American Association for the Advancement of Science, 93–112.

Riewe, R. 1991. Inuit use of the sea ice. *Arctic and Alpine Research* 23: 3–10.

Riewe, R., editor. 1992. *Nunavut Atlas*. Edmonton: Canadian Circumpolar Institute and the Tungavik Federation of Nunavut.

Roberts, M., W. Norman, N. Minhinnick, D. Wihongi, and C. Kirkwood. 1995. *Kaitiakitanga*: Maori perspectives on conservation. *Pacific Conservation Biology* 2: 7–20.

Rocheleau, D. E. 1991. Gender, ecology, and the science of survival: Stories and lessons from Kenya. *Agriculture and Human Values* 8: 156–65.

Roszak, T. 1972. *Where the Wasteland Ends*. Garden City, N.Y.: Doubleday.

Ruddle, K. 1994a. Local knowledge in the folk management of fisheries and coastal marine environments. In *Folk Management in the World's Fisheries: Lessons for Modern Fisheries Management* (C. L. Dyer and J. R. McGoodwin, eds.). Niwot: University Press of Colorado, 161–206.

Ruddle, K. 1994b. A guide to the literature on traditional community-based fishery management in the Asia-Pacific tropics. Rome: FAO Fisheries Circular No. 869.

Ruddle, K., and T. Akimichi, editors. 1984. *Maritime Institutions in the Western Pacific*. Osaka: National Museum of Ethnology, Senri Ethnological Studies 17.

Ruddle, K., E. Hviding, and R. E. Johannes. 1992. Marine resources management in the context of customary tenure. *Marine Resource Economics* 7: 249–73.

Ruddle, K., and R. E. Johannes, editors. 1985. *The Traditional Knowledge and Management of Coastal Systems in Asia and the Pacific*. Jakarta: UNESCO.

Ruddle, K., and R. E. Johannes, editors. 1990. *Traditional Marine Resource Management in the Pacific Basin: An Anthology*. Jakarta: UNESCO.

Sadler, B., and P. Boothroyd, editors. 1994. *Traditional Ecological Knowledge and Modern Environmental Assessment*. Vancouver: Centre for Human Settlements, University of British Columbia.

Said, E. 1994. *Culture and Imperialism*. New York: Vintage.

Sanford, R. L., J. Saldarriga, K. E. Clark, C. Uhl, and R. Herrera. 1985. Amazon rainforest fires. *Science* 227: 53–55.

Schultes, R. E. 1989. Reasons for ethnobotanical conservation. In *Traditional Ecological Knowledge: A Collection of Essays* (R. E. Johannes, ed.). Gland, Switzerland: International Conservation Union (IUCN).

Schultes, R. E., and S. Reis, editors. 1995. *Ethnobotany: Evolution of a Discipline*. Portland, OR: Timber Press.

Scott, C. 1986. Hunting territories, hunting bosses and communal production among coastal James Bay Cree. *Anthropologica* 28: 163–73.

Scott, C. 1989. Knowledge construction among Cree hunters: Metaphors and literal understanding. *Journal de la Société des Américanistes* 75: 193–208.

Shepard, P. 1973. *The Tender Carnivore and the Sacred Game*. New York: Scribner's.

Shipek, F. 1993. Kumeeyay plant husbandry: Fire, water, and erosion management systems. In *Before the Wilderness: Environmental Management by Native Californians* (T. C. Blackburn and K. Anderson, eds.). Menlo Park: Ballena Press, 379–88.

Shiva, V. 1988. *Staying Alive: Women, Ecology and Development*. London: Zed Press.

Shiva, V., and R. Holla-Bhar. 1993. Intellectual piracy and the neem tree. *The Ecologist* 23(6).

Sirait, M., S. Pasodjo, N. Podger, A. Flavelle, and J. Fox. 1994. Mapping customary land in East Kalimantan, Indonesia: A tool for forest management. *Ambio* 23: 411–17.

Siu, R. G. H. 1957. *The Tao of Science: An Essay on Western Knowledge and Eastern Wisdom.* Cambridge: MIT Press.

Skolimowski, H. 1981. *Eco-Philosophy.* London: Boyars.

Slobodkin, L. B. 1968. How to be a predator. *American Zoologist* 8: 43–51.

Smith, A. H., and F. Berkes. 1991. Solutions to the "tragedy of the commons": Sea-urchin management in St. Lucia, West Indies. *Environmental Conservation* 18: 131–36.

Smith, A. H., and F. Berkes. 1993. Community-based use of mangrove resources in St. Lucia. *International Journal of Environmental Studies* 43: 123–31.

Smith, A. H., A. Jean, and K. Nichols. 1986. An investigation of the potential for the commercial mariculture of seamoss (*Gracilaria* spp. Rhodophycophyta) in St. Lucia. *Proceedings of the Gulf and Caribbean Fisheries Institute* 37: 4–11.

Smith, J. G. E. 1978. Economic uncertainty in an "original affluent society": Caribou and caribou-eater Chipewyan adaptive strategies. *Arctic Anthropology* 15: 68–88.

Speck, F. G. 1915. The family hunting band as the basis of Algonkian social organization. *American Anthropologist* 17: 289–305.

Speck, F. G. 1935. *Naskapi: Savage Hunters of the Labrador Peninsula.* Norman: University of Oklahoma Press.

Spencer, J. E. 1966. *Shifting Cultivation in Southeast Asia.* Berkeley and Los Angeles: University of California Press.

Steadman, D. W. 1995. Prehistoric extinctions of Pacific island birds: Biodiversity meets zooarcheology. *Science* 267: 1123–31.

Stevenson, M. G. 1996. Indigenous knowledge in environmental assessment. *Arctic* 49: 278–91.

Steward, J. H. 1936. The economic and social basis of primitive bands. In *Essays in Anthropology Presented to A. L. Kroeber.* Berkeley: University of California Press, 331–50.

Steward, J. H. 1955. *Theory of Culture Change.* Urbana: University of Illinois Press.

Stoffle, R. W., D. B. Halmo, M. J. Evans, and J. E. Olmstead. Calculating the cultural significance of American Indian plants: Paiute and Shoshone ethnobotany at Yucca Mountain, Nevada. *American Anthropologist* 92: 416–32.

Strauss, S. 1992. Historical record be damned, they sell environmentalism by co-opting Chief Seattle. *Globe and Mail,* Toronto, February 8, 1992.

Sturtevant, W. C. 1964. Studies in ethnoscience. *American Anthropologist* 66: 99–131.

Sutton, I. 1975. *Indian Land Tenure.* New York: Clearwater.

Sutton, P. 1995. *Country: Aboriginal Boundaries and Land Ownership in Australia.* Canberra: Australian National University, Aboriginal History Monograph 3.

Suzuki, D., and A. McConnell. 1997. *The Sacred Balance: Rediscovering Our Place in Nature.* Vancouver: Greystone.

Swezey, S. L., and R. F. Heizer. 1993. Ritual management of salmonid fish resources in California. In *Before the Wilderness: Environmental Management by Native Californians* (T. C. Blackburn and K. Anderson, eds.). Menlo Park: Ballena Press, 299–327. (Originally published in *Journal of California Anthropology* 4: 6–29, 1977.)

Taiepa, T., P. Lyver, P. Horsley, J. Davis, M. Bragg, and H. Moller. 1997. Co-management of New Zealand's conservation estate by Maori and Pakeha: A review. *Environmental Conservation* 24: 236–50.

Tanner, A. 1979. *Bringing Home Animals: Religious Ideology and Mode of Production of the Mistassini Cree Hunter.* London: Hurst.

Taylor, R. I. 1988. Deforestation and Indians in the Brazilian Amazonia. In *Biodiversity* (E. O. Wilson, ed.). Washington, D.C.: National Academy Press, 138–44.

Toledo, V. M. 1992. What is ethnoecology? Origins, scope and implications of a rising discipline. *Ethnoecológica* 1(1): 5–21.

Trosper, R. L. 1995. Traditional American Indian economic policy. *American Indian Culture and Research Journal* 19: 65–95.

Trosper, R. L. 1998. Land tenure and ecosystem management in Indian country. In *Social Conflict Over Property Rights: Who Owns America*? (H. M. Jacobs, ed.). Madison: University of Wisconsin Press (in press).

Tuan, Y. 1974. *Topophilia*. Englewood Cliffs: Prentice-Hall.

Turner, B. L., W. C. Clark, R. W. Kates, J. F. Richards, J. T. Mathews, and W. B. Meyer, editors. 1990. *The Earth as Transformed by Human Action: Global and Regional Changes in the Biosphere Over the Past 300 Years*. Cambridge: Cambridge University Press.

Turner, N. J. 1988. The importance of a rose: Evaluating the cultural significance of plants in Thompson and Lilooet Interior Salish. *American Anthropologist* 90: 272–90.

Turner, N. J. 1994. Burning mountain sides for better crops: Aboriginal landscape burning in British Columbia. *International Journal of Ecoforestry* 10: 116–22. (Originally published in *Archaeology in Montana* 32(1991): 57–73.)

Turner, N. J., and A. Davis. 1993. "When everything was scarce": The role of plants as famine foods in Northwestern North America. *Journal of Ethnobiology* 13: 171–201.

Tyler, M. E. 1993. Spiritual stewardship in aboriginal resource management systems. *Environments* 22(1): 1–8.

Vestergaard, T. A. 1991. Living with pound nets: Diffusion, invention and implications of a technology. *Folk* 33: 149–67.

Wallace, A. F. C. 1956. Revitalization movements: Some theoretical considerations for their comparative study. *American Anthropologist* 58(2): 265.

Warren, D. M., editor. 1991a. Indigenous Agricultural Knowledge Systems and Development. Special issue of *Agriculture and Human Values* 8(1/2).

Warren, D. M. 1991b. Using indigenous knowledge in agricultural development. *World Bank Discussion Papers* No. 127. Washington, D.C.: World Bank.

Warren, D. M. 1995. Comments on article by Arun Agrawal. *Indigenous Knowledge and Development Monitor* 4(1): 13.

Warren, D. M., and J. Pinkston. 1998. Indigenous African resource management of a tropical rain forest ecosystem: A case study of the Yoruba of Ara, Nigeria. In *Linking Social and Ecological Systems* (F. Berkes and C. Folke, eds.). Cambridge: Cambridge University Press, 158–89.

Warren, D. M., L. J. Slikkerveer, and D. Brokensha, editors. 1995. *The Cultural Dimension of Development: Indigenous Knowledge Systems*. London: Intermediate Technology Publications.

Watanabe, H. 1973. *The Ainu Ecosystem, Environment and Group Structure*. Seattle: University of Washington Press.

Wavey, R. 1993. International Workshop on Indigenous Knowledge and Community-based Resource Management: Keynote address. In *Traditional Ecological Knowledge: Concepts and Cases* (J. T. Inglis, ed.). Ottawa: Canadian Museum of Nature/International Development Research Centre, 11–16.

WCED (World Commission on Environment and Development). 1987. *Our Common Future*. Oxford and New York: Oxford University Press.

Weinstein, M. S. 1993. Aboriginal land use and occupancy studies in Canada. Workshop on Spatial Aspects of Social Forestry Systems, Chiang Mai University, Thailand.

White, L. 1967. The historical roots of our ecologic crisis. *Science* 155: 1203–07.

Whitehead, A. N. 1929. *Process and Reality: An Essay in Cosmology*. New York: Macmillan.

Wilkins, D. 1993. Linguistic evidence in support of a holistic approach to traditional ecological knowledge. In *Traditional Ecological Knowledge: Wisdom for Sustainable Development* (N. M. Williams and G. Baines, eds.). Canberra: Centre for Resource and Environmental Studies, Australian National University, 71–93.

Williams, N. M., and G. Baines, editors. 1993. *Traditional Ecological Knowledge: Wisdom for Sustainable Development*. Canberra: Centre for Resource and Environmental Studies, Australian National University.

Williams, N. M., and E. S. Hunn, editors. 1982. *Resource Managers: North American and Australian Hunter-Gatherers*. Washington, D.C.: American Association for the Advancement of Science.

Wilson, J. A., J. M. Acheson, M. Metcalfe, and P. Kleban. 1994. Chaos, complexity and communal management of fisheries. *Marine Policy* 18: 291–305.

Wilson, P. 1992. What Chief Seattle said. *Lewis and Clark Law School, Natural Resources Law Institute News* 3(2): 1, 12–15.

Winterhalder, B. 1983. The boreal forest, Cree-Ojibwa foraging and adaptive management. In *Resources and Dynamics of the Boreal Zone* (R. W. Wein, R. R. Riewe, and I. R. Methven, eds.). Ottawa: Association of Canadian Universities for Northern Studies, 331–45.

Worster, D. 1977. *Nature's Economy: A History of Ecological Ideas*. Cambridge: Cambridge University Press.

Worster, D., editor. 1988. *The Ends of the Earth: Perspectives on Modern Environmental History*. Cambridge: Cambridge University Press.

Young, E. 1992. Aboriginal land rights in Australia: Expectations, achievements and implications. *Applied Geography* 12: 146–61.

Zachariah, M. 1984. The Berger Commission Inquiry Report and the revitalization of indigenous cultures. *Canadian Journal of Development Studies* 5: 65–77.

Index